Human–Computer Interaction Series

Editors-in-chief

Desney Tan
Microsoft Research, USA

Jean Vanderdonckt
Université catholique de Louvain, Belgium

More information about this series at http://www.springer.com/series/6033

Phil Turner

HCI Redux

The Promise of Post-Cognitive Interaction

 Springer

Phil Turner
School of Computing
Edinburgh Napier University
Edinburgh, UK

ISSN 1571-5035
Human–Computer Interaction Series
ISBN 978-3-319-82532-8   ISBN 978-3-319-42235-0   (eBook)
DOI 10.1007/978-3-319-42235-0

Printed on acid-free paper

This Springer imprint is published by Springer Nature
The registered company is Springer International Publishing AG Switzerland

Preface

the initial vision of HCI as an applied science was to bring cognitive-science methods and theories to bear on software development (Carroll 2003, p. 3)

The discipline of human-computer interaction (HCI) was originally concerned with the design and evaluation of interactive systems. Its initial aims were to understand their use and to create technologies which were usable. In these early days, to understand the human aspects of HCI was, of course, an appeal to cognitive psychology (and very quickly, 'cognition' and 'cognitive' were adopted to stand for 'psychology' or 'psychological'). Researchers, practitioners and designers were also able to make use of the many cognitive theories, models and methods which were emerging at that time. As for the design aspect of HCI, it was recognised that the best way to create usable and accessible technology was to involve the intended end users, and thus a whole raft of user-centred and user participatory methods were also created. These approaches, in practice, were realised through incremental prototyping, that is, cycles of design, evaluation and redesign which the noted designer David Kelley describes as 'enlightened trial and error'.

However, in all of this excitement, psychology has rather been left behind. While research is still being conducted into understanding and designing for people with special needs or who are very old (old, of course, has been redefined upwards) and those on the wrong side of the 'digital divide', it is now generally expected people are sufficiently familiar with technology to be able to use it or be able to ask their friends how to use it or, failing that, their children. Excepting these groups, there simply isn't a problem to research.

So, what is this book about? We begin by considering some of the things which will not be discussed. For example, we are not concerned with the *design* of interactive systems. There is, after all, no shortage of books, manuals, recommendations, websites, tutorials, online videos and guidelines which will point the interested developer to a good design. So, if you are looking for advice on how to build a better website, app or bot, please look elsewhere, and then come back to understand how and why these recommendations work! Nor will we not discuss why some people appear to use technology compulsively. We read, in the popular press and on technology new sites, about young women checking social media accounts when they first wake up and even during the night (The Telegraph 2016) and that some people check their cell phones as frequently as every 6 s (BuzzFeed 2016). If these bewildering observations are so, they may be better accounted for from the perspective of those studying addiction and the fact that they seem to share many of the characteristics of the partial reinforcement effect that is probably not lost on old behaviourists (and some modern game designers).

So returning to the question of what we will discuss, we are primarily concerned with the role of cognition in HCI, and this discussion is effectively framed by two quotes. The first, which appeared at the outset of cognitive psychology, is from Neisser (1967) who wrote that 'it is apparent that cognition is involved in everything a human being might possibly do; that every psychological phenomenon is a cognitive phenomenon'. So, this establishes cognition as being important. While this kind of all-encompassing observation is not always particularly helpful, we can see why this sort of thinking dominated for decades. Then 40 years later, Clark tells us that cognition is 'whatever mix of problem-solving resources [which] will yield an acceptable result with minimum effort' (Clark 2008, p. 13). This is effectively turning the definition on its head. We have gone from 'cognition is what we use to achieve our ends' to 'whatever it is we are doing to achieve our ends is what we mean by cognition'. And we would add, the greatest problem-solving resource we have invented to date is interactive technology. We can also see that a further problem for psychology is that HCI has emerged as being necessarily multidisciplinary (cf. Clark's 'whatever mix of ...'). Cognitive psychology, as such, is just too narrow in itself to do the job as it has been traditionally concerned with understanding our mental lives. As HCI is about using technology in the world, to account for this extracranial behaviour, we need a wider set of conceptual tools. These tools, in the main, have been developed in the cognitive sciences and, compared with psychology, are a good deal less constrained or confined to the laboratory. It is for these reasons that this book presents a cognitive scientific account of HCI rather than one which is confined to traditional cognitive psychology.

However, to understand the present, we must consider the past.

Suddenly Human

Evolutionary psychology has developed accounts of many of our fundamental characteristics and behaviours (e.g. Barkow et al.1992; Buss 1995; Bereczkei 2000). Cosmides and Tooby (2000) note that evolutionary psychology is not a specific subfield of psychology, but 'It is a way of thinking about psychology that can be applied to any topic within it [...]'. Further, as Buss observes 'Because all behaviour depends on complex psychological mechanisms, and all psychological mechanisms, at some basic level of description, are the result of evolution by selection, then all psychological theories are implicitly evolutionary psychological theories' (ibid, p. 2). For Bereczkei (ibid, p. 185), it involves recognising features of human behaviour that have been selected to be useful for our survival and reproduction. Significantly, he writes 'It claims that cognitive and emotional processes have been selected in our evolutionary environment as devices of solving particular adaptive problems faced by the Pleistocene hunter-gatherers'. In short, the evolutionary psychological perspective is one which supposes that selection pressures on our hunter-gatherer ancestors and the demands of their social lives shaped our contemporary thinking and behaviour. We should note that recognisably modern humans have been around for, perhaps, 250,000 years. It has often been said that if we were to take a man from that time, clean him up and dress him appropriately, he would pass more or less unnoticed amongst us. This similarity is, however, only skin deep as behaviourally and culturally he would be quite different. Yet approximately 50,000 years ago, modern human behaviour appeared almost 'overnight' (e.g. Ambrose 1998; Chase et al. 1990; Klein 2001, amongst many more). We should note that when an anthropologist writes 'overnight', they tend to mean approximately 10,000 years. Despite the uncertainty over the precise dating, a number of prominent authors agree that something remarkable happened to the ways in which we thought and behaved (Klein 2002). Tattersall (2006) agrees and notes that the appearance of the first Cro-Magnons some 40,000 years ago brought with it new behaviours which distinguished them from all that had gone before. These people were able to create sculpture and engraving and were able to paint and add ornamentation to their bodies. They also created musical instruments and buried their dead with care and ceremony (Lewis-Williams 2004, p. 97). They also began to decorate everyday tools. They were recognisably modern humans. Calvin (2006) who attributes these changes to a 'brain specialisation', such as that for language, writes tellingly that these people who looked like us 'finally began acting like us'. Mithen (2002) has argued that '… modern humans had a cognitive advantage which may have resided in a more complex form of language or a quite different type of mentality … Support for the latter is readily evident from dramatic developments that occur in the archaeological record relating to new ways of thinking and behaving by modern humans' (p. 33). He also comments on the sudden change in the archaeological record c.50,000 years ago with the appearance of representational art, religious imagery and rapid adaptations in the design of tools and artefacts. Included in the list of changes in which we can recognise some of the attributes of cognition as we currently understand it are (a) abstract thinking, that is, the ability to act with reference to abstract concepts; (b) planning depth, the ability to formulate strategies [...] and to act upon them in a group context; and (c) behavioural, economic and technological innovation and symbolic behaviour, the ability to represent objects, people and abstract concepts with arbitrary symbols. Thus, the full expression of human cognition is to be found in the savannah of the Upper (Late) Pleistocene. We now jump forward to 1983.

More Recent Origins

The first great HCI text *The Psychology of Human Computer Interaction* (Card et al. 1983) addressed the theory, practice and design of interactive technology, and that theory was almost exclusively the application of cognitive psychology – a position which is still largely (but not wholly) true today. Card and his colleagues, for example, proposed a model of human cognition which could be used to guide the design of technology and to make predictions about its use. This was the first of the many attempts to capture, model, represent and employ accounts of human cognition in HCI which Winograd and Flores (1987) have described as modelling people as 'cognitive machines'. It was assumed that most of what we did was essentially cognitive (cf. Neisser's definition). But this was quite a stretch; psychology had to be broader than just cognition as we were also concerned with understanding how people use technology to do their jobs, interact with other people, have fun and, generally, do all manner of everyday things. These dimensions cannot always be reduced to purely psychological phenomena as other disciplines such as sociology had something of value to contribute here too. To understand how people use technology, for example, is to address the context in which the technology is used which, as we shall see, is often described as 'cognition in the wild' with all the untidiness this implies.

Further, while these endeavours may have begun as different strands of inquiry, they have converged, separated and reconverged at regular but unpredictable intervals against a background of rapidly changing technology. For example, the first IBM personal computer appeared in 1981, Apple Lisa perhaps a year later, the first digital mobile phone about 10 years later again and the Web after a further five or so years. We had to wait until 2001 for Apple to create the first of the i-series of technologies, the iPod. This technological exuberance is not confined to these signal technologies alone as it has changed almost every aspect of our everyday lives.

When the Web was invented in the early 1990s, it was quickly colonised and appropriated by emergent brands such as Google, Amazon and Facebook which have facilitated new ways of working, thinking, socialising and spending money. The Web has changed the ways in which we do business, teach young people and consume entertainment, and products and services have emerged which we could not have anticipated. By the Millennium, mobile technology was becoming ubiquitous with the meteoric rise (and subsequent fall) of Scandinavia chic. These technologies became smaller, more powerful and indispensible and then larger again. Somewhere in there, Apple rewrote how we interact with technology. As I write, apps are the media of choice by which we access, encounter, enjoy and embrace technology. We can be confident that this too will change, for example, Microsoft has just announced that 'bots' are the future (Microsoft 2016), 2 months later Facebook (Facebook 2016) announced something similar, and it is against this background that we seek to outline the promise of a post-cognitive future for HCI, but first let us consider how psychology has fared since 1983.

Guidelines

In *A Guide to Usability* (1990) written for a professional audience by the Open University on behalf of UK's Department of Trade and Industry, we find advice on 'how to apply psychology' to systems design. Its advice includes, for example, help with designing usable screens of information. As a first step, we are encouraged to understand the workings of the visual system. Using this knowledge, we will then be able to ensure that our computer screens are uncluttered and that the content displayed there is meaningfully structured (p. 24). Although linking the workings of the visual (or any other cognitive) system to systems design does seem a little optimistic, we also learn that the overall aim of this is to ensure that the information processing involved completing a task within the capabilities of the users' mental processes (p. 23). This presents the use of psychology as something rather like the application of a coat or two of paint to a garden shed. One coat will help structure information (allow to dry), and a second coat will ensure that the information processing capacity of a user is not exceeded. This, to say the least, is rather naïve, but it is a fine example of the instrumental use of psychology. As we have already observed, psychology was never developed for this use, but this has not stopped people from trying.

Hansen (1971) published arguably the first list of four still perfectly reasonable design guidelines, which were (a) know the user, (b) minimise memorisation, (c) optimise operations and (d) engineer for errors. Shneiderman (1980) amongst his many contributions to HCI doubled the number of guidelines to eight. Both sets of guidelines are a mixture of heuristics, good practice and cognitive psychological principles. So we are not surprised when Shneiderman tells us that we should strive for consistency, offer shortcuts, provide feedback and reduce the load on short-term memory, writing, for example, 'The limitation of human information processing in short-term memory requires that displays be kept simple, multiple page displays be consolidated, window-motion frequency be reduced, and sufficient training time be allotted for codes, mnemonics, and sequences of actions' (Shneiderman 1997).

This was followed by the longest set of guidelines (running to more than 300 pages) which were compiled and published by Smith and Mosier (1986). The guidelines are well referenced, and the psychological bases of the advice have become a matter of good practice. In 1987, Gardiner and Christie published their *Applying Cognitive Psychology To User-Interface Design* in which they systematically derived design principles from cognition. For example, memory was again a popular choice; the limited capacity of short-term memory (which they describe as working memory) prompts them to suggest that we should design our dialogues in chunks so as not to overburden our limited information processing and storage capabilities. It is fair to say that many of these recommendations are still with us today, while others seem very dated. This was not the first instrumental use of cognitive psychology, but it was undoubtedly one of the most grounded and systematic.

In each instance, and there are many others, these principles have not been derived from a psychology of interaction but from off-the-shelf undergraduate-level psychology. Further, there is rarely any evidence presented that the guidelines work. While it is entirely reasonable that an academic discipline should have different emphases, what is surprising about HCI is the dominance of design. This has been noted by Dourish (2006) who writes, 'A common lament to be found in reviews of ethnographic work is, 'yes, it's all very interesting, but I don't understand its implications for design' or the somewhat more subtle (and intriguing), 'this paper does not seem to be addressed towards the CHI [computer-human interaction] audience'. Dourish goes on to consider how theory in its own right has been relegated to a second place behind design. Admittedly he is bemoaning the fate of sociological/ anthropological insights; the same observations also hold true for psychology. Psychology has, in recent years, become an unwilling maidservant to design.

The Promise of a Post-Cognitive Future

The use of the expression 'post-cognitive' should be read as both accurate and descriptive rather than speculative or 'futuristic'. Post-cognitive, like 'post-industrial' or 'post-modern', simply refers to research which has sufficiently diverged from the initial formulations of cognition to merit this label. The foundations of cognition, which include ideas such as mental representation as symbols and the adoption of the computer metaphor (as found in 'human information processing'), have been challenged and, in some cases, rejected by a number of the contemporary accounts of cognition. New ideas have appeared to fill these conceptual gaps, for example, a number of authors have made compelling cases for a role for the body in cognition which, in its classical form, would have been unheard of. Similarly, the use of external representation to supplement or scaffold our thinking has become quite widespread and now appears in a variety of different forms, for example, Donald's suggestion of the exogram (external representations and symbols) to parallel the established idea of the memory engrams is particularly appealing (Donald 1991). New ideas emerging from the work of cognitive scientists and philosophers are not the only source of change, as we have seen in the brief sketch of current interactive technology which itself is the epitome of change. As these technologies are a major defining factor of our society, it is clear that they demand a contemporary, post-cognitive account reflecting their importance, perhaps one which reflects what we developed on the savannah 50,000 years ago rather than in the labs of the 1950s.

The Structure of This Book

Each chapter is independent and can be read in isolation, but the book as a whole has adopted a broadly chronological account of the development of (our understanding of) cognition as applied to the use of digital technology. A consequence of this is that it also begins with a discussion-review of the uncontroversial and slowly becomes more speculative and radical as we approach the modern day.

Chapter 1 starts with a discussion of the *cognitive revolution*. Behaviourism, which had preceded it, had ruled out the possibility of understanding our internal, mental lives, but the advocates of cognition argued that we could indeed access the processes and representations which make up our mental lives. They also adopted the nearly invented digital computer as a model for its operation. With this certainty, they set about not only explaining how we use interactive technology but how we could design it too.

Chapter 2 introduces *activity theory* which we treat from the perspective of mediated cognition. Superficially, activity theory is an alternative to the classical cognition of Chap. 1. It can largely match classical cognition, concept for concept, and then develop the argument further. While classical cognition has a collage-like quality to it, activity theory is coherent, structured and, dare we say, much more complete, but it is also quite foreign to the Anglo-Saxon traditions of the West. We also note that activity theory is not a purely psychological theory particularly in its later revisions or editions (it is currently in its third generation). However, when, in the early 1990s, it was proposed – but not widely adopted – as a theory for HCI, we missed an opportunity. While it is not perfect, it would have met most of our needs at the time and would have continued to do so. While activity theory may not deal with emerging issues in the kind of detail we might like, it does offer a coherent and consistent treatment of tool mediation, context, cognitive distribution, scaffolding, and make-believe – all of which are considered in subsequent chapters.

Chapter 3 addresses the appearance of *situated action*. This arose in the 1980s as one of the most serious challenges to classical cognition. Suchman proposed situated action arguing that the kinds of cognitive models which were being suggested at that time relied on the execution of a plan. The plan might be true to a GOMS-like set of steps or the less structured output from 'running' a mental model: either way for Suchman was not enough because it ignored the nuances and dynamics of the situation. A plan may be appropriate as a kind of starting point for using interactive technology, but it could not account for the social, cultural and historical realities of the everyday world. We are avoiding the word 'context' here, but it is difficult to distinguish between it and 'situation'. So, in short, planning models do not allow for context and as such cannot offer anything like a complete account of HCI.

Chapter 4 finds a place for *the body*. This was one of the first of the post-cognitive initiatives, but it relied on a number of quite different factors coming together. The importance of our corporeality had been identified by Merleau-Ponty in the 1940s. Predating this, the German phenomenologists Husserl and Heidegger in their own, very different, ways had said important things about it, but little of this came to the attention of HCI. When the Media Lab at MIT launched their *tangible bits* initiative, this all changed. However, it was Dourish who was responsible for pulling together these strands of tangible computing and phenomenology to give us a place for the body in HCI. This is still very much a matter of work in progress as if asked 'what is the role of the body in HCI?', we would struggle to give a succinct answer.

However, we would suggest that it is the most likely place to begin (in preference to the brain) if we are to consider technologically augmented and enhanced humans.

Chapter 5 argues that in essence, HCI is about *thinking with technology* or, more fully, thinking and acting with technology. Technology is almost inevitably distributed unless we restrict ourselves to that which is in our reach (which is one reading of Heidegger's famous dictum that technology is often experienced *ready-to-hand*). Technology is also external; it is something which we use to achieve our ends. Vygotski identified this as a defining aspect of purposive behaviour. Technology mediates and technology scaffolds (thinking and) behaviour. This was a start to the argument which persists today and can be found in the work of Scaife and Rogers and of Kirsh. Taking this further, we have Chalmers and Clark suggesting that technology, like the brain, and the body are more or less equal partners in cognition in their extended cognition proposal. Perhaps one day a neural implant will replace the need to master quadratic equations.

Chapter 6 offers an introduction to *enactive cognition*. Enaction is not the product of psychology or of computing but of biology. Its creators see it as self-organising, world creating and embodied. On the face of it, this may seem to be a long way from the everyday use of interactive technology, but it is not. For me, it potentially provides a theoretical rich and highly useful set of concepts which might offer a post-cognitive theory for HCI. Cognition, they tell us, does not exist simply to make copies (internal representations of the world or of technology) and to think with these (poor) copies. Instead, cognition is about enacting a world, and so appealing are these ideas that the European Union funded a research programme to create a new generation of human-computer interfaces or what they described as *enactive interfaces*. Unlike embodied or external cognition, the enactive perspective offers some fascinating insights on the operation of our memories, perception and niche building activities.

Chapter 7 segues to an old debate that cognition may exist in more than one form. In short, cognition may exist as 'fast' or 'slow' thinking. We argue that this is a useful distinction but that fast, intuitive and automatic thinking relies on scaffolding and is better thought of as epistemic coping. In essence, epistemic coping manifests as the smooth, easy, everyday use of technology with scarcely a conscious thought or moment of reflection. If thought-free (or thought-lite) interaction seems unlikely, simply spend 30 min on a rush hour commuter train and observe how people use their cell phones, tablets and e-readers.

Chapter 8 introduces *make-believe* as an unrecognised but complementary cognitive mechanism within HCI. Treating HCI as a set of practices and theoretical positions, we show how make-believe contributes to a better understanding of these. Make-believe involves creating fictional worlds which are not the case and then acting as though they were. We do this every time we create a scenario or prototype or engage in just about any aspect of the design and evaluation of interactive technology – and no one notices that this is make-believe.

Chapter 9 notes that as Gottschall puts it, we are *storytelling animals*. So having presented the current thinking in the cognitive sciences about how we think and behave with interactive technology, we wonder what the story of HCI is. To tell a story about HCI, we must appeal to technology itself. So, what has using interactive technology revealed about us? And you will have to read Chap. 9 to find out what it is. However, we can say that it finds a home for Neisser's definition of cognition and Clark's claim that cognition is a contingent mix of problem-solving resources.

Edinburgh, UK   Phil Turner

References

Ambrose SH (1998) Chronology of the later stone age and food production in East Africa. J Archaeol Sci 25:377–392.

Barkow JH, Cosmides L, Tooby J (eds) (1992) The adapted mind. Oxford University Press, New York

Bereczkei T (2000) Evolutionary psychology: a new perspective in the behavioral sciences. Eur Psychol 5(3):175–190

Buss DM (1995) Evolutionary psychology: a new paradigm for psychological science. Psychol Inq 6(1):1–30

Calvin WH (2006) The emergence of intelligence. Scientific Am Spec 16(2):84–92

Card SK, Moran, TP, Newell A (1983) The psychology of human-computer interaction. LEA, Hillsdale

Carroll JM (ed) (2003) HCI models, theories, and frameworks: toward a multidisciplinary science. Morgan Kaufmann, San Francisco

Chase PG, Dibble HL, Lindly J, Clark G, Straus LG (1990) On the emergence of modern humans. Curr Anthropol 31(1):58–66

Clark A (2008) Supersizing the mind. Oxford University Press, Oxford

Cosmides L, Tooby J (2000) Consider the source: the evolution of adaptations for decoupling and metarepresentation. In Sperber D (ed) Metarepresentations: a multidisciplinary perspective. Oxford University Press, Oxford

Donald M (1991) Origins of the modern mind. Harvard University Press, Cambridge, MA

Hansen W (1971) User engineering principles for interactive systems. AFIPS '71. In: Proceedings of Fall joint computer conference, pp 523–532, 16–18 November 1971

Klein RG (2001) Southern Africa and modern human origins. J Anthropol Res 57:1–16

Klein RG, Edgar B (2002) The dawn of human culture. Wiley, New York

Lewis-Williams D (2004) The mind in the cave. Thames & Hudson, London

Mithen S (2002) Human evolution and the cognitive basis of science. In Carruthers P, Stitch S, Siegal M (eds) The cognitive basis of science. Cambridge University Press, Cambridge, pp 23–40

Neisser U (1967) Cognitive psychology. Appleton-Century-Crofts, New York

Shneiderman B (1997) Designing the user interface, 3rd edn. Pearson Addison Wesley, New York

Smith SL, Mosier JN (1986) Guidelines for designing user interface software. Mitre Corporation, Bedford

Tattersall I (2006) How we became human. Sci Am Spec 16(2):66–73

Winograd T, Flores F (1986) Understanding computers and cognition. Ablex, Norwood

Web Resources

Buzzfeed   http://www.buzzfeed.com/charliewarzel/heres-the-cold-hard-proof-that-we-cant-stop-checking-our-pho#.ddKwzN8aK

Facebook (2016) Available from http://www.bbc.co.uk/news/technology-36021889

Microsoft (2016) Available from http://www.bbc.co.uk/news/technology-35927651. Last retrieved 31 March 2016

Telegraph (2016) http://www.telegraph.co.uk/technology/facebook/7879656/One-third-of-young-women-check-Facebook-when-they-first-wake-up.html

Contents

Chapter 1
Classical Cognition

1.1 The Cognitive Revolution

This book presents a rebooting or (radical) updating of the psychology of human-computer interaction (HCI) but we should begin by admitting that when we say "psychology" we really mean cognition. This is not to suggest that the discussion is limited to *just* cognition, but it is more a recognition that cognition has acquired an extraordinary reach. In part, this is because it is constantly redefining itself, often as a consequence of its encounters with the technology.

This chapter sets the scene. We will define cognition and its origins and describe how it was used by researchers in HCI to understand how people use interactive technology. Not for the last time, we stress that this is cognition in the service of understanding human-computer interaction, rather than cognition in the service of the *design* of the interactive technology. This use-design dichotomy will recur throughout this text.

So, just what do we mean by cognition? To answer this question we need to consider a little history. In everyday usage, of course, cognition is associated with ideas such as mental activity, mind, reasoning, consciousness, intelligence or learning but these are either a little too broad or too specific to be immediately useful here. More detailed definitions present their own difficulties, for example, Enactivism (Chap. 7) defines cognition is "self-organising, self-generating, and self-maintaining" and tells us that "life and cognition" are fundamentally the same phenomena. However, we cannot adopt this rather radical definition in isolation, as it only makes sense in the context of Enactivism. Cognition is also ascribed to a number of animals such as the great apes, elephants and cetaceans and, of course, to those disturbingly intelligent New Caledonian crows (e.g. Jelbert et al. 2014). We also speak of cognition as an expected, hoped for or feared property of all manner of artificial intelligences or of autonomous robots or as an emergent property of a complex network such as the Web.

© Springer International Publishing Switzerland 2016
P. Turner, *HCI Redux*, Human–Computer Interaction Series,
DOI 10.1007/978-3-319-42235-0_1

As for mainstream psychology, Neisser (1967) wrote the first book to be entitled *Cognitive Psychology* and it worth repeating that it he defines cognition as, "all processes by which the sensory input is transformed, reduced, elaborated, stored, recovered, and used". He goes on to tell us that he regards it as being "involved in everything a human being might possibly do; that every psychological phenomenon is a cognitive phenomenon". Here we see psychology and cognitive psychology being treated as synonyms. He is also using the term "cognitive psychology" as a portmanteau to include memory, attention, perception, reasoning, language and so forth. This list, of course, is not exhaustive but cognition, as a collection of faculties, is what we find typically populating the early chapters of many of the standard textbooks on HCI. These books often begin, as we have, by arguing that cognitive psychology is an essential component of HCI before launching into, say, a discussion of the various dimensions of memory and attention, followed by a review of the strengths and weakness of human memory and perhaps ending with an entertaining selection of visual illusions. Having dealt with psychology, the narrative summarily moves on. However, a moment's reflection may leave us wondering what exactly does the transduction of light by the retina or the decay characteristics of short term memory have to do with how, say, we use Facebook on our cell phones?

Despite the importance of cognition to HCI, there is something a little dated about it. It does not present an image of something which is actively and urgently informing our thinking within the discipline. Indeed, at the time of writing, it is hard to identify a unified, much less a recent, account of cognition in HCI. This prompts us to conclude that just because cognition is implicated in "everything a human being might do", it does not mean that it provides a ready-made conceptual platform to reason about human-computer interaction.

Models of cognition were, of course, never developed to serve this purpose. Instead, they have been appropriated on a pretty much *ad hoc*, piece-meal, and "as needed" basis. So, if human-computer interaction was not the primary target domain of cognition, what was?

The study and application of cognition has a complex lineage and its different threads have overlapped, interacted and mutually informed one another to bring us to the mix of concepts and methods that we see today. As space precludes anything like a thorough treatment of the history of cognition, it should be recognised that this introduction is only a sketch at best.

Beginnings

We begin by recognising that cognition is a major paradigm in psychology and became so when it replaced behaviourist thought and practice. A frequently identified trigger for this shift is Chomsky's review (1959) of Skinner's *Verbal Behaviour* (1957).

Historically, Behaviourism had rejected any notion of mental representation and mental life in favour of studying observable behaviour. It chose rats and pigeons as its test subjects as they are readily observable under controlled conditions – and they were cheap. Behaviourism sought to describe low level behaviour in terms of a small set of key concepts, namely, stimulus, response, reinforcement and deprivation. While pigeons pecked at food-dispensing buttons, rats were encouraged to run mazes and if successful were also rewarded with a pellet of food. These animals were systematically exposed to lights, levers, buttons and a variety of other paraphernalia while the effects of different schedules of deprivations and rewards were recorded. In fairness, Behaviourism did a pretty thorough job in mapping these low level behaviours but it was to fail in trying to apply these concepts to higher level behaviours such as language.

So, returning to Chomsky's detailed review of Skinner's book, one key objection was that it was laboratory-bound. Chomsky argued that Skinner's careful definitions simply did not hold up in the complexities of the real world (an argument that we will see again in subsequent chapters). As there was no reply from Skinner, this effectively signalled the end of Behaviourism and established an opening for cognition.

Research into cognition owes a great deal to the Second World War which witnessed the mobilisation of vast numbers of men and women who were to use increasingly complex technology in the pursuit of mutual destruction. At that time, as Wickens and Hollands (2000) observe, the prevailing wisdom was on "designing the man to fit the machine", that is, the emphasis was on training (and on men, rather than people). It was believed that if people were suitably trained, they could then work effectively with complex technology. Experience, however, was to show otherwise. Aircraft, without mechanical problems or having been shot down, were being routinely flown into the ground by well trained pilots. (This became known as "controlled flight into terrain" and remains the leading cause of loss of life in commercial aircraft). As a result, the design of instrument panels on aircraft came under scrutiny (e.g. Fitts and Jones 1947). Not long after the war, the Ergonomic Society was formed by Murrell in the UK (1952), and the Human Factors Society was established in the US (1957) to continue this research. Ergonomics, as the study of work, was to take a variety of forms. For example, the work of Murrell included the design of physical knobs and dials, establishing that, for example, rotating a knob clockwise naturally 'afforded' increasing the volume or the amount, whereas an anticlockwise direction signified a lessening or reduction (Murrell 1965).

Another wartime development was the appearance of the first programmable digital computer in England in the 1940s. These computers proved not only to be a means of breaking German naval codes but were to offer a new way of conceptualising the workings of (human) cognition and ultimately, the possibility of creating artificially intelligent systems (Turing 1950). Post war, two influential researchers, Newell and Simon (1976) were to propose the physical symbol hypothesis which claimed that both digital computers and the human mind could be understood as using strings of bits or streams of neural pulses as symbols representing the external world. Intelligence, they claimed, merely required making the appropriate inferences from these internal representations. As they put it: "A physical symbol system has the necessary and sufficient means for general intelligent action.". A key assumption of this remarkable claim is that cognition can be captured in a formal, symbolic representation which can be manipulated by means of rules – a position which still colours thinking in cognitive psychology today. This also signalled a shift in emphasis from restoring the dimension of "mental life" which cognitivism promised to one of adopting the computer as a central and ultimately dominant metaphor.

In this very brief historical sketch, we have identified three threads of endeavour which have contributed to how we have come to think of cognition but this is only one of many ways of telling this particular story. Here is another.

1956

Miller (2003) has described 1956 as the moment of conception of the cognitive revolution. Quoting Newell and Simon he tells us that, "1956 could be taken as the critical year for the development of information processing psychology". By way of evidence, he notes that 1956 was the year that McCarthy, Minsky, Shannon and Rochester held a conference on artificial intelligence at Dartmouth which "was attended by nearly everyone working in the field at that time". In 1956, signal-detection theory was being applied to accounts of perception and Miller himself published his celebrated, *The magical number seven, plus or minus two* which described some of the limits on our human capacity to process information. He recalls that the legacy of the Second World War was still strong with many of his colleagues who continued to work on applications of information theory, signal-detection theory and computer theory. Finally, he notes that Chomsky was also to publish research which later became his *Syntactic Structures,* itself the trigger for a cognitive revolution in linguistics.

Miller continues that underlining much of this was also the recognition the brain could be thought of as a limited-capacity processor and not unlike the electronic computers which were becoming more available. If computers were information-processing systems then it did not seem unreasonable to suggestion that the brain was (merely) an information processing system too. Having established this of the mind (brain and/or cognition) could then be thought of as a general-purpose, symbol-processing system then the study of cognition simply became the study of these symbolic processes.

Of course, the story does not end in 1956. There were further significant milestones including the appearance of Broadbent's (1958) *Perception and Communication* and Miller et al.'s (1960) *Plans and the Structure of Behavior.* The first of these proved to be a major contribution to the development of human information processing within psychology while the later showed that information-processing psychology could be expressed in the language of computer modelling as evidenced by the appearance of the undergraduate textbook *Human Information Processing: An Introduction to Psychology* (Lindsay and Norman 1972). The 1970s also saw the intersection of work on language and memory (e.g. Anderson and

Bower 1973) while the 1980s ushered in a new approach to representation with the development of connectionism and parallel distributed processing (e.g. Rumelhart and McClelland 1986). Most recently, cognitive neuroscience is offering fresh insights and tools to the psychologist. This brings us, more or less, to where we are today but before we proceed to the first major application of this cognitive theory to HCI, we will consider the imagined behaviour of an ant finding its way home …

Simon's Ant

We borrow the substance of this brief section from John's (2003) introduction to cognitive modelling and task analysis. She tell us that the fundamental assumption was that "both the task structure and the cognitive architecture are necessary to describe and ultimately predict, people's behavior with computer systems – arose from a parable often referred to as *Simon's Ant*". The following extract is from Simon's *Sciences of the Artificial* (1969, pp 63–64 italics and spelling in the original):

> We watch an ant make his laborious way across a wind- and wave-molded beach, He move ahead, angle to the right to ease his climb up a steep dunelet, detours around a pebble, stops for a moment to exchange information with a compatriot. Thus he makes his weaving, halting way back to his home …
>
> He has a general sense of where home lies, but he cannot foresee all the obstacles between. He must adapt his course repeatedly to the difficulties he encounters and often detours uncrossable barriers. His horizons are very close, so that he deals with each obstacle as he comes to it; he probes for ways around or over it, without much thought for future obstacles. It is easy to trap him into deep detours.
>
> Viewed as a geometric figure, the ant's path is irregular, complex, hard to describe. But its complexity is really a complexity of the surface of the beach, not a complexity in the ant. On that same beach another small creature with a home at the same place as the ant might well follow a very similar path …
>
> *An ant, viewed as a behaving system, is quite simple. The apparent complexity of its behaviour over time is largely a reflection of the complexity of the environment in which it finds itself.*

The moral of this tale is that we need to understand both the ant and the beach and, as John observed, the HCI community has not. She notes that while considerable effort has been put into understanding the cognition of the "ant", the same is not quite true of understanding the "beach".

Cognitive modelling, in a variety of different forms, has been developed and applied to understanding the cognitive processes involved in using technology but the equivalent task analytic methods for understanding the technology have not received the same attention. She writes, "with the advent of widespread computer usage, the emphasis in the HCI branch of HIP [human information processing] research changed to understanding the human *and* the environment" because she continues, "HCI is about designing the beach not describing it". The consequences of this insight will be seen in the proceeding chapters.

1.2   Cognitive Modelling

A cognitive model in HCI is an account of the structure, relationships and operation of the supposed cognitive processes we employ when we are using interactive technology. These models are typically used to predict behaviour, for example, how long it will take to complete a task using a computer. In contrast, techniques such as task analysis are concerned with capturing and understanding what people can be observed doing in completing a task using technology (rather than drawing inferences as to what is going on in their heads – though some, of course, do). For the purposes of the current discussion, we have separated and distinguished between cognitive modelling *per se* and mental models (Sect. 1.3). Cognitive modelling tends to be relatively formal, has a computational approach and, as we have already noted, is intended to be predictive. In contrast, mental models are much more informal and discursive. A number of cognitive modelling tools which have been proposed. These models are all predicated on the task as the basic unit of behaviour. That being said, it is remarkably difficult to find a clear definition of a task in the literature. True to form, of course, the first model of human behaviour involving the use of interactive technology is an example of classical psychophysics. It is Fitts' law and this gives a flavour of this kind of thinking.

Fitts' Law

Fitts (1954) developed an equation which can be used to predict how long it will take to hit a target based on its distance and size. This work by Fitts extended Woodworth's original research which was on performance of telegraph operators. This law, which has been shown to be empirically reliable, can predict the time it takes to move a pointer (using, say, a mouse) to a button or other interface element accurately. Unsurprisingly, it takes longer to hit a spot if it is farther away and/or is small. It has also been found to be accurate in predicting the time it takes to hit the emergency shut down button on production line or to apply the brake pedal when stopping quickly in a car. Fitts' law is $MT = a + b.\log_2(2D/W)$. In this equation, t is time, a and b are constants determined empirically, D is distance and W is the width of the target. Mention of this law is made because it is an important element in the thinking behind Keystroke Level Model but perhaps more importantly, it affords insight into the thinking of the time.

KLM: The Keystroke-Level Model

The Keystroke-Level Model (KLM) is a method for predicting user performance. KLM is the simplest model in the GOMS family (below) and operates at the finest level of detail. Using KLM, execution time is estimated by identifying the sequence of a set of operators which are employed and then summing the times it takes to perform an operator. The original KLM had six different kinds of operators: K pressing a key; P pointing with the mouse to a target on the display; H represents moving hands to the home position on the keyboard or mouse and D refers to drawing. These four operators rely on motor skills. KLM also aggregates all perceptual and cognitive function into a single value for the entire task: M is the mentally preparation time and R is the time it takes for the system to respond. So, the time to complete a task can be calculated as follows: $T_{execute} = T_K + T_P + T_H + T_D + T_M + T_R$.

GOMS: Goals – Operators – Methods and Selection

GOMS is the best known of the modelling techniques created to predict human performance (John and Kieras 1996). John (2003, p. 63) describes the GOMS family as consisting of ideas for *analysing and representing tasks in a way that is related to the stage model of human information processing* (italics in the original). GOMS is not a single method but a family of techniques often with fairly obscure names, such as, NGOMSL, CMN-GOMS and CPM-GOMS. These techniques are intimately linked to other important HCI mainstays such as task analysis and evaluation techniques such as the cognitive walkthrough. However, they all remain primarily concerned with modelling tasks and predicting their execution time. The key components of GOMS are:

Goals   are what the user is trying to accomplish which can be defined at different levels of abstraction, from the high-level to the low-goals. Higher-level goals can be decomposed into sub-goals.

Operators Operators are the basic actions that are required to accomplish the goals. Operators, as such, cannot be decomposed into smaller elements. Operators are assumed to take a fixed amount of time to complete, e.g. clicking a mouse button might take 0.20 s.

Methods   Methods are the procedures that describe how to accomplish goals. A method are those steps that the user take to reach their goal.

Selection Selection rules define which method should be used to achieve a goal. As there may usually a number of different ways of achieving the given goal, selection rules reply on the user's knowledge of how to achieve the desired goal.

A GOMS analysis begins by inferring the user's goals and identifying the necessary operators and methods he or she will need to employ to accomplish that/those goals. On those occasions when there is more than one possible means of achieving a goal, a selection rule is applied (e.g. select the operators from a menu or select to use keyboard shortcuts). We should also note that the steps taken by the user are treated strictly sequentially. The example below is taken from John and Kieras (1996, p. 330) and considers one of the goals typical encountered in editing a block of text. Within it are additional goals (sub-goals), one of which is "modify text" which begins with the goal "move-text". The sub-goal of "moving text" is further expanded to reveal some of its detail (Table 1.1).

Table 1.1 A truncated GOMS example

```
GOAL: EDIT-MANUSCRIPT
.        GOAL: EDIT-UNIT-TASK ... repeat until no more unit tasks
.        .        GOAL: ACQUIRE UNIT-TASK
.        .        .        GOAL: GET-NEXT-PAGE ... if at end of manuscript page
.        .        .        GOAL: GET-FROM-MANUSCRIPT
.        .        GOAL: EXECUTE-UNIT-TASK ... if a unit task was found
.        .        .        GOAL: MODIFY-TEXT
.        .        .        .        [select: GOAL: MOVE-TEXT* ...if text is to be moved
.        .        .        .        GOAL: DELETE-PHRASE ...if a phrase is to be deleted
```

```
*Expansion of MOVE-TEXT goal
GOAL: MOVE-TEXT
. GOAL: CUT-TEXT
. GOAL: HIGHLIGHT-TEXT
.                      .        [select**: GOAL: HIGHLIGHT-WORD
.                      .        .        MOVE-CURSOR-TO-WORD
.                      .        .        DOUBLE-CLICK-MOUSE-BUTTON
.                      .        .        VERIFY-HIGHLIGHT
.                      .        GOAL:   HIGHLIGHT-ARBITRARY-TEXT
.                      .        .        MOVE-CURSOR-TO-BEGINNING         1.10s
.                      .        .        CLICK-MOUSE-BUTTON              0.20s
.                      .        .        MOVE-CURSOR-TO-END              1.10s

                                < details removed>

.                      .        MOVE-MOUSE-TO-PASTE-ITEM               1.10s
.                      .        VERIFY-HIGHLIGHT                       1.35s
.                      .        RELEASE-MOUSE-BUTTON          0.10s
                                TOTAL TIME PREDICTED (SEC)            14.38s
```

This GOMS analysis predicts that it will take 14.38 s to move a block of text. Although the GOMS analysis is specified in quite some detail, there is little denying that there is a certain amount of latitude on behalf of the analyst (e.g. in identifying what exactly is a goal) and there are a number of areas where there unavoidable uncertainty such as the extent of "the user's knowledge". John (2003, p. 70) herself admits "three critical restrictions" on the kinds of tasks that GOMS can be used for. The first is that the task should be analysed in term of procedural knowledge; the second is that GOMS can only represent skilled performance and thirdly, the analyst must begin with a list of top-level tasks or goals. We might add to this list that GOMS assumes the error free execution of tasks by an expert (despite the evidence that experts do not work in this manner) and GOMS makes no allowance for fatigue, boredom, urgency, disinterest and learning for that matter. Perhaps more importantly, GOMS does not have clearly defined semantics which means that it is likely to be unreliable (i.e. two analysts considering the same issue can arrive at quite different but equally valid models). Overall, while GOMS may some restrictions, it has received sustained attention over the years and does underline some of the very real problems in trying to model user behaviour (and cognition) in this way. In an attempt to address the problem of semantics and to improve the general ease of use of GOMS, NGOMSL – Natural GOMS Language and CCT were created. In addition to the use of natural language in the analysis, innovations such as the use of production rules were also introduced.

CCT: Cognitive Complexity Theory

Cognitive Complexity Theory (Kieras and Polson 1985) provides a framework for modelling the complexity of a system but from the perspective of its usability rather than providing performance estimates. CCT is built on a representation of the user's knowledge of how to operate the artefact (which they describe as the "job-task representation"), and a representation of the artefact itself in the form of a transition network. Interestingly the use of production rules to represent the user's job-task was also adopted. A production rule at its simplest has the following form: *IF condition THEN action*. The condition part of the rule acts as a template that determines when the rule may be applied. The action component defines the problem-solving step. This simple form of knowledge representation has been used by early expert systems such as Mycin (Shortcliffe 1976). However Kieras and Polson do not offer a discussion of whether they believe that cognition works in this way. The authors also confine themselves to modelling text processing (in due course, text-editing was to be described as the "white rat" of HCI research) but these "toy problems" are often been regarded as too limited as they fail to reflect real world complexity.

TAG: Task Action Grammar

Task Action Grammar (TAG) is a modelling technique proposed by Payne and Green (1986) as a means by which a user's understanding of an interactive system can be mapped onto what they do with it. They write, "The central aim of TAG is to formalize (the mapping from task to action) in such a way that simple metrics over grammar, such as the number of rules, will predict aspects of the psychological complexity of the mapping".

They argue that by using a task grammar it is possible to represent tasks, or complex commands, in terms of the basic underlying actions necessary to perform those tasks. As is evident, TAG was created to exploit the parallels between how we complete a task with a device, construct a natural language sentence or write a computer program. They also tell us that the use of grammars offers a number of advantages: firstly, the number of rules offers a measure of the complexity of the language itself, and a measure of the difficulty in learning it. Further, the ease with which tasks are constructed/deconstructed is potentially a measure of how simple it is to understand. So, instead of enumerating a set of rules, a grammar allows us to create a general rule, thus: *Task[Direction, Unit] --> symbol[Direction] + letter[Unit]*. This has an undoubted economy but, unhappily, there is scant empirical support: there is no evidence to suggest that tasks have this grammatical structure.

All of these cognitive modelling tools broadly share the same "fact" and "rule" approach to representing human cognition and, it should be said, really very little empirical support for the operation. What evidence is presented tends to be limited to simple, non-real world problems such as those involving a text editor.

While it would be wrong to suggest that these forms of cognitive modelling are no longer used, it is fair to same that they may have fallen out of favour, excepting the use of keystroke level modelling, which has experienced something of a renaissance in predicting user behaviour with small, portable devices such as cell phones. Fitts' law and KLM are still useful and are being used to predict user behaviour with touch screens (e.g. Abdulin 2011; El Batran and Dunlop 2014), in gaming (Song et al. 2013), using in-vehicle information systems (e.g. Pettitt et al. 2007) and with other handheld devices (Luo and John 2005).

Task Analysis

Task analysis was, and remains, a considerable field of endeavour in its own right. This very brief summary is intended to simply to place task analytic techniques along side the broader domain of cognitive modelling.

As we indicated earlier, task analysis is very much a complement to cognitive modelling. Diaper (2004, p. 14) defines it as, "the collective noun used in the field of ergonomics, which includes HCI, for all the methods of collecting, classifying, and interpreting data on the performance of systems that include at least one person as a system component". Less formally, Hackos and Redish (1998) tell us that it helps us understand what your users' goals are, and what they actually do to achieve them. A thorough task analysis should also reveal what users think about their work, and the extent of their previous knowledge. Finally, details of the context in which the work is being performed should emerge including the social and cultural dimensions. Task analysis is undertaken to create a model or an account of how and where (broadly, the context) work is done. Diaper (2004) reiterates that at the core of any task analytic model are a description of the world and an account of how work is performed in the described world.

Despite its importance, task analysis is not without its problems. Firstly, people are difficult: here is one illustration. One of the major reasons we undertake task analysis is in the service of design. To design a better system we should first understand the current one, the context, how the technology is used and so forth. So, in effect, not only do we need to create a model of the world as-is, but we need to speculate as to how the new world will look and behave after employing our innovations. Faced with creating this new description of the world, Diaper tells us that it can be "virtually impossible" because people make it difficult. For example, they may adapt their behaviour to the proposed changes; or alter other aspects of their world to accommodate what has been designed for or even appropriate and subvert the designed changes to their own ends. Secondly, although a task is treated as "the work which is performed in order to reach a goal", this is a very loose definition. Tasks can range from the very highly abstract to one which is concrete and action-oriented. In practice this might take the forms of "This nation should commit itself to achieving the goal, before the decade is out, of landing a man on the moon and returning him safely to the earth (Kennedy 1961) to "I must remember to wash the dishes before I go to work" – which we might quantify as perhaps two million person years of effort versus 15 min. What is more, the term "task" is often used interchangeably with the words such as "activity" or "process". And a third problem is that task analysis itself can and does take very many different forms. It might, for example, be represented as a hierarchy (as found in a hierarchical task analysis) depicting the steps an individual actually takes to perform a task. Or it might take one of the various forms of collaborative task analysis reflecting the fact that that people work together (e.g. Pinelle et al. 2002) and the choice of method is very much the analyst's.

1.3   Mental Models

Craik in his *The nature of explanation* (1943) wrote that, "if the organism carries a "small-scale model" of external reality and of its own possible actions within its head, it is able to try out various alternatives, conclude which is the best of them, react to future situations before they arise, utilize the knowledge of past events in dealing with the present and the future, and in every way to react in much fuller, safer and more competent manner to the emergencies which face it" (p. 61). This description of a small-scale model is, of course, a description of a mental model.

From an empirical perspective, Tolman (1948) reported observing something similar in rats. A rat's behaviour in a particular environment (typically a maze) indicated that its responses had, over time, become integrated into a map-like representation of the space. He wrote, " … information impinging on the brain, worked over and elaborated […] into a tentative cognitive-like map of the environment indicating routes and paths and environmental relationships." A cognitive map is, of course, a specific kind of mental model. Tolman proposed that the rats create a cognitive map of the maze to which they had been exposed and this, he argued, was a more plausible and simpler explanation than arguing for chains of stimulus and response as required by Behaviourist theory. Curiously, despite the persuasiveness of his argument, this first stirrings of cognition failed to gain traction within the wider community at that time.

Two Books Entitled "Mental Models"

Mental models were to re-appear in the 1980s with Johnson-Laird's *Mental Models* (1983) and Gentner and Stevens' publication of the same name (1983) which quite independently adopted the concept to describe complex cognitive representations in the service of deductive reasoning and the use of technology respectively. While the names were the same, and their purposes apparently similar, that is, they are concerned with reasoning, their structure and content could not have been more different. Johnson-Laird proposed mental models as the basis of *logical* reasoning (of the

"A or B, not A, therefore B" variety), while for Gentner mental models provide the means of everyday reasoning (to use one of her examples, "Which can you throw further, a potato or a potato chip?"). Johnson-Laird's work was to be hugely influential within cognitive psychology but it was Gentner's (and Norman's too – see below) use of the term which was readily adopted by HCI researchers. Mental models were used to describe how people reasoned about and used a wide range of systems and devices including pocket calculators (Norman 1983), the operation of mechanics (McCloskey et al. 1980) and electrical circuits (e.g. Gentner and Gentner 1983).

The Psychology of Everyday Things

It was Norman's (1988) landmark *The Psychology of Everyday Things* which popularised mental models in HCI. He introduced them by way of a description of the operation of his two compartment home refrigerator. He found this difficult to use because it did not support an unambiguous mapping between its operation and the mental model he had acquired (or sought to acquire) of it. Indeed he claimed that the refrigerator supplied a false conceptual model.

This example also served to illustrate the overlap in the language of cognitive psychology and design in HCI. In an article entitled, "Some Observations on Mental Models", Norman distinguished between mental models and conceptual models, writing, "Conceptual models are devised as tools for the understanding or teaching of physical systems. Mental models are what people really have in their heads and what guides their use of things." Thus the designer embodies a conceptual model into the system (named the target system) so that its operation appears comprehensible and coherent to a user. In turn, if the user of the system grasps the conceptual model, the "correct" mental model (in the mind of the user) is acquired (Norman 1983).

A little later Norman revised this account and renamed a number of the different systems and models and adding physical and other components of the system such as its input/output devices, documentation, training, error handling, and so forth. Despite the change in terminology, a good design ultimately depended on the quality of mapping between the technology and the user's mental model. Despite the somewhat volatile language, this was compelling and is still regularly quoted as a key design principle. In the light of this, it is perhaps unsurprising that Norman's *The Psychology of Everyday Things* was reissued as *The Design of Everyday Things*.

Despite their apparent usefulness, there is no agreement on the precise nature, function, or composition of mental models. Norman has proposed this (widely quoted) list to summarise the state of understanding:

(a) mental models are incomplete and unstable, since people forget details of the system;

(b) people's abilities to 'run' their models (in the sense of running an internal simulation) are severely limited and do not have firm boundaries, that is, similar devices and operations get confused with one another;

(c) mental models are unscientific, exhibiting "superstitious" behaviour; and

(d) mental models are parsimonious. People are willing to undertake additional physical operations to minimize mental effort; for example, people will switch off the device to reboot and start again rather than trying to recover from an error.

Similarly, Rouse and Morris (1986, p. 360) comment that, "At present, this area of study is rife with terminological inconsistencies and a preponderance of conjectures rather than data. This situation arises, to a great extent, because a variety of sub-disciplines have adopted the concept of mental models, and proceeded to develop their own terminology and methodology, independent of past or current work in this area in other sub-disciplines". Indeed, Rips (1986) was unconvinced of the mental model explanations of deduction, and dismissed them as "mental muddles".

Some Reflections on Mental Models

One of the things which should be apparent from this discussion of mental models is that it is a little dated. Not having undertaken a detailed bibliographic analysis, I am reluctant to estimate the average age of these publications but they do appear to be very *eighties* and this is very old from the perspective of HCI. They pre-date, for example, the Web and mobile communications technology.

We now consider Payne's (2003) interesting review of *"Users' Mental Models: The Very Ideas"*. Payne begins by contrasting mental models with mainstream theorising in cognitive psychology. He claims that theorising focuses on the cognitive *structures* whereas proponents of mental models do the reverse as they seek to understand the *contents* of these structures (and are generally unconcerned about how it is structured). The clear problem with this is that the content of a mental model is peculiar to that individual and this is very much at odds the desire to make generalisable statements about the cognition involved in the use of technology.

Next, Payne considers mental models with respect to skills. A skill is a collection of methods which we can draw upon to achieve our goals. Early in learning a skill, the selection of the appropriate method is a matter of searching through the mental constructed problem space of possible states. With practice this becomes more automatic or routine. Payne tells us that when we apply this model to the use of interactive technology we end up with something of a mixture: a measure of routine, automatic skills and some other methods identified by searching the possible states in the problem space. If this is so, then there is a role for mental models as a means of elaborating the problem space an individual creates. Thus a mental model allows us to participate in "mental simulation" which involves stepping though possible courses of action, evaluating their effectiveness and if necessary deciding on another path.

Payne's final proposal is that mental models are representational artefacts. He elaborates this in his yoked state space (YSS) hypothesis (Payne et al. 1990). His argument is that the user must construct and maintain two separate state spaces, a goal space and a device space, and a mapping between the two. The goal space represents the possible states of the external world that can be manipulated with the device while the device space represents the possible states of the computer system. A mapping is then maintained to yoke the contents of the two space. The device space in this account is an example of a surrogate model which was introduced by Young (1983). Although this approach is not without its appeal particularly when applied to simple technology, there is a question as to whether it would scale to more complex systems.

The Continuing Appeal of Classical Mental Models

Although the popularity of mental models in their original form has tended to diminish in recent years, they have maintained a loyal following in some quarters notwithstanding their age.

Nersessian (2008), for example, comments that a mental model is a "structural, behavioral, or functional analog representation of a real-world or imaginary situation, event or process. It is analog in that it preserves constraints inherent in what is represented", while Crampton Smith tells us that a good mental model is important in the design of interactive technology, writing, "… we need a clear mental model of what we're interacting with" (quoted in Moggridge 2007 , p. xv).

Very contemporary applications of mental models, among other reports, in the work of Cunningham et al. (2015) and Huang and Cakmak (2015).

Demand Characteristics and Black Boxes

As we have already noted, the contents and operation of a mental model remain unclear and consideration of some of Payne's earlier work is helpful here. He has reported a "descriptive study" of mental models which involved interviewing a number of participants with respect to their beliefs and understanding of the mechanisms behind ATMs (Payne 1991). He was specifically interested in whether people create explanatory mental models as required by the situation ("on demand") as to the ATM's operation. Applying what he described as "an informal content analysis" to a transcript of the interviews with the participants, Payne suggests that " … many subjects had already constructed mental models of bank machines – they had speculated about the inner working of the system in advance of being promoted to do so by a curious psychologist" (1991, p. 18). In all, he concluded that mental models can be used to predict behaviour and to support inferences by "mental simulation" and that they relied on analogy to function. However mention of the role of the curious psychologist suggests that there may an element of the "demand characteristic" about the elicited mental models (see Turner et al. 2009 for a discussion).

But what if the user or curious psychologist, for that matter, has no access to the workings of the interactive device. Here the American philosopher of technology Albert Borgmann provides some useful vocabulary as he has distinguished between commodities and things (1984). He defines a *commodity* is a an entity isolated from traditions and customs while a *thing*, in contrast, is capable of engaging and connecting with us. So, for example, a hamburger bought from a fast food restaurant is a commodity because it is uniform, prepared to a carefully specified formula and is largely free of local context. A hamburger bought and enjoyed in Paris, will be very similar to one bought 10,000 miles away in Canberra. In contrast, a home cooked meal in either location will be very different as it relies on the skill of the cook, the availability of ingredients, time, effort and so forth. This same reasoning can be applied to interactive technology: mobile phones, laptops, games consoles can be purchased from the local supermarket along with the groceries. These technologies are safe, reliable and usable without their owner necessarily having the remotest of idea as to how they work. Interactive technologies have become commodities and there is a growing dichotomy between the user interface and the "black box" which lies beneath. So, having been excluded from their workings, it is reasonable to suppose then the mental model the users form of them will become correspondingly *shallow* and potentially "magical" or superstitious (recalling the behaviour of pigeons in a Skinner box) as we may resort to older ways of thinking.

"Old Brain" Mental Models

Johnson et al. (2008, p. 169) have written that, "The ascription of human-like characteristics to computing technology has become integral to our design, use, training, and communications with regard to computing technology and it has been argued to be the most common metaphor used in computing discourse". This observation stands in contrast to the focus we have given cognition so far. For this is an alternate perspective we turn to Reeves and Nass who recognised that we treat interactive technology, television, and other new media in a manner which is essentially social. In their *The Media Equation* (1996), they show that people tend to blur real and mediated life along social lines. Reeves and Nass proposed that we are using the same old "rules" that govern face-to-face interpersonal interactions to make sense of these technologies. This is both remarkable and counter-intuitive, particularly since no one believes that these media remotely resemble other people. The argument runs that we are polite (and rude) to interactive technology as the product of our "old brains" which had evolved to deal with other humans but which (apparently) are misled by media. The mental models formed in these circumstances appear to be primarily anthropomorphic. Nass and Moon (2000, p. 86) have examined what they describe as the "fundamental truth" that "the computer is not a person and does not warrant human treatment or attribution" and point out that computers do not have faces or bodies which make them unresponsive to human affect, and do not express emotion themselves. Yet for all of this, there is abundant evidence that people mindlessly (their term) apply social rules and expectations to interactive media. In a series of experiments, they also found that people tend to "overuse human social categories" such as gender and ethnicity, politeness and reciprocity, and behave as though computers have a personality traits, such as friendliness (ibid, p. 82). People have been also been found to use social rules and respond to computers with different voices (Nass and Steuer 1993), to feel psychologically close to or connected with a computer (e.g. Lee and Nass 2005), to respond to computer "personalities" in a similar manner as they respond to human personalities (e.g. Brave et al. 2005), and even to respond to flattery from the computer (e.g. Fogg and Nass 1997). In a similar vein, Turner (2008) have shown that webpages can be reliably distinguished by means of their "personality". This applies beyond screen-based interaction as Marks (2008) found. He reported that people treated their Roomba, a robot vacuum cleaner, socially; they "dressed him [the vacuum cleaner] up, they have also given him a name and gender." While there are fewer studies of this kind than the corresponding classical cognitive accounts, their findings do appear to be robust and reliable.

But, of Course, It Wasn't That Neat

In reviewing the development of cognitive accounts of interaction it is tempting to paint a coherent picture of scholarly endeavour but, of course, it wasn't that neat. There were (at the very least) two more contributions which we should mention before moving on. In the first of these examples we see the "brain is a computer" metaphor taken a step or two further forward and the second says a little about the overlap between cognition and design. Together they illustrate from this diversity in thinking.

Barnard's Interacting Cognitive Subsystems (ICS) is a proposal which, as the name suggests, has us consider cognition operating as a series of subsystems interacting over a "data network" (Barnard 1987). Barnard regards ICS as, in some respects, an extension to the human information processor account of Card and his colleagues and adding significant detail as to the structure of cognition itself without necessarily tying it to a particular psychological theory. The ICS model is different from those accounts we have considered so far in that it was intended to describe the workings of the human information processing system rather than making predictions about task completion. It is based on the assumption that "perception, cognition and action can usefully be analysed in terms of well-defined and discrete information processing modules". Of these, Barnard proposed two sensory subsystems, acoustic and visual; four representational subsystems, morphonolexical (the production of speech), propositional, implicational and object; and two effector subsystems, articulatory and limb. Each subsystem has its own "record structure", and methods for "copying records" both within and across other subsystems. (The information processing flavour of this model is plain to be see.) While there are, of course, a number of questions regarding this model such as the nature and location of the "general data network", there are arguments for a common format of the "data" itself, for example both Prinz (1997) and Hommel et al. (2001) – with their *Theory of Event Coding* (TEC) have argued for a common perception and motor coding.

The second contribution is the Cognitive Dimensions framework developed by Green and his colleagues (Green 1989). This was created as a practical tool for designers based on "cognitively-relevant" properties such as "viscosity" and "premature user commitment". Green writes that the cognitive dimension framework applies to, "notations (such as music, dance, Morse (code) and programming languages), and to all kinds of information-handling devices (spreadsheets, databases, word-processors, and the famously-difficult video cassette recorder or VCR). [...] It is a small vocabulary of about 12 terms which describe aspects that are cognitively-relevant" (Green Web, no date). Here the idea is that the cognitive dimensions are a set of heuristics such as stickiness, viscosity and premature commitment which the designer ought to consider rather than blindly apply (Green and Petre 1996). It should be noted that the evidence supporting the attribution of "cognitive" is a little vague.

1.4 Affordance

An affordance is an invitation do to something which is picked up by our perceptual systems (e.g. Gibson 1977, 1986; Norman 1988; Turvey 1992; Reed 1996; Chemero 2009; Noë 2004; Kaptelinin 2014; Rietveld and Kiverstein 2014 among very many). Examples of affordances include a knife which invites us to use it to cut, or a cup which invites us to drink from it. Affordances have their origin in the Gestalt School of psychology and cannot be described as cognitive phenomena. However, affordance has acquired a great deal of prominence as a concept within HCI, as it is treated as a powerful explanatory device, as a *deus ex machine* and as an inconvenience often in equal measure. While the debate continues as to precisely where affordances are to be found, everyone agrees that are not in our heads which rather rules out classical cognition. Further, there is no broad agreement on what they are or how they work, they are the antithesis of what is normally considered cognitive. There is no mention of affordance in cognitive modelling; and there is little or no mention of affordance in discussions of mental models, yet for all that, they are an unavoidable concept within HCI.

Origins

The Gestaltists working in Europe in the 1920s and 1930s argued that we perceive the function of a thing as quickly as its colour or shape. Gibson quotes Koffka, who publishing in 1935, writes, "Each thing says what it is … a fruit says eat me, water says drink me", Gibson (1986, p. 138). Lewin, again quoted by Gibson, preferred the term *Aufforderung-scharakter* (invitation character). These properties were seen as being phenomenal in nature and not the physical properties of objects – that is, we see directly what these objects are for and how to use them, without having to reason about it. Gibson adopted the term "affordance" to denote the relation between the organism and its environment. "The affordances of the environment are what it offers the animal, what it provides or furnishes, either for good or ill." (Gibson 1986, p. 127). Specifically on tool use, Gibson wrote, "An elongated object, especially, if weighted at one end and graspable at the other, affords hitting or hammering (a club). A graspable object with a rigid sharp edge affords cutting and scraping (a knife)". Further examples of affordances include surfaces that provide support, objects that can be manipulated, substances that can be eaten and other animals that afford interactions of all kinds. Gibson extended the idea to include post boxes which invite posting letters.

Norman (1988) agreed, writing "Affordances provide strong clues to the operations of things. Plates are for pushing. Knobs are for turning. […] When affordances are taken advantage of, the user knows what to do just by looking: no picture, label, or instruction needed." Given the power of affordance it is perhaps unsurprising that Norman sought to adapt this original, direct unlearned formulation of affordance with one which is at one remove, namely *perceived* affordance. He suggested that an individual could be said to perceive the intended behaviour of, say, interface widgets such as sliders and buttons. The intended and perceived behaviours of such widgets are, of course, very simple, including sliding, pressing and rotating leaving him to conclude that "real affordances are not nearly as important as perceived affordances; it is perceived affordances that tell the user what actions can be performed on an object and, to some extent, how to do them" (ibid). He continues, "… the perceived or actual properties of the thing, primarily those fundamental properties that determine just how the thing could possibly be used … A chair affords ('is for') support and therefore affords sitting. A chair can also be carried. Glass is for seeing through, and for breaking."

However, as Kaptelinin (2014) has recently noted, "[it is] a common assumption about affordances is that perceiving them does not usually require much (or even any) learning; an ability to directly understand affordances is something that we all have. Without any instruction we can see that cliffs afford falling off, small stones afford throwing, and chairs afford sitting. The assumed independence of learning has probably been one of the reasons behind the popularity of affordances among designers". However as he goes on to demonstrate, this is a misconception. He observes that most animals are born with limited perceptual and motors skills which then develop in a given ecological niche and it is this leaning we should consider when determining whether or not an animal can pick up an affordance. We simply cannot assume that an individual animal can perceive a given affordance as this ability is (to some extent) a product of their individual development.

Like Gibson, Norman subsequently modified his position on perceived affordances to observe that they are "often more about conventions than about reality" (Norman 1999 p. 124) citing scrollbars as examples of such a convention. While he has remained resolute that perceived affordances are not real affordances this discussion opened the door to the widespread adoption of the term. Affordance can be found across the literature and its use has been expanded well beyond its original formulation.

As affordances are very clearly not cognitive, I am happy to step over them for the moment (aside from a brief mention in the context of HCI) and to suggest that there is a strong case for treating them as an example of thinking with things (Chap. 5) or as a part of the case for enactive cognition (Chap. 6).

1.5   The Cognitive Revolution – A Reprise

It would be easy to dismiss classical cognition as being incomplete, dated, and, if we are honest, occasionally inconsistent. We have described in the preceding pages a number of different approaches, accounts and models and how they were developed for HCI. However it is upon these uncertain foundations that a generation of increasingly usable and accessible technologies have been constructed. It is difficult to imagine the word processor I am using to write this as being as usable as it is without it. So, while it is not without its faults, it has proved itself fit for at least one of its purposes, though whether that continues to be the case has been a central motivation in writing this book.

Offering these words of summary does afford the opportunity to introduce two of the most important critiques of classical cognition, namely, Winograd and Flores' *Understanding Computers and Cognition* (1986) and Dreyfus' (originally, 1972 but the edition referenced here, 1999) *What computers still can't do* (originally published without the "still" in the title).

Winograd and Flores' book has quite rightly been described as ground breaking. Although it is an out-and-out critique of the rationalist tradition in Artificial Intelligence (AI) which had been adopted pretty much wholesale by HCI, we should also note that their book is subtitled, "A new foundation for design". While the book is a trenchant criticism of the treatment of the mind/cognition as a device which can be modelled using symbols and rules, it does propose alternatives. Although their main argument hinges on the importance of what was to become Enaction (see Chap. 7), it was also to introduce the HCI community to the work of Heidegger.

Heidegger

Heidegger's major work – Being and Time (1927/1962) is primarily concerned with the question of being. This is the unanswered question which Descartes posed in his famous, "I think therefore I am". Having established that all he could be certain of was that he was thinking, Descartes fails to discuss the consequences, namely, that he was (the "I am" in his question). Heidegger's reply to this question is to tell us that we-are-in-the-world, not separate from it, not separable from it and to-be-in-the-world is to be involved with it and all it comprises. This, then, is an holistic account as it necessarily abandons any subject-object dualism – which is so prevalent within cognitivism. By addressing the nature of being from this perspective, Heidegger shifts the focus of attention from the theoretical to the practical; from the reflective to the phenomenological; from abstract knowledge to the practical and everyday. So, despite the fact that his approach was philosophical, and specifically, ontological, it is firmly based in the real, everyday world experiences of people.

For Heidegger, all human activity is located in a "web of significance", or "context of equipment" comprising inter-related items of technology which are perceived as being useful. From this reading, we are involved with technology as an inevitable, unavoidable consequence of being-in-the-world. So, being-in-the-world, how do we encounter technology? Dreyfus and Wrathall (2005, p. 4) tell us, "we first encounter worldly things as available", that is, available for use. This availability means that we encounter it *ready-to-hand*. Being available means that it can be used in-order-to [complete tasks], indeed for Heidegger, equipment is essentially something *in-order-to* and this in turn is pretty much equivalent to an affordance. Very neatly Heidegger brings together affordances (which is not a term he used), tools and tasks but tells us that this is not the result of detached reflection but it is simply the way we encounter the world.

In answering the question, "why we are using this technology?", Heidegger replies it is *for-the-sake-of*-something or other. We do things for a purpose and it is this purpose which provides context. So, more fully, Heidegger tells us that we encounter technology as offering possibilities for use (*in-order-to*'s) which we exploit *for-the-sake-of* the tasks we need to complete. What Heidegger has done here is to account for tasks and the purpose behind them and seamlessly linked them to affordance without recourse to cognition or mental representation (or psychology for that matter). Given this, we should not be surprised to find that Heidegger regarded psychology as something which is less direct (less "primordial" to use his expression) than these encounters and which only arises to account for the present-at-hand[1]. We now consider Dreyfus' *What computers still can't do*.

---

[1] We should add at this point that Heidegger's work is generally regarded as pretty much unreadable but the interested reader is directed to Dreyfus' excellent commentary on the former's work *Being-in-the-World: A Commentary on Heidegger's Being and Time, Division I.* We should also note that Heidegger's work also carries a taint: he was a member of the Nazi party and it is perhaps this, as much as anything, which has prevented wider interest in his work.

What Computers Still Can't Do

Dreyfus has contributed more than anyone else to our understanding of Heidegger particularly from the perspectives of cognitive science and artificial intelligence. He is also a longstanding critic of GOFAI – "good old fashioned AI" (e.g. Dreyfus 1991, 1996, 2002), but here we will consider one chapter from probably his most famous book – *What computers still can't do*. This was originally published without the "still" in the title but the passage of time has taken care of this. This is a much revised and reprinted work – the edition used here has several (historic) introductions which collectively run to more than 130 pages alone.

Dreyfus writes that after 50 years of effort that, "it is now clear to all but a few diehards that this attempt to produce general intelligence has failed" (p. *ix*). He continues, that this does not mean that artificial intelligence is not achievable but that the approach which assumes that intelligence is based on "facts and rules" is a dead end and there is no reason to think that it could ever succeed. His book offers a long, complex and tightly argued case against GOFAI which shares many of the same assumption, concepts, and researchers of classical cognition. There are a number of chapters which examine the biological and epistemological assumptions which underlie AI's "persistent optimism" but we will focus on the psychological assumptions.

Dreyfus begins by telling us that he aims his criticisms at the supposed information-processing level of operation of the mind. At this level it is claimed that the mind engages in comparing, classifying, searching and so forth to produce intelligent behaviour. He admits that the mind may indeed process information but there is no reason to suppose that it functions like a digital computer. However much of his argument centres on the word "information". Dreyfus quotes Weaver as follows:

> The word *information*, in this theory, is used in a special sense that must not be confused with its ordinary usage. In particular, *information* must not be confused with meaning. In fact, two messages, one of which is heavily loaded with meaning and the other of which is pure nonsense, can be exactly equivalent, from the point of view, as regards information. It is this, undoubtedly, that Shannon means when he says that "the semantic aspects of communication are irrelevant to the engineering aspects.

For Dreyfus, this unjustified transformation of information into meaning, carries with it the presumption that the theory and language of computing and with this the assertion that experience can be analysed into "isolable, atomic, alternative choices" (Dreyfus, p. 165). We will consider one further example before we leave Dreyfus and it is when he takes issue with the language used by Miller, Neisser and Fodor. In particular he dislikes the following sentence, which he claims one can find on almost every page of their work, "When an *organism executes* a Plan *he* proceeds step by step, completing one part and then moving to the next" (italics in the original). Dreyfus analysis of this is as follows, " … *organism* [biological] *executes* [machine analogy borrowed from a human agent] a Plan *he* [the human agent] …". He characterises this sentence as "the organism being personified" or the "mind mechanized" (ibid, 179). He describes these sentiments as "bizarre" and "gibber-ish" and revealing of "serious underlying conceptual confusion" (*ibid*). He con-cludes this chapter on the psychological assumptions underpinning AI (and HCI) by suggesting that there is quite a simple test of whether the mind works like a com-puter and it is this – if an intelligent machine can be created which works on these principles then we can gauge its likelihood by considering the actual achievements within the field. On the basis of this Dreyfus concludes that the most plausible answer seems to be, "No" (p. 187).

1.6   In Conclusion

We began this chapter with the recognition that cognition had become the dominant paradigm within post-war psychology and that it had adopted a human-information processing perspective. We have seen how researchers sought to deconstruct tasks into manageable atoms of behaviour, knowledge or skill and to recombine them to predict a user's performance at the user interface. These cognitive models were complemented by task analytic account telling us about the context in which our cognition was at work. We should also remember that although the task is central to both approaches it is (generally) neither justified nor defined. In parallel with this we have seen the use of various forms of mental models, which emphasize mental content, as an alternative. And there is the small matter of affordances which, despite being so important within HCI, feature in neither cognitive nor mental mod-els or, for that matter in task analysis. Finally, we considered the apparently uncon-troversial notion of human information processing only to find that philosophers find the very idea of it ridiculous. Classical cognition supposes that our use of tech-nology is mediated by a plan or model which we either execute or use to guide our actions to achieve our goals. However, while we may have created models of cogni-tion in action for HCI, there are no corresponding models of technology – so we have only been dealing with the first half of HCI. In addition to having neglected the issue of technology, context has not received its due attention. We cannot locate context in many of these models. In all, this all seems a very long way from solving the problems faced by a user of interactive technology. As we have described it so far, HCI is very much a product of the cognitive revolution of the 1950s and 1960s. The next chapter describes quite a different approach to the same problems.

References

Abdulin E (2011) Using the keystroke-level model for designing user interface on middle-sized touch screens. CHI'11 extended abstracts on human factors in computing systems. ACM, New York. pp 673–686

Anderson JR, Bower GH (1973) Human associative memory. Winston & Sons, Washington, DC

Barnard PJ (1987) Cognitive resources and the learning of human-computer dialogs. In: Carroll JM (ed) Interfacing thought: cognitive aspects of human-computer interaction. MIT Press, Cambridge, MA

Borgmann A (1984) Technology and the character of contemporary life. The University of Chicago Press, Chicago

Brave S, Nass CI, Hutchinson K (2005) Computers that care: investigating the effects of orientation of emotion exhibited by an embodied computer agent. Int J Hum-Comput Stud 62(2):161–178

Broadbent D (1958) Perception and communication. Pergamon Press, London

Chemero A (2009) Radical embodied cognitive science. MIT Press, Cambridge, MA

Chomsky NA (1959) A review of Skinner's verbal behavior. Language 35(1):26–58

Craik K (1943) The nature of explanation. Cambridge University Press, Cambridge

Cunningham L, Kirkscey R, Reynolds-Dyk A, Small N, Tran C, Tucker V (2015) Rhetorical grounding and an Agile attitude: complex systems, multi-genre testing, and service learning in UX. J Usability Stud 10(4):182–194

Diaper D (2004) Understanding task analysis for human-computer interaction. In: Diaper D, Stanton NA (eds) The handbook of task analysis for human-computer interaction. Lawrence Erlbaum Associates, Mahwah

Dreyfus HL (1991) Being-in-the-world: a commentary on Heidegger's being and time, division I. MIT Press, Cambridge, MA

Dreyfus HL (1996) The current relevance of Merleau-Ponty's phenomenology of embodiment. Electron J Anal Philos 4 (Spring 1996)

Dreyfus H (2002) Intelligence without representation – Merleau-Ponty's critique of mental representation the relevance of phenomenology to scientific explanation. Phenomenol Cogn Sci 1(4):367–383

Dreyfus HL, Wrathall MA (2005) Introduction. In: Dreyfus HL, Wrathall MA (eds) A companion to Heidegger. Blackwell Publishing, Malden

El Batran K, Dunlop MD (2014) Enhancing KLM (keystroke-level model) to fit touch screen mobile devices. In: MobileHCI'14: proceedings of the 16th international conference on human-computer interaction with mobile devices & services, ACM Press, New York, pp 283–286

Fitts PM (1954) The information capacity of the human motor system in controlling the amplitude of movement. J Exp Psychol 47(6):381–391

Fogg BJ, Nass C (1997) Silicon sycophants: the effects of computers that flatter. Int J Hum Comput Stud 46:551–561

Gentner D, Gentner DR (1983) Flowing water or teeming crowds: models of electricity. In: Gentner D, Stevens A (eds) Mental models. Lawrence Erlbaum Associates, Hillsdale

Gentner D, Stevens A (eds) (1983) Mental models. Lawrence Erlbaum Ass, Hillsdale

Gibson JJ (1977) The theory of affordances. In: Shaw R, Bransford J (eds) Perceiving, acting and knowing. Wiley, New York, pp 67–82

Gibson JJ (1986) The ecological approach to visual perception. Houghton Mifflin, Boston

Green TRG (1989) Cognitive dimensions of notations. In: Sutcliffe A, Macaulay L (eds) People and computers V. Cambridge University Press, Cambridge, pp 443–460

Green TRG, Petre M (1996) Usability analysis of visual programming environments: a 'cognitive dimensions' framework. J Vis Lang Comput 7(2):131–174

Hackos JT, Redish JC (1998) User and task analysis for interface design. Wiley, New York

Heidegger M (1927/1962) Being and time. (trans: Macquarrie J, Robinson E). Harper Collins, New York

Hommel B, Müsseler J, Aschersleben G, Prinz W (2001) The Theory of Event Coding (TEC): a framework for perception and action planning. Behav Brain Sci 24:849–937

Huang J, Cakmak M (2015) Supporting mental model accuracy in trigger-action programming. In: Proceedings of the 2015 ACM international joint conference on pervasive and ubiquitous computing, ACM Press, New York, pp 215–225

Jelbert SA, Taylor AH, Cheke LG, Clayton NS, Gray RD (2014) Using the Aesop's fable paradigm to investigate causal understanding of water displacement by New Caledonian crows. PLoS ONE 9(3):e92895. doi:10.1371/journal.pone.0092895

John BE (2003) Information processing and skilled behaviour. In: Carroll JM (ed) HCI models, theories and frameworks. Morgan Kaufmann, San Francisco

John BE, Kieras DE (1996) The GOMS family of user interface analysis techniques: comparison and contrast. ACM Trans Comput-Hum Interact (TOCHI) 3(4):320–351

Johnson RD, Marakas GM, Palmer JW (2008) Beliefs about the social roles and capabilities of computing technology: development of the computing technology continuum of perspective. Behav Inform Technol 27(2):169–181

Johnson-Laird PN (1983) Mental models: towards a cognitive science of language, inference, and consciousness. Cambridge University Press, Cambridge

Kieras DE, Polson PG (1985) An approach to the formal analysis of user complexity. Int J Man Mach Stud 22:365–394

Lee KM, Nass C (2005) Social-psychological origins of feelings of presence: creating social presence with machine-generated voices. Media Psychol 7:31–45

Lindsay PH, Norman DA (1972) Human information processing: an introduction to psychology. Academic, London

Luo L, John BE (2005) Predicting task execution time on handheld devices using the keystroke-level model. In: Proceedings of the SIGCHI conference on human factors in computing systems (CHI2005), Portland. ACM, New York, April 2–7

Marks P (2008) The rise of the emotional robot. New Scientist Magazine, April 2008, 24–25

McCloskey M, Caramazza A, Green B (1980) Curvilinear motion in the absence of external forces: Naïve beliefs about the motions of objects. Science 210:1139–1141

Miller GA (2003) The cognitive revolution: a historical perspective. Trends Cogn Sci 7(3):141–144

Miller GA, Galanter E, Pribram KH (1960) Plans and the structure of behavior. Holt, New York

Moggridge W (2007) Designing interactions. MIT Press, Cambridge, MA

Murrell KFH (1965) Ergonomics – man in his working environment. Chapman and Hall, London

Nass C, Moon Y (2000) Machines and mindlessness: social responses to computers. J Soc Issues 56(1):81–103

Nass C, Steuer J (1993) Voices, boxes, and sources of messages. Hum Commun Res 19(4):504–527

Neisser U (1967) Cognitive psychology. Appleton, New York

Nersessian NJ (2008) Creating scientific concepts. MIT Press, Cambridge, MA

Newell A, Simon HA (1976) Computer science as empirical enquiry: symbols and search. Commun ACM 19(3):113–126

Noë A (2004) Action in perception. MIT Press, Cambridge, MA

Norman DA (1983) Some observations on mental models. Ment Model 7(112):7–14

Norman DA (1988) The psychology of everyday things. Doubleday, New York

Norman DA (1999) Affordance, conventions, and design. Interactions 6(3):38–43

Payne SJ (1991) A descriptive study of mental models. Behav Inform Technol 10(1):3–21

Payne SJ (2003) Users' mental models: the very ideas. In: Carroll JM (ed) HCI models, theories and frameworks: toward a multidisciplinary science. Morgan Kaufmann, San Francisco, pp 135–156

Payne SJ, Green TRG (1986) Task-action grammars: a model of the mental representation of task languages. Hum-Comput Interact 2(2):93–133

Payne SJ, Squibb HR, Howes A (1990) The nature of device models: the yoked state space hypothesis and some experiments with text editors. Hum-Comput Interact 5:415–444

Pettitt M, Burnett G, Stevens A (2007) An extended keystroke level model (KLM) for predicting the visual demand of in-vehicle information systems. In: Proceedings of the SIGCHI conference on human factors in computing systems (CHI'07). ACM Press, New York, pp 1515–1524

Pinelle D, Gutwin C, Greenberg S (2002) Task analysis for groupware usability evaluation: modeling shared-workspace tasks with the mechanics of collaboration. ACM Trans Comput-Hum Interact (TOCHI) 10(4):281–311

Prinz W (1997) Perception and action planning. Eur J Cogn Psychol 9:129–154

Reed ES (1996) Encountering the world: toward an ecological psychology. Oxford University Press, Oxford

Rietveld E, Kiverstein J (2014) The rich landscape of affordances. Ecol Psychol 26(4):325–352

Rips LJ (1986) Mental muddles. In: Brand M, Harnish RM (eds) The representation of knowledge and belie. University of Arizona Press, Tucson, pp 258–286

Rouse WB, Morris NM (1986) On looking into the black box: prospects and limits for mental models. Psychol Bull 100(3):349–363

Rumelhart DE, McClelland JL (1986) Parallel distributed processing, vols 1 & 2. Bradford Books, Cambridge, MA

Simon HA (1969) The sciences of the artificial. MIT Press, Cambridge, MA

Skinner BF (1957) Verbal behavior. Copley Publishing Group, Acton

Song K, Johoon K, Cho Y-H, Lee A, Ryu H, Choi J-W, Lee YJ (2013) The fingerstroke-level model strikes back: a modified keystroke-level model in developing a gaming UI for 4g networks. CHI '13 extended abstracts on human factors in computing systems. ACM Press, New York, pp 2359–2362

Tolman EC (1948) Cognitive maps in rats and men. In: Downs RM, Stea D (eds) Image and environment, cognitive mapping and spatial behaviour. Edward Arnold, Chicago, pp 27–50

Turing AM (1950) Computing machinery and intelligence. Mind 59:433–460

Turner P (2008) Towards an account of intuitiveness. Behav Inform Technol 27(6):1–8

Turner P, Wilson L, Turner S (2009) Do web pages have personalities? In: Proceedings of the 2009 European conference on cognitive ergonomics. ACM Press, New York, pp 62–70

Turvey MT (1992) Affordances and prospective control: an outline of the ontology. Ecol Psychol 4:173–187

Wickens CD, Hollands JG (2000) Engineering psychology and human performance, 3rd edn. Prentice Hall, Upper Saddle River

Winograd T, Flores F (1986) Understanding computers and cognition. Ablex, Norwood

Young RM (1983) Surrogates and mappings: two kinds of conceptual models of interactive devices. In: Gentner D, Stevens AL (eds) Mental models. Lawrence Erlbaum Ass, Hillsdale, pp 35–52

Web Resources

Fitts PM, Jones RE (1947) Psychological aspects of instrument display. Analysis of 270 "pilot-error" experiences in reading and interpreting aircraft instruments (Report No. TSEAA-694-12A). Dayton: Aero Medical Laboratory, Air Materiel Command, U.S. Air Force. Available from www.dtic.mil/cgi-bin/GetTRDoc?AD=ADA800143

Kaptelinin V (2014) Affordances. In: Soegaard M, Dam RF (eds) The encyclopaedia of human-computer interaction, 2nd edn. Interaction Design Foundation. https://www.interaction-design.org/literature/book/the-encyclopedia-of-human-computer-interaction-2nd-ed/affordances. Last accessed 27 Apr 2016

Kennedy JF (1961) Available from http://www.jfklibrary.org/JFK/JFK-Legacy/NASA-Moon-Landing.aspx

Shortcliffe EH (1976) Computer based medical consultation. Elsevier, New York. Available from http://people.dbmi.columbia.edu/~ehs7001/Shortliffe-1976/MYCIN%20thesis%20Book.htm. Last retrieved 29 July 2015

Chapter 2
Mediated Cognition

To be able to analyse such complex interactions and relationships, a theoretical account of the constituent elements of the system under investigation is needed ... Activity Theory a strong candidate for such a unit of analysis in the concept of object-oriented, collective and culturally mediated human activity. (Engeström and Miettinen 1999, p. 9)

2.1 Introduction

In this chapter we will consider Activity Theory and we will do so from the perspective of *tool mediation*. Although ostensibly Activity Theory addresses the same issues as classical cognition, it really is quite different and this is largely attributable to its complex origins. Engeström (1999) has observed that its aetiology is three-fold. Firstly, he identifies the contribution of classical German philosophy ranging from Kant to Hegel; secondly, the political writings of Marx and Engels and finally, the cultural-historical psychology of Vygotski, Leont'ev and Luria (the so called "Vygostskian" school). This is a heady mix of Continental thought which stands in sharp contrast to the Anglo-Saxon tradition of classical cognition. Engeström laments, parenthetically, that the contribution from Marxist thought is often lost in modern treatments and we should also remember that Stalin suppressed the publication of Vygostki's work for the two decade after his premature death. Indeed, Activity Theory was not well known in the West before the 1980s so it was aptly described by Engeström and Miettinen (1999) as "a well kept secret". Just to add to this complexity, the name Activity Theory itself is something of a misnomer as it is not a theory, in the sense that it is not falsifiable or predictive in character, instead it is a conceptual framework and vocabulary for describing human purposive behaviour – or activity.

The work of Vygotski and his colleagues still lie at the heart of Activity Theory, and their contribution is the observation that human behaviour is a matter of historical development and not a product of evolution or biology. These historical

© Springer International Publishing Switzerland 2016
P. Turner, *HCI Redux*, Human–Computer Interaction Series,
DOI 10.1007/978-3-319-42235-0_2

Fig. 2.1 The basic mediation triangle

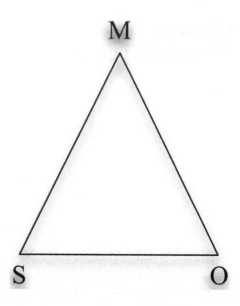

developments, in turn, rely on tools. Luria (1928), in what has been described as the first English language publications of the Vygotskian school, writes, "Man differs from animals in that he can make and use tools" and he continues, "… the tools used by man not only radically change his condition of existence, they even react on him in that they effect a change in him and his psychic condition". This places tool mediation at the heart of our actions, behaviour, and cognition.

Luria (1928, p. 495) places the first appearance of tools in the hands of children when he writes, "instead of applying directly its natural function to the solution to a particular task, the child puts between that function and that task a certain auxiliary means … by the medium of which the child manages to perform the task".

The importance of tool mediation in Activity Theory is thus revealed – it is species wide, it is central to just about everything we do, we begin to use tools in childhood and this use is not simply a matter of achieving our ends but we should recognise the ability of tools to "change our minds" – quite literally. And all of this is usually and remarkably represented as a simple triangle, thus (Fig. 2.1).

The triangle comprises a subject or subjects (s), an object (o) and a mediating tool (m). Unmediated functions (s-o) are represented along the base of the triangle, and examples of these tend to be very simple and often biological – digesting food comes to mind. Just about everything else, the arguments goes, is mediated and this is easy to recognise when we appreciate that tools are not limited to physical artefacts like hammers but include "psychological" tools such as language which Clark has described as "the ultimate artefact" (Clark 1997a, b) – please see Chap. 6.

Despite the remarkable power of this simple triad, Leont'ev (1981) was to extend this, as it failed to account for the social (collective) nature of most of our endeavours. This was to be further elaborated by Engeström (1987). The extended triangle, which is by no means a universally popular form of representation for an activity, adds community, division of labour and praxis to the original formulation.

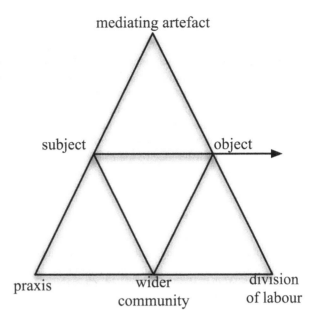

Fig. 2.2 An (extended) activity triangle

Community should be understood as standing for all other groups with a stake in the activity which, of course, can be potentially very large. The division of labour is the recognition of "horizontal" and "vertical" lines of division of responsibilities and power within any activity. Finally, there is praxis which is a neat way of representing the great array of formal and informal rules and social and cultural norms which govern the relationships between yje subjects and the wider community for a given activity. As we can see this is a very "broad-brush" approach. These relationships are illustrated here (Fig. 2.2).

Since the 1980s Activity Theory has moved beyond the specialist scholar to be embraced by researchers in disciplines as diverse as human computer interaction, cultural psychology, computer supported cooperative working, information systems and, of course, pedagogy. As a consequence of this dissemination, Activity Theory was quite readily identified as a potential theoretical framework for HCI (e.g. Bødker and Bannon 1991; Kuutti 1996) and within this community a number of key players have been responsible for both developing and promoting it. Bødker (1991) and Kuutti (1991) have broadly, but not exclusively, established a Scandinavian perspective with a focus on user-centred and participative design, while Bannon (1991), Grudin (1990), Kaptelinin (1996), Nardi (1996b), Engeström (1999) and others have made significant contributions to Activity Theory's acceptance and uptake within HCI. The appearance of Nardi's *Context and Consciousness* (1996a, b) brought Activity Theory to the attention of many within HCI and it remains a particularly important collection. Finally, Activity Theory should very much be seen as a continuing project as, for example, Bødker's recent work on artefact ecologies demonstrates its continued relevance to new and emerging fields within HCI. We now examine the anatomy of an activity.

2.2   Object-Orientedness

The principle of object-orientedness is one of the most important in Activity Theory; it is also said to be the most difficult to articulate. Leont'ev (1978, p. 4) tells us that "The basic, constituent feature of activity is that it has an object. In fact, the very concept of activity (doing, Tätigkeit) implies the concept of the object of activity. The expression "objectless activity" has no meaning at all". Kozulin (1986) underlines this by telling us that, "the main thing which distinguishes one activity from another [...] is the difference of their objects".

Object as Objective

The simplest understanding of the object of an activity is that it is held by the subject, motivates and gives it direction (Leont'ev 1974). The object is the need or desire to which the activity is directed. Christiansen (1996) uses the term "objectified motive" and Nardi (1996a) writes of it as the *object* of the "object lesson" or the "object of the game". However, objects are not fixed but can be transformed in the course of the execution of an activity.

Object as Intentionality

Perhaps a more sophisticated understanding of an activity's object is it that refers to an activity's intentionality. Intentionality refers to the about-ness or directed-ness of many of our mental and bodily states. An activity is intentional in that it is about something. This may seem an entirely obvious observation but it is conspicuously absent in, say, the description of a task. The concept of intentionality can be traced back to the philosophical writings of St. Thomas Aquinas, who introduced the concept in the thirteenth century, by recognising that most of our mental states (including attitudes, beliefs and emotions) are directed towards things and events in the world. Brentano (1874) revived the idea when he defined intentionality as the main characteristic of mental phenomena (i.e. as a "mark of the mental") and the means by which they could be distinguished from physical phenomena. In much the same vein but more recently Searle has written, "Intentionality is that property of many mental states and events by which they are directed at or about or of objects and states of affairs in the world" (1983, p. 1).

Leont'ev writes of this in the following (fairly obscure) way when he tells us that the object appears in two forms: first, in its independent existence, commanding the activity of the subject, and second, as the mental image of the object, as the product of the subject's "detection" of its properties, which is effected by the activity of the subject and cannot be effected otherwise". To understand this we must recognise that Activity Theory is a materialist account which recognises that human beings live in an objective reality which gives rise to subjective phenomena, a consequence of which is that an activity's intentionality is necessarily bi-directional. While every activity is oriented towards something in the real world it must also be pointing back to the person or persons who gave rise to it. As Kaptelinin (2005, p. 5) puts it, "The object of activity has a dual status; it is both a projection of human mind onto the objective world and a projection of the world onto human mind". Kaptelinin continues that this bi-directionality anchors and contextualises subjective phenomena in the objective world. So, "Instead of being a collection of 'mental processes' the human mind emerges as biased, striving for meaning and value, suffering and rejoicing, failing and hoping, alive, real. On the other hand, the world is no longer just a collection of physical bodies, organizational structures, and so forth, but a place full of meaning and value, a place that can be comfortable or dangerous, restricting or supporting, beautiful or ugly, or (as it is often the case) all of these at the same time" (*ibid*).

From Kaptelinin's description we can see that there are very clear similarities between the definition of an Activity's object and what Merleau-Ponty calls the "intentional arc" which he describes as the means by which we are bound to the world. Dreyfus (2002) offers a clearer definition of this when he describes the intentional arc as the tight connection between the agent and the world. He writes that, for example, as the agent acquires skills, these are not held as mental representations but as "dispositions to respond to the solicitations of situations in the world". This again emphasizes the bi-directional quality of an activity's object.

2.3   The Structure and Dynamics of an Activity

The extended triangle representation we considered above is only a partial representation of an activity, indeed, it might be better thought of as a nexus, existing as it does in a continuum of development and learning while at the same time masking its internal structure.

An activity is realised by a collection or aggregation of behaviours called *actions*. An action is similar to a task in that it is directed at achieving a particular goal, except that it is always mediated by an artefact or tool. Actions, in turn, have their own fine grain internal structure as they are executed by means of unconscious *operations*. Although this is quite hierarchical in structure, an activity is not fixed as it may be flexibly reconfigured as a consequence of learning, context or both. Table 2.1 is reproduced from Bødker and Klokmose 2012, p. 202, illustrates these relationships.

By way of example, it is something of a convention to consider how people learn to drive a motorcar at this point in the discussion. The object of the activity is likely to be quite complex and might include the need to be able to drive to work; to take the family on holiday or to participate in an armed robbery. The activity is realised by means of an aggregation of actions (i.e. taking driving lessons; obtaining a car;

Table 2.1 The structure of an activity

Levels of activity	Mental representation	Realises	Level of description	Analytical question
Activity	Motive – not necessarily conscious	Personality	The social and personal meaning of activity …	Why?
Action	Goal – under conscious control	Activities (systems of actions organised to achieve goals)	Possible goals, critical goals, particularly relevant sub-goals	What?
Operation	Conditions of actions – normally not under conscious control	Actions (chains of operations organised by goals and concrete conditions)	The concrete way of executing an action in accordance with the specific conditions surrounding the goal	How?

Fig. 2.3 The activity hierarchy

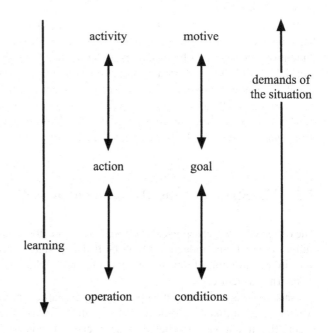

buying petrol and so on). These individual actions in their turn are realised by a set of operations – (i.e. steering, indicating at junctions, changing gear and so forth). This, of course, is very much a static account of the activity whereas humans are constantly learning with practice, so when first presented with the intricacies of the gear-stick (manual gear shift) it is likely that the process of disengaging the engine, shifting gear and re-engaging the engine are under conscious control. With practice this becomes automatic and unconscious. Unless, of course, circumstances demand otherwise. If the driver were to find themselves driving in icy conditions, gear changing and braking may become more consciously controlled and with it a shift in our attention depending upon the competence of the driver. In such circumstances our attention becomes focused at the level demanded by that context (Fig. 2.3).

The Dynamics of an Activity

While Activity Theory differentiates between internal and external activities it also emphasize their inter-relatedness, so internal activities cannot be understood independently of external activities (and vice versa). Further, Bertelsen and Bødker (2003) tell us not to assume a fixed separation between these representations as they are prone to mutual transformation (and swap places) with each other.

Internalisation is the transformation of external activities into internal ones and in doing so it provides a means for people to practice, rehearse, simulate and generally try out potential interactions with the real world without committing to them. These internal states might include make-believe and various forms of "what-if" thinking. In turn, externalisation is the process by which internal activities become externalised which is often necessary when an internalized action needs to be coordinated between people. For Vygotski, internalisation-externalisation is a key mechanism in a child's cultural development, writing "Every function in the child's cultural development appears twice: first, on the social level, and later, on the individual level; first, between people (inter-psychological) and then inside the child (intra-psychological). This applies equally to voluntary attention, to logical memory, and to the formation of concepts. All the higher functions originate as actual relationships between individuals".

For such an important mechanism, Activity Theory offers only relatively few examples of internalisation-externalisation. We are invited to consider, for example, mental arithmetic which can be thought of as internalised "counting on our fingers". The external counting on our fingers, which a child learns, is internalised with practice but if this becomes too demanding, it may be externalised by prompting the child to use pencil and paper or, more likely, resort to the calculator on her mobile phone.

Development

Activity Theory is perhaps unique among accounts of how we use technology in placing such a strong emphasis on the role of learning. The most famous aspect of this is Vygotski's "zone of proximal development" (ZPD). He defines this as, "The distance between the actual development level as determined by independent problem solving and the level of potential development as determined through problem solving under adult guidance or in collaboration with more capable peers" (1978, p. 88). Consider a child trying to tie her shoe laces (I suppose I should update this to "downloading an app"). We can imagine the struggle she might have if this challenge were a little beyond her abilities. Naturally she turns to a parent or teacher to help. We might expect the adult to demonstrate the process, or guide the child through the process with a running dialogue ("left over right"). Later when the child needs to retie a loose lace she can repeat what she was instructed but this time to herself. The public language of the adult, having been successfully internalised, now functions to guide behaviour. Vygotski has argued, using examples such as this, that the use of public language has profound effects on cognitive development.

The ZPD is not merely a product of child-adult relationships as it is always with us. Every time we ask for help from a more skilled, knowledgeable, or for that matter, the nearest available person, we can see this mechanism at work. Indeed when we fail to cope with a situation or technology, we do not simply experience an all or nothing breakdown, instead we rely on epistemic[1] nudges to allow us to continue to engage with the technology.

This is can be seen in the following example (a form of which I have quoted elsewhere – Turner 2013). I witnessed a pair of young backpackers at the Centraal railway station in Amsterdam trying to use a left luggage locker. They selected the picture of the British flag on the system's user interface and the display was promptly rendered into English. The instructions told them to choose a locker of the appropriate size, put the luggage inside, close the door, insert money (or credit card) and then wait for a receipt. The receipt providing the number they would need to unlock the locker and retrieve their luggage. This sequence is a familiar one and from a usability perspective the sequence was clearly logical. However for these backpackers, the situation appeared to be fraught and uncertain. However within a few seconds the situation was resolved by the pair asking a nearby user of the system whether it was "ok". He replied,"*Yeah, it's ok*".

The concept of the ZPD has been widely accepted by educationalists but has also been adopted by those who see this as the basis of scaffolding – please see Chap. 5. More recently, Engeström (1987) has proposed expansive learning, which for some, marks the appearance of the third "generation" of Activity Theory. Engeström has demonstrated the applicability of expansive learning with its cycles of internalisation, questioning, reflection and externalisation in the development of activities in a variety of domains (Engeström 1990, 1999; Engeström et al. 1997). The drivers for these expansive cycles of learning and development he calls contradictions – an explicitly Marxist concept – which arise within and between activities. While this is something of a departure from Vygotski, it has proved of interest to information scientists and CSCW researchers.

2.4 Mediation

The artefactual world into which children are born contains the accumulated knowledge of our species. Harari (2014, p. 48) writes "Over the course of his or her life, a typical member of a modern affluent society will own several million artefacts – from cars and houses to disposable nappies and milk cartons. There's hardly an activity, a belief or even an emotion that is not mediated by objects of our

---

[1] In this instance, the contribution of a little "know that" to our "know how". We pick up on the epistemic in more detail in Chap. 7.

own devising." He goes on to suggest that our eating habits, play, romantic and sexual relations and religions are all comfortably defined as examples of mediated behaviour.

Artefacts are created by people to mediate and, to an extent, control their own behaviour. These have been are developed over time and are local to the community which created them, so that they have an historical and cultural lineage. Modes of acting within an activity system may be realised or crystallized into artefacts – "Artifacts can be characterized as "crystallised" knowledge, which means that operations that are developed in the use of one generation of technology are later incorporated into the artefact in the next" (Bannon and Bødker 1991, p. 342). Wartofsky (1979, p. 205) has also observed that, "the artefact is to cultural evolution what a *gene* is to biological evolution." Cole (1996) adds that artefacts embody their own "developmental histories" which is a reflection of their use, i.e. these artefacts have been manufactured or produced and continue to be used as part of, and in relation to, intentional human actions. Cole stresses another aspect of tool mediation and this is with respect to the affordances they offer. He identifies, for example, the affordance offered by a variety of mediating artefacts including the personal histories of recovering alcoholics in AA meeting (affording rehabilitation), patients' medical charts in a hospital setting (afford access to a patient's medical history), and poker chips (inviting gambling). Sellen and Harper (2002) have written in detail of the affordances of paper in an office setting which include reading, offering easy navigation through a [paper] document; one being able to read more than one document at once; and writing notes upon/annotating; ease of filing; portability; joint viewing and so forth. (Please see Sect. 2.5 for a different view of "affordances").

Vygotski (1930) recognised the importance of tool mediation and was the first to offer an extended definition of tools to include language, algebraic symbolism, works of art and writing. He distinguished between what he calls "psychological tools" from the "means-to-an-end" variety of tools such as hammers and garden furniture. He writes that psychological tools are artificial, social "formations", not individual devices and tells us that they are directed toward the mastery of [mental] processes – one's own or someone else's. Of these tools, language is the most important and as they are intrinsic to our behaviour, their use modifies our cognition.

As we have seen, one of the great insights offered by Activity Theory is that most of what we do is mediated and the substance of this mediation is artefactual – the product of human, purposive endeavour which has, and which continues to develop over time. So cognition, for example, can only be understood with respect to this cultural – historical mediation. Cole and Engeström (1993, p. 9) have very conveniently created a list of the key issues with respect to this mediation. We offer an edited summary of their work (we preserve their numbering):

1. The naturally occurring psychological functions we share with the great apes are different in kind to those which are the product of "tools and rules";
2. Tool mediation has created a structure for the human mind. It has also shaped the ways in which we use the tools themselves;
3. Tool mediation is bi-directional and modifies both mind and environment;

4. Tools are both material and "symbolic". The master tool is language.
5. The benefits of tool mediation are transmitted culturally from one generation to another.
6. The historical effects of tool mediation are with us in the present and are a species-specific mode of development.
7. Tool mediation highlights the importance of the social, again because this is the medium of transmission for these developments.

As we can see, Activity Theorists are at pains to underline our intimacy with tools.

Functional Organs

Finally, Kaptelinin (1996) writes of the *two interface boundary problem* which arises with the use of tools. He points out that there is a boundary/interface between (i) the user *and* her computer and (ii) the user and her computer *and* the world. He tells us that Activity Theory has provided a means to reason about this in the concept of the "functional organ". Leont'ev coined this term to describe, "functionally integrated, goal-oriented, configurations of internal and external resources". External tools function to support and complement human abilities which, when working in concert, are more effective. He gives examples of notebooks enhancing memory and eyeglasses enhancing sight (*ibid*, p50). When the use of these external tools is well integrated they are experienced as a property of that person, though they are experienced as separate while we are learning to use them.

Kaptelinin tells us that these original observations about tools also apply to digital technology and writes that a problem within HCI lies with integrating these technologies into functional organs. He suggests that an integrated technology has the potential to be a *transparent technology*. He also notes that computers are a special form of tool which are not limited to a single, fixed function and because of this they can give rise to a special kind of functional organ. In this instances, he is writing of the IPA – the inner plane of action. The IPA is said to arise during child development and provides for a new form of interaction between internal and external activities. Initially, a child only has control over things in the external world as a consequence of an action and feedback loop. Through the processes of internalisation-externalisation which transform external activities into internal ones, the child acquires the ability to perform or rehearse some of these activities in their "mind's eye" – or IPA. This, of course, has significant advantages in rehearsing or considering a plan of action in the real world without committing to it with all of the unfortunate consequences that might attract. Finally, we note that technology often supports the IPA in exploring the what-if (*cf.* the what-if analysis functions in spreadsheets or the print preview facilities in word processors).

We conclude this brief introduction to Activity Theory with an illustration of its power to provide the necessary concepts to explain intriguing and problematic issues in HCI. We offer an alternative treatment of affordance.

2.5   Affordance – Soviet Style

It should be noted that the author published "Affordance as Context" which appeared in the journal Interacting with Computers, in 2005. This chapter, like the paper before it, draws heavily on Bakhurst's excellent commentary on the work of Ilyenkov where he makes a difficult topic, lucid (1991).

Ilyenkov has offered a materialist account of an interesting non-material phenomena, namely, significances. Significances closely resemble affordances but are collective rather than individual. Ilyenkov begins by identifying two classes of non-material phenomena namely: mental phenomena such as thoughts, beliefs and feelings and phenomena that are neither material nor mental such as meaning and values, an example of which might be goodness. It is this second class which are of interest which he calls ideal. Ilyenkov then considers how we might account for them. One account might argue that such ideal phenomena are external to us individually, for examples, religions often present their teachings such as the importance of charity as 'God-given'. Alternatively, we could argue that these phenomena are product of human nature and have no independent existence. But there is a third possibility, as Ilyenkov proposes a dialectic position arguing that a thing can be *objective* without being *independent* of us. He reasons that we have idealised the world, that is, endowed it with meaning and in so doing we also endow it with properties that come to exist completely independently of us. These properties are the product of our labour and are not defined by nature. (Ilyenkov, 1977). Indeed we have seen reference to this already when we recognised that artefacts are "crystallised actions". These established ideal phenomena are objective but as to the independence from an individual mind, the key is the word "individual" rather than "mind". The ideal exists in the collective not the individual mind – a concept reminiscent of distributed cognition (Chap. 5) and it is also quite *meme*-like (Dawkins, 1976). So our social lives are a product of the dealings with others, experienced individually as a formal – informal set of rules, practices, tools and artefacts. We, individually, grow up among pre-existing and apparently objective phenomena. From this perspective human development can be seen as the process of becoming enculturated into this objectified, historically developed world. Ilyenkov offers a specific example of this: ancient mariners saw the stars as a pre-existing navigational aid, while priests regarded them as pre-existing guides to future events (astrology). These interpretations, that is, the need to find one's way at sea or the need to predict future events, were subsequently attached to the stars as the result of their incorporation into human activity.

Ilyenkov (1977) describes the creation of artefacts as a further illustration of how ideal properties could be held to exist objectively in the world. He uses the example of a table. A table is part of objective reality and yet can be distinguished from a block of wood because it has been objectified by the human activity responsible for shaping it. Indeed, this is how we distinguish wood from tables. Wood itself affords a variety of uses, for example, burning, throwing, shaping, trading and so forth, but through purposive use it acquires significance. So, for example, shaping a block of wood into a pair of clogs, endows the clogs with the significances of working footwear, or as a souvenir, or as a means of looking ridiculous when worn with socks. In a sense, these significances make a thing knowable. For Ilyenkov, nothing about the physical nature of a thing in itself explains how it is possible that it can be knowable and it is perhaps this point which allows us to distinguish between significance and affordance. In order to be knowable some significance has to be attached to the thing through the process of the object's incorporation into the sphere of human activity. This is not necessarily true of an affordance – particularly simple affordances. The ideal properties of an artefact represent to the individual a reification or embodiment of the practices of the human community that has historically developed the thing. In other words, objects acquire this ideal content not as the result of being accessed by an individual mind, but by the historically developing activities of communities of practice.

Activity Theory as a Theory of HCI

Activity Theory is complex, demanding and occasionally obscure, but it is remarkably comprehensive and coherent. As we noted earlier, Activity Theory has been proposed by a number of people as a platform or theory for HCI and we can but agree. It not only offers its own version of task analysis and cognitive modelling which parallel that of classical cognition but it does so while recognising that cognition is tool mediated. Further, its treatment of mediation is not confined to physical artefacts such as hammers or keyboards or Photoshop® but also includes psychological tools too. Activities are not just recognised to be situated but (a) they are made meaningful by recognising that they are the expression of peoples' motivation or purpose; and (b) an activity explicitly includes the other people with whom we work and play; and (c) activities does not just appear, they have a history – they have come from somewhere and are likely to change and develop in the course of their execution. Activities are also distributed across other people, across time, and across a range of tools and artefacts. This social distribution has an immediate face validity. We do not work alone, we rely on others, nor are we confined to the bounds of our individual cognition.

Activity Theory has all the qualities to provide a solid, extensible and theoretically rich platform for human-computer interaction but yet it is not. Why not? Two possible answers present themselves. The first answer is very simple, it is not because it is at odds with the Western, Anglo-Saxon tradition. The Western cognitive psychology tradition which is embedded in HCI is predicated on single users. In contrast, Activity Theory is based on the collective (or the group or the soviet) rather than the individual and favours Kant, Hegel and Marx to Descartes, Hume and Locke. These difference are rarely addressed. Secondly, we can draw a parallel with what Dreyfus has to say about the "facts and rules" approach to creating artificially intelligence systems (as discussed at the end of the last chapter). He notes that if this hasn't worked after all of this effort, it probably never will – perhaps the same is true for Activity Theory. Thirty years ago, it was not well known and had only a small number of advocates. This is not true now. Activity Theory has become well known and is well respected but it is still not widely used. It is not that it is too complex or obscure because its supporters have done an excellent job in promoting and demystifying it but because (I suspect) HCI is much more concerned with *designing* interactive systems than it is understanding how they are used. Activity Theory focussed publications in HCI are not primarily about how to design a system which embodies its principles but are more concerned with using it to describe how the technology was used. Learning, breakdowns (as contradictions), mediation, internalisation, the role of the zone of proximity will all be regularly, and completely properly, invoked to *explain* technology use but are rarely used prospectively to contribute to its design. The psychological aspects of Activity Theory are still largely confined (mistakenly) to education or perhaps organisational learning. It may be that HCI is pretty much *a*theoretic at heart and a design discipline in practice to find a place for Activity Theory.

References

Bannon LJ (1991) From human factors to human actors. In: Greenbaum J, Kyng M (eds) Design at work: cooperative design of computer systems. Lawrence Erlbaum Associates, Hillsdale, pp 25–44

Bannon LJ, Bødker S (1991) Beyond the interface: encountering artifacts in use. In: Carroll JM (ed) Designing interaction: psychology at the human–computer interface. Cambridge University Press, Cambridge, pp 227–253

Bertelsen OW, Bødker S (2003) Activity Theory. In: Carroll JM (ed) HCI models, theories and frameworks. Morgan Kaufmann, San Francisco

Bødker S (1991) Through the interface: a human activity approach to user interface design. Lawrence Erlbaum Associates, Hillsdale

Bødker S, Bannon L (1991) Beyond the interface: encountering artifacts in use. In: Carroll JM (ed) Designing interaction: psychological theory at the human-computer interface. Cambridge University Press, New York, pp 227–253

Bødker S, Klokmose CN (2012) The human-artifact model – an activity theoretical approach to artifact ecologies. Hum-Comput Interact 26(4):315–371

Brentano F (1874) Psychology from an empirical standpoint. (transl: Rancurello AC, Terrell DB, McAlister L, 1973). Routledge, London (2nd edn, intr. by Peter Simons, 1995)

Christiansen E (1996) Tamed by a rose: computers as tools in human activity. In: Nardi BA (ed) Context and consciousness: activity theory and human computer interaction. MIT Press, Cambridge, pp 175–198

Clark A (1997a) The dynamical challenge. Cogn Sci 21(4):461–481

Clark A (1997b) Being there: putting brain, body, and world together again. MIT Press, Cambridge, MA

Cole M (1996) Cultural psychology. Harvard University Press, Cambridge, MA

Cole M, Engeström Y (1993) A cultural-historical approach to distributed cognition. In: Salomon G (ed) Distributed cognitions – psychological and educational considerations. Cambridge University Press, Cambridge, pp 3–45

Dawkins R (1976) The selfish gene. Oxford University Press, Oxford

Dreyfus H (2002) Intelligence without representation – Merleau-Ponty's critique of mental representation The relevance of phenomenology to scientific explanation. Phenomenol Cogn Sci 1(4):367–383

Engeström Y (1987) Learning by expanding: an activity-theoretical approach to developmental research. Orienta-Konsultit, Helsinki

Engeström Y (1990) Learning, working and imagining: twelve studies in activity theory. Orienta-konsultit, Helsinki

Engeström Y (1999) Expansive visibilization of work: an activity theoretic perspective. CSCW 8(1–2):63–93

Engeström Y, Miettinen R (1999) Introduction. In: Engeström Y, Mittinen R, Punamäki R-L (eds) Perspective on activity theory. Cambridge University Press, Cambridge

Engeström Y, Miettinen R, Punamäki RL (1997) Introduction. In: Perspectives on activity theory. Cambridge University Press, Cambridge, pp 1–16

Engeström Y, Miettinen R, Punamäki RL (eds) (1999) Perspectives on activity theory. Cambridge University Press, Cambridge, pp 1–16

Grudin J (1990) The computer reaches out: the historical continuity of interface design. In: Proceedings of the SIGCHI conference on Human factors in computing systems. ACM, New York, pp 261–268

Harari YN (2014) Sapiens: a brief history of humankind. Random House, New York

Ilyenkov E (1977) The concept of the ideal. In: Philosophy in the USSR: problems of dialectical materialism, pp 71–99

Kaptelinin V (1996) Activity theory: implications for human- computer interaction. In: Nardi BA (ed) Context and consciousness: Activity theory and human-computer interaction. MIT Press, Cambridge, MA, pp 103–116

Kaptelinin V (2005) The object of activity: making sense of the sense-maker. Mind Cult Act 12(1):4–18

Kozulin A (1986) The concept of activity in Soviet psychology. Am Psychol 41(3):264–274

Kuutti K (1991) Activity theory and its applications in information systems research and design. In: Nissen H-E, Klein HK, Hirschheim R (eds) Information systems research arena of the 90's. Elsevier, Amsterdam

Kuutti K (1996) Activity theory as a potential framework for human-computer interaction research. In: Nardi B (ed) Context and consciousness. MIT Press, Cambridge, MA, pp 17–44

Leont'ev AN (1974) The problem of activity in psychology. Sov Psychol 13(2):4–33

Leont'ev AN (1978) Activity consciousness, and personality. Prentice-Hall, Englewood Cliffs

Leont'ev AN (1981) Problems of the development of the mind. Progress, Moscow

Nardi B (1996a) Studying context. In: Nardi B (ed) Context and consciousness. MIT Press, Cambridge, MA, pp 69–102

Nardi B (1996b) Some reflections on the application of activity theory. In: Nardi B (ed) Context and consciousness. The MIT Press, Cambridge, MA, pp 235–246

Searle J (1983) Intentionality. Cambridge University Press, Cambridge

Sellen AJ, Harper R (2002) The myth of the paperless office. MIT Press, Cambridge, MA

Turner P (2013) How we cope with digital technology. Morgan & ClayPool, San Rafael

Vygotski LS (1930/1990) Imagination and creativity in childhood (trans; Smolucha F). Sov Psychol 28(1);84–96 (Original work 1930)

Vygotski LS (1978) Mind in society: the development of higher psychological processes. Harvard University Press, Cambridge, MA

Wartofsky M (1979) Models: representation and scientific understanding. Reidel Publishing Company, Dordrecht/Holland

Web Resources

Ilyenkov E (1977) Problems of dialectical materialism (trans: Bluden A). Progress Publishers. Also available from http://www.marxists.org/archive/ilyenkov/works/ideal/ideal.htm. Last retrieved 23 June 16

Luria AL (1928) The problems of the cultural behaviour of the child. J Gen Psychol 35:493–506. Available from https://www.marxists.org/archive/luria/works/1928/cultural-behaviour-child.pdf

Chapter 3
Situated Action

A fundamental problem for cognitive modellers is to interleave internal and external states in order to achieve naturalistic behaviour. (Vera and Simon 1993, p. 12)

3.1 Introduction

In a sense, all cognition is situated, or so Robbins and Aydede (2009) would have us believe. They observe that cognition has become associated with terms like embodiment, enaction, distributed cognition, and the extended mind. Of these, three stand out. These are, firstly, that cognition depends not just on the brain but on the body too (cognition is "embodied"); secondly, cognition is not merely a biological phenomenon as it exploits aspects of the natural and social environments (cognition is "embedded"); and finally, the boundaries of cognition extend beyond the individual (cognition is "extended"). Together, they suggest, that these different forms comprise situated cognition. So cognition is situated. We should also note that that this is an unusually broad definition, so for the purposes of this book we have maintained a broadly cognitive science partition of embedded/embodied/extended/enactive.

As we noted in the opening pages of this book, HCI called upon psychology to answer two questions. Firstly, it was to answer the questions surrounding how people use and think about or think with interactive technology; and, secondly, how people complete their tasks using this technology – where does the technology fit in with the other things we need to do to achieve our goals. To these ends various forms of cognitive modelling and task analytic approaches were developed but the 1980s and 1990s were to witness challenges to this goal-task focus within HCI. The first of these, which we will consider in this chapter, is Suchman's situated action proposal (note – situated action, not situated cognition).

Norman (1993), in an introduction to a volume on situated action, offers some interesting insights which we now borrow. He tells us that researchers with a

© Springer International Publishing Switzerland 2016
P. Turner, *HCI Redux*, Human–Computer Interaction Series,
DOI 10.1007/978-3-319-42235-0_3

background in cognitive psychology or artificial intelligence, are primarily concerned with the study of "internal representations" whereas these are of "limited relevance" to anthropologists – and, of course, Suchman is an anthropologist. He goes on to tell us that her interest is on "constructing accounts of relations among people, and between people and the historically and culturally constituted worlds that they inhabit together". He emphasizes the phrase: "the historically and culturally constituted worlds that they inhabit together" noting that as we are sense-making entities, and nothing we do, including the use of interactive technology, can be understood outside the situation in which it has occurred. So, to understand the use of technology, we need to understand the context of that use too. This, of course, sounds very much like an appeal to task analysis but Norman concludes that these situations are also the product of significant historical and cultural influences which we should not ignore. This final flourish may have unwittingly extended Norman's introduction to include Activity Theory, but the point is not developed. So we can see from these sentiments that an account of how we use technology based solely on a "goal-task" perspective or the simple execution of plans may not be enough.

Plans Are Not Enough

Suchman (1987) demonstrated that the planning models which were proposed by Artificial Intelligence and HCI researchers to account for our use of technology were unable to do so in real situations. There is nothing wrong with a plan, indeed there are frequently useful but they are, all too often, not enough in themselves. Nardi (1996a, b), for example, tells us that work in psychology, anthropology and computer science has shown that it is not possible to understand how people learn or work by only considering the isolated individual engaged in an isolated task – we need to consider situation too.

Suchman's work was followed by Dourish's (2001) *Where the action is* in which he tells us that we are find "the action" in our everyday dealings with the world. These dealings with the world, he observes, have taken the form of social computing and tangible computing. The former was building on the recognition that work is socially organised; the latter that there is more to interaction than a keyboard and a mouse and that our bodies offer a range of interesting alternatives. But it is not a matter of either-or as he writes, "I want to argue that social and tangible interaction are based on the same underlying principles" (p. 17) and this principle is embodiment. This, however, is not the embodiment of flesh and blood alone but the recognition that cognition embodies the everyday realities of our social and corporeal worlds. Embodiment, used in this way, is peculiar to Dourish and appears to be his way of saying that action (and cognition) is situated.

A Second Challenge

The Suchman – Dourish challenge to the HCI of the time is still very much with us, but a second challenge was to appear from studies of "cognition in the wild" as its creator characterised it. The argument here is that in many situations, cognition operates in a manner which draws upon resources which are distributed across our brains, other people, and a whole host of information-rich sources. This "cognition in the wild" was so-called because (1995a) developed the idea from watching people working together in real world situations, particularly the operation of US naval vessels and specifically how they were navigated. He found that analysing the behaviour of a single individual offered an incomplete picture of how navigation was accomplished. He concluded that the ship was successfully navigated only as a result of a set of actors (naval personnel) interacting with each other and using different forms of technology. The resulting account became known as *distributed cognition* and was seen as another significant challenge to the classical cognition paradigm and we discuss this in more detail in Chap. 5.

The idea that our actions are, in some sense situated, is now a widely accepted within HCI however, as we can see, the precise nature of this situated-ness remains a matter of debate.

3.2 Beyond the Isolated Individual

In 1987 Suchman published *Plans and Situated Action: A critique of human computer communication*. This was to become, at least for a time, the most cited text in all of academic HCI. She describes the theme of her book as centred on an "obvious proposition" that "insofar as actions are always situated in particular social and physical circumstances, the situation is crucial to action's interpretations". She adds although this is obvious, it has been overlooked (p. 178). This problem, she tells us, arises from classical cognition's pre-occupation with abstract structural accounts.

Her book is not about HCI as such but concerns the mutual intelligibility of humans and computers. She tells us that as the social sciences are built on the shared understanding among people and now that machines are being thought of and treated as "being alive" or "intelligent", there is a case for including these artefacts in this understanding. Suchman cites the work of Turkle (specifically, her *Second Self*) as evidence for the blurring of perceptions between machine and person.

At the time, planning was central to AI. A plan is a script for the sequences of actions to be undertaken by an intelligent agent (machine or person) and a plan, of the kind which AI researchers believed were the product of our cognition, was thought to comprise a set of procedures. Beginning with a goal, we successively execute the procedures associated with goals and sub-goals. As we can be seen this resembles the workings of a GOMS model. So we might imagine an agent who might want to withdraw some money from an automated teller machine, or may wish to cross a room without colliding with the furniture. The agent, in executing a plan, steps though it and takes an action or makes a decision as demanded by the plan. One final point – plans need not be too specific so that they can be generalized to other situations, for example, different automated tellers and different room layouts.

Suchman's contribution was to recognise that since our behaviour is situated, so too must be our plans. The situation, of course, has the potential to interfere with neat execution of a plan by introducing a messy unpredictability to this process to which a plan is unable to respond. Unpredictability might take the form of the cash dispenser running out of a particular denomination of notes, or discovering that we have insufficient funds in our account, or we have forgotten our passcode, or we are being mugged at gunpoint. All of this unpredictability is, by definition, difficult to anticipate.

These preceding paragraphs summarise what many people would recognise as Suchman's position on situated action. However, it would be a mistake to think it was that simple, for example, AI had not ignored the problems of context, indeed researchers have made strenuous, though not entirely successful, attempts to capture this everyday knowledge.

3.3 Everyday Knowledge

Early AI was interested in creating machines or computer programmes which had some of the attributes of intelligence. Here intelligence tends to be confined to specific domains such as rule-based medical reasoning (as employed by expert systems such as Mycin (e.g. Shortcliffe 1976), language and story comprehension (e.g. Charniak 1972), and scene comprehension using SHRDLU (Winograd 1972). Then, despite some early promise, AI researchers encountered problems in getting their systems to function in the everyday world. As we have already noted, a key approach to developing intelligent machines was to make use of planning. Plans, it was assumed, are responsible for the behaviour of people and by extension, could be used by artificial intelligences (*cf.* Miller et al.'s *Plans and the Structure of Behavior,* 1960). Further, it was believed that not only do plans guide behaviour, they also enable us to make sense of behaviour in others, for example, Schank and Abelson's (1977) note that when people are presented with the disconnected sentences, such as, John knew that his wife's operation would be very expensive/There was always Uncle Harry.../He reached for the suburban phone book, people use plans to make sense of John's problem. People are able to make sense of these sentences by matching them against a possible plan. So, while we can easily imagine what John needs do to pay for this wife's operation, it also serves to highlight the problem of telling an AI about the complexity of a particular social world. In this example, we need to explicitly tell the AI about the need for a telephone number to be able to contact uncle Harry; and that Harry is a wealthy and a generous man. This kind of knowledge would be familiar to a typical Harry or John (as a consequence of living in the world) but they need to be made explicit to an artificial intelligence. Thus we are then faced with the problem of communicating this information to an AI (and, of course, Suchman's work). Minsky's (1974) response to this was to propose *frames* as means of doing just that.

Schemata, Frames and Scripts

A frame is a knowledge structure which Minsky appropriated from Bartlett's work on human memory. Bartlett was interested in everyday memories and this was very different from the work of his predecessors, such as Ebbinghaus who was interested in "pure memory". In contrast, Bartlett was interested in how and what we remembered in real world situations and he found that when he asked people to recall an unfamiliar story (they had just been told), they recast the story to match their existing knowledge. From this he argued that memory is an active, sense-making process which was liable to change its contents to match the participant's expectations. He concluded that people store and retrieve information in complex cognitive structures which he described as *schemata*. This idea was, in turn, adopted and defined by Piaget as "a cohesive, repeatable action sequence possessing component actions that are tightly interconnected and governed by a core meaning" (Piaget 1952). Piaget argued that schemata were crucial to cognitive development as they functioned as a set of linked mental representations of the world, which we use both to understand and to respond to situations.

Given this pedigree, Minsky adopted this approach to organising and communicating knowledge to an AI and he renamed his version, *frames*. A frame is an elaboration of a schema to which has been added the idea of a "slot", or a number of slots. These slots are able would accept a range of different values including a "default". So, to use a familiar example, we all know – to great or less extent – how a restaurant works and it is very likely that we have a default restaurant which might involve the sale of hamburgers or pizza or sushi. In a further development, Schank and Abelson's (1977) were to propose scripts, which reflect a possible sequence of events (that is, knowledge of what to do) in a given context and as such provide templates of how to respond appropriately. Their most famous and widely quoted example is the restaurant script. This script describes how we should behave in a variety of different restaurants by simply changing the contents of the "slots" from, say, Chinese to Indian and "order at the table" to "order at the counter" depending on the venue. Scripts were described by their creators as stereotyped, simplified and abstracted from the complexities of the real world and as, "a very boring little story". Frames only represent the world in miniature and may lack key background knowledge such as your fellow diners' food allergy, or the dispute over who had the garlic mushrooms when dividing up the bill at the end of the evening. So, AI researchers were more than aware of the need to represent everyday, contextual knowledge in their artificially intelligent systems but found it frustratingly difficult.

Articulation and Immutability

Despite these efforts, neither frames, scripts nor schemata have proved to be a solution to the problem of representing everyday knowledge. There are a number of reasons why they were less than successful. Here are two. Firstly, there is the articulation problem. While a script may be able to guide the ordering of dinner, they may not offer guidance on how to make small talk, or how eat soup, or how to choose and drink wine. Some of these actions are so intrinsic to eating in a restaurant that they are unspoken because they cannot be articulated. Polanyi (1966) has described this as tacit knowledge – or as he put it, "we know more than we can tell". Examples of tacit knowledge include how to tell a joke, or ride a bicycle or how to look suave or graceful or how to eat soup. Scripts and other similar forms can only, by definition, represent knowledge which can be articulated.

Secondly, there is the problem that the world we deal with are not stable, immutable and objective and as Suchman reminds us, the world is dynamic. Of course it is dynamic. The wind blows, seasons change, currencies fail but here she is describing the everyday worlds of work, school and leisure. This dynamism is evidenced by the constant interpretation and re-interpretation by intelligent agents and this interpretation depends upon the situation. For example, walking home from the office is safe during the day but not at night – here we observe the same actions in a different situation but with very different interpretations. Given this, she argues that a plan is better thought of as a resource which helps an agent to achieve their goals (in conjunction with the resources offered by the situation) rather than treating it a set of instructions which are slavishly executed. And, of course, as we have already noted there was no place for the unpredictable in idealised accounts of human cognition we described in Chap. 1. She concluded that we do not plan our action in the world, but respond to external cues on a moment by moment basis.

Dourish on Embodiment

Dourish's *Where the action is* has proved to be hugely influential in developing the idea of our action being situated, or as he prefers, embodied. The evidence he was to offer for embodiment was the emergence of "two recent trends", namely the appearance of tangible and social computing (it should be recalled that this book was published in 2001).

Tangible computing relies on direct interaction with the physical (graspable, tangible) user interface elements rather than pictures of them (e.g. icons). Dourish observes that tangible computing has its origins in ubiquitous computing which was concerned with moving computation into the environment and the user interface to the physical world. This research gave rise to a variety of new physical forms of interaction and notable among these were Marble Answering Machine (Bishop 1992) and Live Wire (Jeremijenko 1995). The Marble Answering Machine was a telephone answering machine which represented incoming calls as marbles which the user can pick up and drop to play the message. This is an elegant example of a physical interface to a digital system. Live Wire, in contrast, comprised LED cables which lit up relative to the volume of Internet traffic it monitored. Tangible/ubiquitous computer is continuing to receive attention under the loose heading of the "Internet of Things". We return to tangible interaction in the next chapter.

Dourish also notes that in parallel with tangible computing, social computing emerged with the realisation that people work together, and so CSCW – computer supported cooperative working – was born (*cf.* Grudin 1988). CSCW introduced a new discipline, a new vocabulary and a new set of challenges for designers, developers and theorists. From the off, sociological (rather than psychological) methods and thinking were adopted as a means of gathering and interpreting data from the workplace and as a consequence, ethnomethodology (the study of everyday social interactions) became a mainstream technique (e.g. Bentley et al. 1992). CSCW is distinguished from HCI in that it relies on groups of people using technology rather than single-user interaction and these groups are necessarily situated within cultural, social and organisational milieu (e.g. Whittaker 1996; Mark 1997). Consequently, Heath and Luff immersed themselves in the operation of a London underground control room (Heath and Luff 1992, 2000); while Hughes and his colleagues spent extended periods of time observing the operation of an air traffic control centre (Hughes et al. 1994) and there have been very many studies of the everyday workings of offices (e.g. Orlikowski 1992). CSCW signalled a shift to the study of "cognition in the wild" which provides significant overlap with Hutchins' socially distributed cognition proposal.

Despite the manifold differences between tangible and social computing, Dourish argues that they both rely on "embodiment". To substantiate this, he introduces an explicitly phenomenological dimension citing the work of Heidegger, Merleau-Ponty and Shultz as important sources. He reasons that embodiment has an important role in phenomenology as it refers to not just having, and acting through, a physical instantiation, but recognising that the particular shape and nature of one's physical, temporal and social immersion is what makes meaningful experience possible. In other words, we need our bodies to have all manner of experiences including the ability to make appropriate decisions, thus "embodiment is the property of our engagement with the world that allows us to make it meaningful". Thus "Embodied interaction is the creation, manipulation, and changing of meaning through engaged interaction with artifacts" (ibid, p. 126). So embodiment is not just about the body (indeed he has surprisingly little to say about our corporeality) instead he is interested in emphasizing our relationships with others and being situated in the real world (Dourish 2013). Heidegger wrote something similar when he recognised that "being-in-the-world" and "being-with [others]" are effectively synonyms. We are in the world, physically and existentially, but that world is social – it is a "lived world" (Heidegger 1927/1962; Merleau-Ponty 1945/1962).

3.4   A Challenge to Situated Action

In a special issue on situated action in the journal *Cognitive Science*, Vera and Simon (1993) contest the central tenets of situated action. They identify situated action as the claim that real world interactions with technology which cannot be understood using symbol based models and for which planning and representation are irrelevant. They also note that situated action is not a single body of thought but better described as "a whole congeries of closely related views that share a deep scepticism about the dominant role of symbol systems" and they write that situated action is not clearly defined – "there is no official credo to which all those usually associated with SA (situated action) subscribe" (p. 8). A little unfair, perhaps, as the classical view of cognition itself also reflects a number of different theoretical positions.

Their argument begins with a reiteration of the physical symbol hypothesis before consider the situated action proposal. They write that Suchman and Winograd and Flores both advocate the adoption of the methods and vocabulary of situated action by HCI. This, they note, would shift the focus of our interest from "what goes on in our heads" (cognition) to what and how people actually use technology and interact with each other in the real world (situated action). As part of their argument they summarise the SA position as follows: situated action requires no internal representations, does not use symbols and, does not use production (IF-THEN) rules *and* situated action operates directly between the agent and the environment without the mediation of a plan; instead it makes use of the available "affordances" offered by the environment which itself is defined socially. From this new perspective, the interpretation of how technology is used would be "non-symbolical" (p. 11). However, Vera and Simon actually see little incompatibility between a situated action and a symbolic approach in modelling cognition, indeed they argue that the former is actually an instance of the latter. We should note that Vera and Simon are fairly liberal with their definitions at times: for example, they write, "that the symbols in question are both goal-dependent and situation-dependent does not change their status. They are genuine symbols in the traditional information-processing sense." (p. 37). This statement appears to equate symbols in the head (goal-dependent) with symbols in the world (situation-dependent) simply by asserting that they are both symbols. This is quite a step.

Skipping ahead a little, Vera and Simon are also critical of Suchman's rejection of planning. They quote her when she writes, "I argue that artifacts built on the [cognitivist] planning model confuse plans and situated actions, and recommend instead a view of plans as formulations of antecedent conditions and consequences of actions that account for action in a plausible way. As ways of talking about action, plans as such neither determine the actual course of situated action nor adequately reconstruct it". A little later they remind us of the example Suchman suggests to illustrate this. She proposes that when facing a set of rapids with a canoe, a person would plan a course down the river but this plan would serve no purpose when the rapids were finally run. Vera and Simon reply to this by noting that stunt men usually assert that 99 % of the work that goes into a stunt is in the planning. A stunt, by definition, is situated and dynamic. However, it is the planning which protects stunt workers from injury. Abandoning a plan in such a situation is a recipe (which is a kind of plan) for disaster. They conclude that Suchman does not to understand that a plan is not a fixed sequence of actions, but is better thought of as a strategy enabling us to determine what to do as a function of the current information about the situation. This is a little surprising as it is not very different from Suchman's own conclusions.

A number of advocates of situated action were, of course, quick to rebuff this critique. Greeno and Moore (1993), for example, identify situated action with ecological psychology; the ethnographic study of activity (including the work of Hutchins) and philosophical theory (e.g. Barwise and Perry's development of situation semantics). For them the key question is whether (1) to treat cognition that involves symbols as a special case of cognitive activity, and that *situativity*[1] is fundamental in all cognitive activity or (2) to treat situated activity as a special case of cognitive activity, with the assumption that symbolic processing is fundamental in all cognitive activity. Greeno and Joyce favour the first option, while Vera and Simon prefer the second. Needless to say, these issues were not resolved.

3.5   The Problem with Context

While situated action has posed an important challenge to classical cognition, it is not clear that a situated approach had proposed a workable alternative. The AI/HCI planning models may not be able to account for the everyday use of technology, but does simply adding the prefix "situated" help?. After all, what do we mean when we insist that the use of technology is situated? Isn't this just a different way of saying we need to understand context? Dourish (2004) agrees and describes it as "a central issue for HCI design and for interactive systems" but also regards it as "a slippery notion". So, although it is now generally recognised that what we do and how we think need to be studied in context, we are still missing an agreed definition of this slippery notion. This is made more difficult as context is not something which can be readily captured even if we had the right tools. Despite this, positivist tools and definitions have been created and are popular.

Context is often treated as a form of information which can be elicited from the physical or cognitive engagement we might have with technology. According to this perspective, context surrounds activities, or at least comprises a number of elements which might impact on it and which can be readily identified and quantified. This is context as a "container". Many researchers cite the definition proposed by Dey et al. (2001) which considers context as "typically the location, identity and state of

---

[1] They use the term "situativity" and "situativity theory", rather than situated action, because they believe that the latter expression implies that it is different from a treatment of cognition which is not situated.

people, groups and computational and physical objects". Other elements identified include that great catch-all "culture", as in Oshlyansky et al. (2004), who describe the "cultural" differences between the UK and the US in the affordances offered by light switches. Interestingly, their discussion is an exemplar of context-as-container, observing that "We learn the names, properties and uses of objects within a context of use". However, the most thoroughly operationalised approach to context has found form as a methodology entitled *Contextual Design* (Beyer and Holtzblatt 1998). Here context is treated as a collection of objective data detailing work practices, workers and their tools and motivations which can be systematically captured, modelled, interpreted and shared – which, of course, is highly reminiscent of the aims and practices of task analysis.

As practical and useful as this might be, it has little to say about cognition. So, as context or situated-ness remain unresolved, there has been a shift from psychology to design – so it is case of "we may not be able to agree on a definition but we can still design for it" – or not.

The Lasting Impact of Situated Action

The impact of situated action has been two-fold, both methodologically and theoretically. Carroll observes that it helped expand the outlook of the HCI community, thus facilitating the subsequent acceptance of Activity Theory, participatory design, and ethnographically-driven design (Carroll 2003, p. 273). This observation echoes Norman's about psychologists look within, anthropologists look about. Rogers (2012) has also added that the impact of situated action on HCI was to foreground the importance of context. She writes, "it changed the way researchers thought of computer interactions and work activities, taking context to be a focal concern" (p. 47). More generally, the appearance of situated action was seen by many as a "turn to the social" for HCI. Effectively, Suchman, Dourish and Winograd and Flores have ushered in methods and ways of thinking from anthropology, sociology and philosophy which have gone some way to enable us to deal with the situated use of tools, artefacts, representation and other people. They have also invited is to think differently about cognition.

3.6   Situated Cognition

We end this chapter on situated action with a discussion of situated cognition. Clancey's very individual account of situated cognition draws upon domains as diverse as neurobiology, anthropology and ethology and he begins with the observation that researchers are now "reading each others' work". From this mix, he claims that a new treatment of cognition has emerged which emphasizes the roles of "feedback, mutual organization and emergence in intelligent behaviour" (Clancey 1997,

p. 1). His definition of situated cognition is revealing when he writes, "... it is a philosophical perspective and an engineering methodology that acknowledges the value of descriptive models of knowledge as abstractions but attempts to build robots in a different way" (*ibid*, p. 3). By "descriptive models of knowledge" he means the pairing of "descriptions of how the world appears" and "descriptions of how to behave". He regards the use of descriptive models of knowledge as being appropriate to a range of situations which include, for example, discovering patterns in medical databases, controlling manufacturing plants and auditing spreadsheets. Indeed this kind of representation of knowledge has proved to be useful in a range of applications (including expert systems) but are limited in that "they do not capture the full flexibility of how perception, action and memory are related in the brain" and have proved to be better suited to routine applications. Although he recognises the value of this form of representation, his perspective on situated cognition, if anything, highlights the differences between human and artificial reasoning. He regards every human thought and action as being specifically adapted to their environment. He writes that what people perceive, and think about their activity, and what they do physically necessarily develop in concert. This insight is the basis of his account which involves re-coordination and coupling. So for example, when we ride a bicycle we are not consciously applying the laws of physics pertaining to balance, momentum and centre of gravity, instead we are engaged in the reuse or re-coordination of previous postures and sequences of motion.

Clancey extends this observation to claim that all human action is partially improvised through the coupling of perceiving, conceiving and moving all of which he describes as self-organisation "with a memory" (ibid, p. 2). He develops this further. Memory, he argues, is neither fixed and nor is it responsible for the generation of perception or behaviour nor is a storehouse of symbolic structures, but it is better thought of as the re-composition and re-coordination of perceiving and acting. He writes, "There is no correspondence between mental processes and the world because both our habits and what we claim to be true arise dialectically, by the interaction of mental processes and the environment". Thus we are not following scripts or executing procedures instead we act, in whatever form, at the time of our acting. Thus, for Clancey, situated action, as a consequence of situated cognition, emerges in response to requirement of the situation.

Let's not forget robots. The engineering aspect of Clancey's definition of situated cognition concerned building robots. He asks, "what should a robot builder put inside the head of a robot?" (ibid, p. 76). We can, and have, built robots with "maps" – that is, representations of the environment and rules telling the robots what to do when a door or wall is encountered. These robots can, in a very limited manner, navigate themselves across a room but this is less than optimal. Essentially we are back to the issue of how we represent knowledge. Clancey reminds us that human knowledge and behaviour cannot be defined by or limited to symbolic representation. Instead he introduces the idea of *transactional* knowledge. His argument is as follows, if human knowledge is not held as symbolic, stored descriptions, then Clancey asks what is the relationship between what we say and what we do? He reasons that when we speak or describe something we are not making explicit what is stored in the brain, instead we are engage in the *activity of representing* and in doing so we necessarily changing that which we know. Knowledge, then, cannot be seen as fixed but as something which develops as a consequence of our speaking about it or, for that matter, perceiving, or trying to understand it. The interaction between and among these cognitive processes is mutually shaping and is what he describes as the *transactional perspective*. In the light of this position, he then refines his definition of situated cognition as "the study of how human knowledge develops as a means of coordinating activity within the activity itself". True to the spirit of the transactional perspective, the recursion is deliberate.

His conclusions are striking and quite individual but are similar in tone to those of Suchman and Dourish. It makes sense that cognition necessarily has a recursive quality if it is not the application of fixed rules. If cognition is the ability to respond effectively to the situation, then it cannot exclude it from a description of the situation itself.

As a bridge between this and the next chapter, we should note that Shapiro (2011) writes that it is the nervous system which is embodied and the body is situated.

References

Bentley R, Hughes JA, Randall D, Rodden T, Sawyer P, Shapiro D, Sommerville I (1992) Ethnographically-informed systems design for air traffic control. In: Proceedings of the ACM conference on computer supported cooperative work, Toronto, Ontario. ACM Press, New York, pp 123–129

Beyer H, Holtzblatt K (1998) Contextual design. Morgan Kaufmann, San Francisco

Bishop D (1992) Marble answering machine. Royal College of Art, London, Interaction Design

Carroll JM (ed) (2003) HCI models, theories, and frameworks: toward a multidisciplinary science. Morgan Kaufmann, San Francisco

Clancey WJ (1997) Situated cognition: on human knowledge and computer representations. Cambridge University Press, Cambridge

Dey AK, Salber D, Abowd GD (2001) A conceptual framework and a toolkit for supporting the rapid prototyping of context-aware applications. Hum Comput Interact 16(2–4):97–166

Dourish P (2001) Where the action is. MIT Press, Cambridge, MA

Dourish P (2004) Where the action is: the foundations of embodied interaction. MIT press, Cambridge, MA

Dourish P (2013) Epilogue: where the action was, wasn't, should have been, and might yet be. ACM Trans Comput-Hum Interact 20(1):2

Greeno JG, Moore JL (1993) Situativity and symbols: response to Vera and Simon. Cogn Sci 17:49–59

Grudin J (1988) Why CSCW applications fail: problems in the design and evaluation of organization interfaces. In: Proceedings of CSCW'88, ACM Press, New York

Heath C, Luff P (1992) Collaboration and control: Crisis management and multimedia technology in London Underground Line Control Rooms. Comput Support Coop Work 1:69–94

Heath C, Luff P (2000) Technology in action. Cambridge University Press, Cambridge

Heidegger M (1927/1962) Being and time (trans: Macquarrie J, Robinson E). Harper Collins, New York

Hughes JA, King V, Rodden T, Anderson H (1994) Moving out from the control room: ethnography in system design. In: Furuta R, Neuwirth C (eds) Proceedings of CSCW'94. ACM, New York, pp 13–21

Jeremijenko N (1995) The dangling string. Artistic exhibit, p 104

Mark G (1997) Merging multiple perspectives in groupware use: intra- and intergroup conventions. In: Hayne SC, Prinz W (eds) Proceedings of Group'97. ACM Press, New York, pp 19–28

Merleau-Ponty M (1945/1962) Phenomenology of perception (trans: Smith C). Routledge Classics, London

Miller GA, Galanter E, Pribram KH (1960) Plans and the structure of behavior. Holt, New York

Nardi B (1996a) Studying context. In: Nardi B (ed) Context and consciousness. MIT Press, Cambridge, MA, pp 69–102

Nardi B (1996b) Some reflections on the application of activity theory. In: Nardi B (ed) Context and consciousness. The MIT Press, Cambridge, MA, pp 235–246

Norman DA (1993) Cognition in the head and in the world: an introduction to the special issue on situated action. Cogn Sci 17:1–6

Orlikowski WJ (1992) Learning from notes: organizational issues in groupware implementation. In: Proceedings of the 1992 ACM conference on Computer-supported cooperative work. ACM, New York, pp 362–369

Oshlyansky L, Thimbleby H, Cairns P (2004) Breaking affordance: culture as context. In: Proceedings of the 3rd Nordichi conference. ACM Press, New York, pp 81–84

Piaget J (1952) The origin of intelligence in children. International University Press, New York

Polanyi M (1966) The tacit dimension. University of Chicago Press, Chicago

Robbins M, Aydede P (2009) A short primer on situated cognition. In: Robbins M, Aydede P (eds) The Cambridge handbook of situated cognition. Cambridge University Press, Cambridge, pp 3–10

Rogers Y (2012) HCI theory: classical, modern, and contemporary. Synth Lect Hum Cent Inform 5(2):1–129

Schank RC, Abelson RP (1977) Scripts, plans, goals and understanding. Earlbaum Associates, Hillsdale

Shapiro L (2011) Embodied cognition. Routledge, Oxford

Suchman L (1987) Plans and situated actions. Cambridge University Press, Cambridge

Vera AH, Simon HA (1993) Situated action: a symbolic interpretation. Cogn Sci 17:7–48

Whittaker S (1996) Talking to strangers: an evaluation of the factors affecting electronic collaboration. In: Ackerman MS (ed) Proceedings of CSCW'96. ACM Press, New York, pp 409–418

Winograd T (1972) Understanding natural language. Academic, New York

Web Resources

Charniak E (1972) Towards a model of children's story comprehension. Technical report 266. MIT Artificial Intelligence Laboratory Report. Available from ftp://publications.ai.mit.edu/ai-publications/pdf/AITR-266.pdf. Last retrieved 29 July 2015

Minsky M (1974) A framework for representing knowledge, MIT-AI Laboratory Memo 306. Available from https://web.media.mit.edu/~minsky/papers/Frames/frames.html. Last retrieved 6 July 2015

Shortcliffe EH (1976) Computer based medical consultation. Elsevier, New York. Available from http://people.dbmi.columbia.edu/~ehs7001/Shortliffe-1976/MYCIN%20thesis%20Book.htm. Last retrieved 29 July 2015

Chapter 4
Embodied Cognition

We have to admit that the body is the organism whose states regulate our cognition of the world. (Whitehead 1925, p. 91)

4.1 Introduction

This chapter offers a discussion of embodied cognition and its consequences for HCI. Embodied cognition is treated very differently from author to author and between disciplines but here we are concerned with how the body shapes our cognition. We should also be aware that embodiment as such is a feature of enactive cognition and of extended cognition which we consider in subsequent chapters. We should recognise that while situated action represented a challenge to classical cognition and its treatment of human-computer interaction, the very idea of embodiment is essentially post-cognitive. We should also note that there is not a whiff of the corporeal in classical cognition.

So, how can the body contribute to thought when it is the brain which is the organ of thought? There is no "psychology" of the body, indeed any such proposal seems oxymoronic. Interestingly, a recent publication in *Frontiers of Psychology* describes embodiment as an "exciting hypothesis". Wilson and Golonka (2013) write that it is the "radical hypothesis that the brain is not the sole cognitive resource we have available to us to solve problems. Our bodies and their perceptually guided motions through the world do much of the work required to achieve our goals, replacing the need for complex internal mental representations. This simple fact utterly changes our idea of what "cognition" involves …". It is difficult to gauge whether this attitude is typical of the psychological community as a whole but it is, nonetheless, a little surprising given the work of, for example, Piaget and Vygotski. They, in their own very distinctive and different ways, recognised the importance of bodily interaction with the world and its consequences for our cognitive development. This they

© Springer International Publishing Switzerland 2016
P. Turner, *HCI Redux*, Human–Computer Interaction Series,
DOI 10.1007/978-3-319-42235-0_4

described as "sensorimotor" and they both treat this as a stage which is either subsequently lost, internalised or becomes very much unimportant to adult cognition.

However, embodied cognition as we currently understand has its roots in the Continental philosophy of Merleau-Ponty, more obscurely in the work of Heidegger, which he manages without mentioning the body, and in the phenomenology of Husserl. At its simplest, to recognise that cognition is embodied is to appreciate the body plays a significant and active role in how we think and with HCI in mind, this prompts us to consider tangible interaction.

The goal of tangible computing, which first appeared in the 1990s, was to replace the "painted bits" of the graphical user interfaces (GUI) with "tangible bits". The Media Lab at MIT, one of the early centres of this research, described the use of tangible bits as *"giving physical form to digital information"*. From this position they set about designing *"tangible user interfaces" which employ physical objects, surfaces, and spaces as tangible embodiments of digital information. These include foregrounding interactions with graspable objects and augmented surfaces, exploiting the human senses of touch and kinaesthesia"*. (MIT, nd). Tangible user interfaces (TUI) differ from GUIs in a variety of ways. Firstly, TUIs use physical representations – such as modelling clay, plastic bricks and physical drawing boards rather than representations (pictures) of them. Secondly, and as a consequence of this, TUIs tightly couple representation and control. In traditional GUIs, these are kept separate as we use devices such as a mouse or keyboard to control a digital representation of what we are working with, the results of which are then displayed on a screen or some such device which prompts us to work on it. Finally, as these tangible components cannot perform computation on their own they must be explicitly linked to an underlining digital representation.

Why Tangible Interaction?

So, why did tangible interaction arise? There are a number of reasons for this, for example, if we were to remove the divide between the digital and physical worlds we potentially have the benefits of both. Ullmer and Ishii (1997) note that, "TUIs (tangible user interfaces) couple physical representations (e.g. spatial manipulable physical objects) with digital representations (e.g. graphics and audio), yielding interactive systems that are computationally mediated but generally not identifiable as 'computers' per se". This enables the user to exploit the full range of affordances offered by a variety of physical objects. The Bricks system is an early example of a TUI, so early in fact that it was called a "graspable" user interface. Bricks was developed by Fitzmaurice et al. (1995) to facilitate the manipulation of digital objects by way of physical 'bricks'. The bricks, which are approximately the size of LEGO® pieces, are placed and operated on a large, horizontal computer display surface called *Active Desk*. A brick is an object composed of both a physical and a virtual component. The physical bricks are designed to act as the "handle" of the corresponding virtual object. The bricks are tightly coupled with the corresponding digital objects, so that moving a physical brick moves the corresponding digital object, rotating the brick, rotates the digital object. A further example of a TUI is *Illuminating Clay*. This is a specialist example of tangible computing which is described in the following scenario.

> *A group of road builders, environment engineers and landscape designers stand at an ordinary table on which is placed a clay model of a particular site in the landscape. Their task is to design the course of a new roadway, housing complex and parking area that will satisfy engineering, environmental and aesthetic requirements. Using her finger the engineer flattens out the side of a hill in the model to provide a flat plane for an area for car parking. As she does so an area of yellow illumination appears in another part of the model. The environmental engineer points out that this indicates a region of possible landslide caused by the change in the terrain and resulting flow of water. The landscape designer suggests that this landslide could be avoided by adding a raised earth mound around the car park. The group tests the hypothesis by adding material to the model and all three observe the resulting effect on the stability of the slope.* (Piper et al. 2002)

Ordinarily, people working with landscapes would create digital models using computer aided design (CAD) software and then run simulations to examine, for instance, the effects of wind flow, drainage and the position of power-lines and roads. With Illuminating Clay, people simply create a model using the clay itself, this model is then scanned and a digital copy made of it. Calculation of wind flow, for example, can be superimposed on the physical model using a projector. The interaction with this system simply relies on our ability to model clay with our hands rather than a complex graphical model which is manipulated indirectly.

The clear advantage that the user of a TUI can enjoy is the ability to manipulate multiple affordances simultaneously. So, for example, when presented with clay as the user interface he or she can make use of everything that this physical medium has to offer: it can be pressed thin and shaped to reproduce the flow of the landscape – multiple manipulations in one fluid movement. This is said to break the shackles of "enforced sequentiality" (Dourish's term). To reproduce this operation with a GUI, the user would have to select the graphical object representing the feature on screen, select menu item to manipulate it, select next item …) and so on. Tangible interaction offers true direct manipulation (e.g. Fishkin et al. 2009). From these beginnings, Shaer and Hornecker (2010) tell us that research into tangible interaction has diversified into a number of different forms including wearable technology, whole body interaction and performative tangible interaction.

4.2 Corporeality

In Chap. 3 we noted that Dourish's treatment of embodiment was couched in terms of the use of technology embodied or embedded in the everyday which he saw expressed in social and tangible computing. Although this usage is common throughout HCI, the use of embodiment in this chapter follows the cognitive science pattern and refers to our corporeality. Sheets-Johnstone tells us that she instigated the "corporeal turn" in the 1980s in response to what she describes as 350 years of Cartesian misrepresentation. She describes this misrepresentation as portraying the body as the "material handmaiden of an all powerful mind, a necessary but ultimately discountable aspect of cognition, intelligence and affectivity" (Sheets-Johnstone 2009, p. 2).

So if we are not to disregard the body we should begin by recognising that it is an active partner in cognition and which, as we shall see, provides the very foundations of our intelligence, our self-awareness, skilled behaviour, affectivity and cognitive regulation. This is no small list and it cannot be surprising that the discussion of embodiment is a sea of competing and conflicting accounts, attributes and terms, but a number of common issues do emerge. We begin, perhaps a little unexpectedly, with the role of the body in our experience of affect.

Somatic Markers

Historically, emotion has been treated as the antithesis of rationality. Plato, for example, argued that our emotions arose from a lower part of the brain and perverted reason while Darwin tells us that emotion was a vestige of our animal past and lacked any functional value because it had been superseded (by reason). However, emotion has undergone something of a renaissance as it is now recognised to lie at the root of our intelligent action in the world.

Oatley and Johnson-Laird (1996), for example, have recognised that any living being has to constantly choose between different courses of action. Fight or fly, go to work or stay in bed, pizza or burger. They argue that our emotions guide our actions in situations of multiple conflicting goals or imperfect knowledge, in short, "bounded rationality" (Simon 1957). In these circumstances, it has been argued that emotions alter our brain states and make available the repertoire of appropriate actions which have been previously useful in similar situations. Thus our emotions obviate the need to work through every possibility. Further, when undertaking any task we typically set ourselves a number of goals and sub-goals (consciously and unconsciously). If we achieve them our emotional systems signal us to feel happy, or if we have failed to achieve them to feel sad, frustrated or disappointed. This primarily computational account offers an interesting complementary perspective to that of Damasio's neurological work.

Damasio (1994, 1999) has written widely on the neuroscience of self, affect and cognition and our interest here is his work on affect and decision making. Damasio tells the now famous story of Phineas Gage who had an iron bar shot through his head. Gage was a railroad construction worker charged with preparing the ground for track laying and which required the blasting of outcrops of rock. The blasting itself involved making a hole, adding blasting powder, a fuse, and sand then compacting this with a tamping iron. On this particular occasion a spark detonated the charge prematurely and launched the metre long iron bar through Gage's head. It passed through his left eye, and emerged at the top of his head. While he survived the trauma, his injuries reportedly affected his personality and behaviour, so much so that friends described him as "no longer Gage". Gage experienced blunted emotions and had considerable difficulty in planning everyday activities, for example, he was said to have made poor social choices as evidenced by mixing with the "wrong" people; he was also given to endless dithering over inconsequential decisions and generally showed poor manners and a lack of concern for others.

At this point we need to consider what Damasio has proposed regarding the function and purpose of our emotions. He tells us that emotions are changes in both body and brain states in response to stimuli which, with repeated exposure, become associated. He calls these patterns of association "somatic markers" and he argues that we use these markers to guide our decision making. These markers are available during decision making, so that any outcome that has been previously bad for us is associated with "an unpleasant gut feeling" (p. 173). Naturally, of course, we tend towards those decisions which are associated with reward and avoid those which have unpleasant consequences.

Returning to the unfortunate Gage, Damasio has suggested that the changes in his behaviour and decision making were due to him no longer having access to these somatic markers which were destroyed in the accident.

4.3   The Embodied Mind

Unlike mainstream psychology, the concept of embodiment is well established in the cognitive sciences and by way of evidence, we briefly introduce four key texts.

The first to be considered is Merleau-Ponty's *Phenomenology of Perception* (1945/1962). Though this was not his first book, it is undoubtedly the most influential. In it we learn that the body is responsible for our experience of space, "far from my body's being for me no more than fragment of space, there would be no space at all for me if I had no body" (ibid, p. 102). To feel our body (kinaesthesia) and to feel its surroundings are not merely exercises in self-reflection but the means by which we 'prehend' the world. This kinaesthetic feedback is the means by which we both objectify the world and orient ourselves within it. Thus, for Merleau-Ponty, we need bodies to both create the world and to orientate ourselves within it.

Merleau-Ponty (1962, p. 144) illustrates this nicely, telling us that, "To know how to touch type is not [...] to know the place of each letter among the keys, nor even to have acquired a conditioned reflex for each one, which is set in motion by the letter as it comes before our eye ... what then is it? It is knowledge in the hands, which is forthcoming only when bodily effort is made, and cannot be formulated in detachment from that effort". This "knowledge in the hands" is a form of embodied knowledge in that it is not represented mentally but which is available to the body alone when it is needed or practiced. So, the knowledge of how to touch type is said to be "lived" by the hands or by the body. Merleau-Ponty calls it "knowledge bred of familiarity". Finally, we note that these two forms of knowledge are independent of each other and that we learn how-to before we learn that. He also tells us that it is only through our lived bodies that we have access to what he describes as the *primary world*, As he puts it, "I observe objects with my body, I handle them, examine them, walk around them but as for my body, I do not observe it in itself ..." (ibid, 91) and Gallagher and Zahavi (2008, p. 145) confirm that, "the body tries to stay out of the way so that the we can get on with our task".

Next, in Varela, Thompson and Rosch's *The Embodied Mind* (1991) we find the claim that embodied cognition is a product of the kinds of experiences that come from having a body with the kinds of sensorimotor capacities that it has. Further, these individual sensorimotor capacities do not exist in isolation but are embedded in a biological, psychological and cultural context. They also emphasise that sensory and motor processes (perception and action) are "fundamentally inseparable in lived cognition". (ibid, p. 173). We act in order that we perceive new opportunities for action (affordances) and in turn, acting on these affordances, new opportunities are revealed. For Valera and his colleagues, cognition is essentially the result of these recurrent patterns of action-perception coupling which in turn are necessarily products of our embodiment. We can characterise their position as (i) a direct rejection of the traditional dualistic view of cognition and (ii) an enthusiastic endorsement of Gibson's view of the world. Finally, we should note that this initial work has provided the foundations of enactive cognition.

This important volume was followed by Clark's (1997) *Being There* with its revealing subtitle "putting the brain, body and world together again". Interestingly he begins his discussion by noting that this unity had been expressed decades earlier in the writings of Heidegger and Merleau-Ponty though many of the examples in his book are from contemporary robotics. He cites the work of Brooks and his colleagues who, at that time, were building robots. These robots were called "mobots". "Allen" was the first, "Attila" and "Herbert" followed (see Chap. 6). By way of example, Attila weights only 1.5 kg and uses multiple special purpose "mini-brains" to control local behaviours such as moving individual legs and the feedback from the terrain to compensate for slopes. Attila can get about on its own and it was said to display insect-level intelligence. A key feature of Attila (and other mobots) is that they are highly decentralised, self-organising, and have a "no one in charge" form of intelligence.

Finally, we introduce Lakoff and Johnson's (1999) *Philosophy of the Flesh*. This is a substantial work which offers a "challenge to Western thought". They state that the three key findings from cognitive science (to date) which, if they were to be taken seriously, would require this radical rethink. These are: the mind is inherently embodied; thought is mostly unconscious; and, abstract concepts are largely metaphorical. Lakoff and Johnson describe how we use bodily "projections" to orientate ourselves in space, for example, the projections "in front of" and "to the right of" are, of course to be understood in terms of having a body as we have inherent front and backs. We see from the front, normally move in the direction our fronts are oriented, and interact with objects and other people at our fronts. We also project fronts and backs onto objects (*ibid*, p. 34). These projections, in turn, are a consequence of the corresponding sensorimotor experiences of something being in front of us – and so on. They go on to tell us that with continued exposure to the world, these embodied experiences become conceptualised as metaphors and its is these embodied metaphors which underpin our conceptual knowledge of the world thought itself. Our experiences of the world are not, of course, limited to spatial relationships but also afford direct experience of such concepts as FULL-EMPTY and BIG-SMALL and it is the knowledge of these and other relationships which enables us to make sense of the world.

Hurtienne (2009) agrees writing that the mind is often portrayed as an "information processing device" made up from dedicated modules for perception, cognition, and action and these, in turn, rely on a set of symbols and their manipulation. As symbols are amodal they and their associated processing can be instantiated on any kind of hardware, or software, or brain. However as the body influences and constrains cognition, it is impossible to see how human experience and symbol manipulation can be incompatible. Together this suggests that the mind simply cannot be viewed as an information processing device. Human cognition is dependent on its concrete implementation in a human body with specific experiences of the world.

The Uncertain Consequences of Embodiment

What are the consequences of embodiment? Well, this really depends upon how we define it. For example, in a widely cited review, Wilson (2002) found an array of competing and overlapping claims about the nature of embodiment. She notes that "embodied cognition" was being used as an umbrella term to capture the ideas that cognition is situated, time-pressured, off-loaded (onto/into the environment), and extended (that is, the environment is treated as part of a larger cognitive system). She also found that the purpose of cognition was revealed to be "for action" and finally, when operating in its "off-line" mode, it is embodied. She finds the last claim to be the most compelling but concludes that embodied cognition should not be treated as a single viewpoint. From quite a different perspective Klemmer et al. (2006) produced a similar review though their interest was in the consequences of embodiment for the designers of interactive technology. They found evidence that embodied cognition was often associated with "thinking through doing". They describe this in terms of how thought (mind) and action (body) are deeply integrated and how they "co-produce learning and reasoning". For example, they write that humans learn about the world and its properties by interacting with it and this simple truism is supported by evidence from pedagogic approaches such as the Montessori method. This method employs, for example, bodily engagement with tangible "manipulatives" (such as Cuisenaire rods) to facilitate the learning of an abstract discipline such as mathematics. Finally, Anderson (2003), in his *Embodied Cognition: A field guide* which offers a substantial review, suggests that rather than emphasizing the classical cognition position of formal operations on abstract symbols, embodied cognition has foregrounded cognition as a situated activity, and suggests that thinking beings ought therefore be considered first and foremost as "acting beings". So, no real consensus.

4.4 How the Body Shapes the Mind

When I reach for my morning cup of tea, as I have just done, I do so without looking and I do so successfully. I am a skilled and highly practised tea drinker. I am able to do this, not because I consciously keep track of where my hands are and the location and orientation of the things on my desk but because I have a model of my body and the peripersonal space about me which is constantly being updated. This model is the *body schema*, a concept which is used by a variety of disciplines and, inevitably, in a variety of different ways. Among the first to propose this schema were Head and Holmes (1911) who identified two aspects of it, noting firstly that it comprised a "postural schema" which represents details of the position and the movement of the body. This postural schema is created and maintained by the action of the pro-prioceptive and kinaesthetic nerves. They also identified a further schema based on afferent impulses from the skin which provided the location of tactile stimuli on the surface of the body. These schemata are independent from, though related to, con-scious 'images' of the body – that is, how one perceives or feels about one's own body (of the "I could lose some weight" variety). Although this initial classification of Head and Holmes has been superseded it continues to offer a good starting point for any discussion of these bodily schemata.

The Body Schema

We now consider the recent work of Gallagher in his well-received, *How the body shapes the mind* (2005). We pick up his account with the question, how is the body represented by our cognition? He writes that at present there are a number of differ-ent, often conflicting, accounts of this – to which he adds his own. He tells us that the body can be described in terms of a body schema and a body image. He defines a body schema as, "a system of sensory-motor capacities that function without awareness or the necessity of perceptual monitoring" and as the "non-conscious performance of the body", and again as "a non-conscious system … of motor-sensory capacities that function below the threshold of awareness, and without the necessity of [conscious] perceptual monitoring" (Gallagher 2005, p. 234, 1986, p. 548). As our skills and capacities change so too does the body schema. As chil-dren grow and learn the body schema also adjusts itself to these long term changes. These adjustments are also triggered at the other end of life too. The body schema adjusts itself to account for our arthritic fingers and bent backs.

The Body Image

The body image "consists of a system of perceptions, attitudes, and beliefs pertain-ing to one's own body". (ibid p. 24). The evidence for this distinction between body image and schema is based on neurological and pathological evidence. Stroke patients, for example, may neglect one side of the bodies which may be evidence of damage to their body image. In contrast, people who may have broken their necks or suffered some form of neuropathy which effectively "cuts them off" from their bodies, that is, they no longer receive tactile or proprioceptive information from their bodies and as a result may be unable to move if they do not directly observe what they are doing. In such cases, the body schema may be impaired. Despite their very clear differences, Gallagher claims that the body image and body schema share a number of features, firstly, they both rely on the integration of visual, propriocep-tive and tactile information to construct a sense of bodily ownership. Secondly, both body image and body schema are partly innate. He has deduced this from evidence of phantom limbs in people afflicted with the congenital absence of limbs. Overall, he concludes quite succinctly that the body schema is for action while the body image is for everything else (e.g. bodily states). This established, he then argues that the ways in which our body allows us to interact with the environment structures the way we perceive the self, the world and others. Gallagher concludes by suggesting that once we have established how the body schema shapes perception, we will be able to extend this to understand how it shapes the whole of cognition (p. 137).

Four Different Bodies

Gallagher also tells us that there are, at least, four ways in which the body shapes the mind (while this is not explicitly defined, he includes cognition and affect). These are:

1. *The organic body*. Here Gallagher highlights, for example, the importance of upright posture in developing new capabilities;
2. *The spatial body*. Gallagher regards the body as a kind of spatial anchor. He also argues that perception is encoded relatively to the location of the body in space, while the external world is encoded in egocentric frames of reference, which can be either eye-centred, head-centred or trunk-centred;
3. *The body schema*, as we have seen, structures our interactions with the world and with ourselves. Gallagher appears to regard the world, like Gibson, as being made up from affordances ready to be exploited by this schema;
4. *The affective body*. The emotions provide a *tonality* to our perceptual experi-ences. If this were missing, one may be unable to recognize perceptions for what they really are. This is a little mysterious though it does resemble what both Dewey and Heidegger have written about the role of affect.

So, we can see that for Gallagher there is no simple "embodiment" as the body is experienced in a variety of different ways but the effects of the body schema seems to the most important means by which cognition is regulated.

4.5   Barely a Sense of Self

Metzinger is a German philosopher who has created his own treatment of embodiment which draws on a wide range of sources including robotics, neurological studies, artificial intelligence among others. Metzinger, in his *Being No One: The Self-Model Theory of Subjectivity*, makes a convincing case for there being no such thing as a self which in some sense exists in the world. Indeed, he also tells us that nobody ever had or was a self. This (for me) echoes the words of the Sixth Patriarch in the seventh century who famously wrote, "from the beginning nothing is". Metzinger goes on to say that all that exists are phenomenal selves as they appear in conscious experience and these selves are not things but processes.

Metzinger proposes three different forms or orders of embodiment which are: the morphology of the body, the body schema, and the body image respectively. As we can see there are some distinct overlaps with the aspects of Gallagher's position.

Morphology

Morphology belongs to the first order of embodiment and its definition is familiar. He observes that the human body has a number of distinct characteristics, including the number, kind, and location of limbs, muscles, and sensory receptors, that distinguish it from the bodies of other animals. These characteristics both enable and constrain the animal's behaviour. Wings are needed to fly and it is difficult (but not impossible) to fly without them. Thus the morphological and physiological characteristics of the body both enable and constrain the animal's repertoire of actions. So, for example, we all find scratching our own backs can be difficult, because of the length and flexibility of the arm, as well as the degrees of freedom offered by of its joints. A further example, and my particular favourite, is that the walking speed of a typical adult human is about the same as a farmyard chicken. He also notes that as we humans all have similar morphologies (more or less) it is reasonable to assume we have/or are capable of having similar experiences (more or less). Metzinger concludes that this first-order embodiment is important to the design of biologically inspired-robotics and some formulations of artificial intelligence.

The Body Schema

Metzinger's own definition of the body schema includes that it belongs to the second order of embodiment and that it is a model or representation which we maintain of our corporeal capabilities. Metzinger tells us that second-order embodiment can develop in a system (note the word system) that satisfies the following three conditions (these criteria are quoted from Self-models 2007):

(a) We can successfully understand the intelligence of its behaviour and other "mental" properties by describing it as a *representational system*,

(b) This system has a single, explicit and coherent self-representation of itself *as being an embodied agent*, and

(c) The way in which this system uses this explicit internal model of itself as an entity possessing and controlling a body helps us understand its intelligence and its psychology in *functional* terms. Some advanced robots, many primitive animals on our planet, and possibly sleepwalking human beings or patients during certain epileptic absence seizures could be examples. (italics in the original).

Leaving this definition of the second-order of embodiment, we move on to the final and highest order.

The Body Image

Finally, the body image belongs to the third-order of embodiment and is relatively rare in that it is consciously experienced. When we experience ourselves as being embodied, it is the phenomenal self-model (PSM) of which we are conscious. Metzinger is careful to differentiate between (everyday) bodily self-knowledge and bodily self-consciousness. He tells us that the phenomenal contents of the PSM are available after all internal properties of the central nervous system become fixed, for example, human beings are able to experience themselves as fully embodied selves, even when input from the physical body is minimal, for instance during dreams.

Support fro Metzinger's proposals can be found in the work of other. Very strikingly, Brugger et al. (2000) have reported on A.Z., a 44-year-old woman who was born without forearms and legs but who experiences "vivid phantom sensations of all four limbs". Specifically, "For as long as A.Z. can remember, mental images of forearms (including hands and fingers) and legs (with feet and first and fifth toes) have been experienced as integral parts of her own body" (p. 6168). Yet, despite the fact that A.Z.'s body has not developed fully, a variety of empirical investigations indicate that those missing elements are still represented at a neural level.

Staying with the body image for a moment longer, Edelman (2003) claims that it can best be described as a part of consciousness. For Edelman, consciousness is the result of neural processes which integrate multimodal sensory information, with the contents of our memory. This synthesis gives rise to a unified experience of perceptual scene, affect and memory. He also tells us that there are two types of consciousness which he calls *primary* and *higher-order*. All organisms that have a body image have primary consciousness which means that they are able to discriminate themselves from the environment at any particular moment but this is not sustained. Edelman calls that moment "the remembered present". However unless this organism has higher-order consciousness it will be unable to link the remembered present with the remembered past, and an anticipated future. Thus, any organism with primary consciousness might be limited to the experience a succession of discrete, unconnected bodily states, whereas those who enjoy higher-order consciousness have a continuous or longer lasting conception of its bodily existence. This longer lasting conception of its bodily existence we generally describe as self-consciousness. A popular means of determining whether an animal is self-conscious is the rouge test (Gallup 1970). For this the animal is anesthetized and a patch of skin on the head or ear is marked with rouge. After the animal has fully recovered from anaesthesia, a mirror is placed in front of it. If it, after seeing the marks in the mirror, attempts to remove the marks from its body, then we can infer is that it recognises itself and, thus, is likely to be self-conscious. Currently, only human beings, chimpanzees, bonobos, orang-utans, and perhaps dolphins, elephants and magpies have passed the test, and as such can be expected to have higher-order body images.

Finally, a compelling aspect of Metzinger's work is that some of his ideas have been realised in robotic form.

A Robot Starfish

Metzinger tells us that self-models can be entirely unconscious as they can be present in many (simple) animals but they can be also instantiated in artificial systems, such as robots, too. Bongard et al. (2006) have created an artificial "starfish" which is able to develop its own unconscious internal self-model. Their starfish uses its actuators and its sensors to infer its own self-model. This structure is then used drive the motors (actuators) to generate locomotion. Perhaps the most compelling evidence of this self-model is when a part of a leg is removed, the Starfish updates its self-model and learns to limp. It does this by using the actuator – sensor pairing to iteratively test optimal body structures. When this optimal body schema has been found, the robot re-structures its body-representation and adapts its behaviour accordingly. Metzinger concludes that this suggests that this self-model is the product of dynamic self-organisation, not conscious thought. This self-model, perhaps most significantly, it is not limited to living beings.

4.6   Cyborgs

There is a vivid demonstration of the plastic and extensible nature of the body schema in that we are able to incorporate foreign objects, including tools of all kinds, into it. One such demonstration is the so-called rubber-hand illusion. This was originally reported by Botvinick and Cohen (1998) who had found that when participants viewed a rubber hand being stimulated in synchrony with their own unseen hand, they misperceived the position of their hand as being closer to the rubber hand than it really was. This body schema illusion is typically induced by having a person watch a fake rubber hand being stroked and tapped in precise synchrony with his or her own concealed hand. After a few minutes of this synchronous stimulation, the effect is achieved, namely that the body schema as incorporated the fake hand, that is, it is now treated as though it is part of one's own body. This has been verified by asking the participants to judge the position of their real hand which is reported to be closer to the rubber hand, as if their real hand had drifted toward the fake. Interestingly this illusion also works in virtual environments too (IJsselsteijn et al. 2006). This effect has been reproduced many times and is now a feature on popular psychology TV programmes.

Limanowski (2014) has observed that illusions such as this have become a useful tool for investigating our sense of corporeal ownership. The rubber hand illusion has been extended and applied to other parts of the body including even the face and most strikingly, to the entire body, producing the same pattern of responses including anxiety, ownership of the fake body, and the misperception of one's physical location (Ehrsson et al. 2007; Lenggenhager et al. 2007; Maselli and Slater 2013). All of this seems to lend weight to Clark's observation that: "There is no self, if by self we mean some central cognitive essence that makes me who and what I am. In its place there is just the "soft self": a rough-and-tumble, control-sharing coalition of processes—some neural, some bodily, some technological …". If we were to accept this position we must recognise that there is no special or unique factor which makes us human. A further consequence is that these observations effectively reduce us to a collection of bits, or body parts which are open to enhancement or "cyborgisation". Clark's thoughts on cyborgs naturally complement Metzinger's three layers of embodiment particularly the latter's description of second order embodiment. A "cybernetic organism" has "deliberately incorporated exogenous components extending the self-regulating control function of the organism in order to adapt it to new environments." (Clark 2003, p. 14 quoting the original definition by Clynes[1]). Since this definition, "cybernetic organism" has become "cyborg" and "self-regulating control" has been simplified into "a notion of human-machine merging". So the study of our embodiment may lead to technological dis-embodiment.

Tools, Space and Morphology

As Clark recognised, we are "natural born cyborgs" in that we have always used tools and technological artefacts to extend, improve, or repair the perceptual and motor functions offered by our unenhanced human bodies. Examples are plentiful: a hammer allows us to generate enough force to drive a nail into a piece of wood; a bio-mechanical prosthesis can replace a lost limb; and, of course, a magnifying glass (or reading glasses) allows us to see things otherwise too small for our own ageing visual system. Thus people who have learned to use a white stick claim that they are no longer aware of it as it has become "part of their body". Heidegger famously noted that when we have learned to use a hammer effectively all that

---

[1] While the notion of a cyborg carries with it a sinister science fiction aura, the original work by Clynes was benign. He was responsible for the design and development of a variety of self-regulating hospital equipment such as those devices which assist patients to control their heart rate.

remains is hammering as the tool-body dichotomy is lost. The proficient use of these temporary extensions of our bodies relies on our the ability to switch rapidly between tools and this requires not just a body, but a dynamic body schema too. Thus fluent tool use requires an organism to be second order embodied.

We keep track of the disposition of our bodies so that we can scratch own noses in the dark and are able to extend our body schema to seamlessly incorporate a prosthetic hand and to this we can add proximal space. We constantly monitor what is going on all around us, with a special interest in the space immediately surrounding us (Kirsh 2013). We do this to ensure, for example, that we can make our way across a room without walking into furniture or avoid knocking a cup of tea over our computer's keyboard. Kirsh argues that we avoid this clumsiness by maintaining a model of proximal space which he describes as "peripersonal space". His observations are supported by a number of neurological studies which have provided evidence that we, with other animals, construct representations of space and have specialist neurons which fire when objects enter the peripersonal. So, for example, the next time you wave a fly away from your face you are doing just that. Heidegger would, no doubt, delight in this neurological evidence which appears to support his most famous construct, namely, that we experience tools as being ready-to-hand. One last thought on this, when we use a tool to reach for a object we are effectively extending our motor capability. It is as though our fingers have been stretched to the end of the tool. Kirsh offers examples of this, including fly-swatter distance, tennis and fencing reach distance, distance and estimates of "pole-vault-able height" (*ibid*, p. 7). Though pole-vault-able may in itself be stretching language a little - perhaps an alternative formulation might be to speak of tele-operation which is a natural partner to tele-presence as can be found in the title of the journal *Presence: Teleoperators and Virtual Environments* whose appearance announced the academic study of presence.

4.7 Our Ties with the World

Intentionality, as we discussed in Chap. 2, is our tie with the world. The one great difference between humans and computers is that most of our bodily and cognitive states are intentional. They about things in the world; they have the quality of *about*-ness or *of*-ness. They are typically directed at things in the world – like an activity's object. Computers do not demonstrate intentionality. For Merleau-Ponty it is the body which is responsible for intentionality, or as he put it, the only way to access the *primary world* is though our lived bodies. More than this, the world and the lived body form an *Intentional Arc* which binds them together. He writes that "the life of consciousness – cognitive life, the life of desire or perceptual life – is subtended by an 'intentional arc' which projects round about us our past, our future, our human setting, our physical, ideological and moral situation". The intentional arc can be seen in action with the maximal grip. According to Merleau-Ponty, higher animals and human beings are always trying to get a maximal grip on their situation. When we are looking at something, we tend, without thinking about it, to find the best

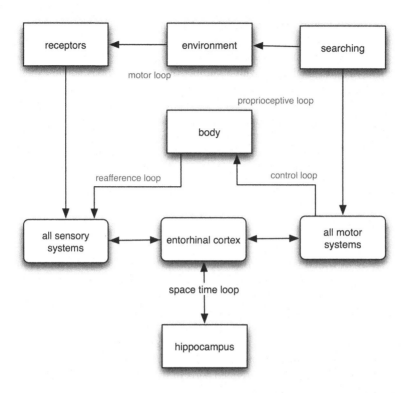

Fig. 4.1 A dynamic architecture of the limbic system (Redrawn after Freeman 1999 p. 150)

distance for taking in both the thing as a whole and its different parts. When grasping something, we tend to grab it in such a way as to get the best grip on it (think about we hold a tea cup or a hamburger or a child's hand). "For each object, as for each picture in an art gallery, there is an optimum distance from which it requires to be seen, a direction viewed from which it vouchsafes most of itself: at a shorter or greater distance we have merely a perception blurred through excess or deficiency. We therefore tend towards the maximum of visibility, and seek a better focus as with a microscope." (p. 352).

As interesting as these observations are, they are not readily translated into something a psychologist or cognitive scientist could readily locate in a model of cognition except for Freeman's highly original work which locates the intentional arc in the limbic system. The limbic system, it will be recalled, is where our emotional response to the world originates.

Freeman begins his discussion of this by describing the philosophical treatment of intentionality as "anaemic". For him, intentionality is 'the process of the brain in action' (p. 18) which has "the properties of unity, wholeness and intent (the intension of taking in by stretching forth) …". Freeman sees intentionality as an outward push, an "élan vitale" mediated by the neural circuits represented schematically in Fig. 4.1.

In this (highly) simplified diagram the intentional arc is shown originating in the mammalian forebrain where purposive behaviours are generated. The global pattern of interaction between the motor, sensory and associational areas pattern is transmitted to the brain stem and spinal cord, with a number of feedback loops acting as a control mechanism. Additional feedback is delivered proprioceptively and monitors action and evaluates the performance with respect to the intent. These loops serve to specify and realise the intended action. Simultaneously the sensory consequences of the intended action are predicted by corollary discharges sent to all sensory cortices via the pre-afferent loop. While this is no simple matter (sic), Freeman has established the possible neurological basis for intentionality and what (perhaps) HCI calls context.

Mirror Neurons

Another way in which we are tied to the world is by way of *mirror neurons* which have been reported in a number of primates (e.g. Rizzolatti and Sinigaglia 2006) – but not yet conclusively in humans. Mirror neurons, which are a form of motor neuron, are active ("fire") when an animal acts (e.g. when it reaches for an apple) and they are also active when the animal observes the same action in another (another monkey reaching for an apple) – hence their name. In humans, brain activity consistent with mirror neurons has been found in the premotor cortex, the supplementary motor area and other related parts of the brain but these findings rely on indirect measurements only.

The function of the mirror system is a subject of considerable discussion and have been proposed to be implicated in the understanding (and interpretation) of action (e.g. Rizzolatti and Craighero 2004); imitation and empathy (e.g. Iacoboni et al. 1999); emotion (e.g. Wicker et al. 2003); and in mediating social interaction in their role in the theory of mind (Ramachandran and Oberman 2006). While Ramachandran (2000) has gone so far as to claimed that they may be the basis of imitative learning and as such have allowed us to create culture. These are all pretty broad claims but an insight into their operation can be had from Iacoboni and his colleagues when they reported that mirror neurons allow us to discern if another person picking up a cup of tea intended to drink it or was simply lift it from a table (Iacoboni et al. 2005).

4.8 Playing Cricket with Aliens

If our cognition is embodied, then this observation goes someway towards accounting for why our thinking and language are the way they are. The fact of our embodiment does not have new, unexpected consequences for shaping the design of interactive technology because it always has. We have been shaping stone tools to match our needs and the shapes of our hands for as long as we Hominids have been around.

However, our understanding of embodiment has moved well beyond simply fitting technology and humans together using anthropometric and ergonomic principles. We now recognise that our bodies are the basis of who and what we are but our ownership of this most intimate possession is easily attenuated and even misplaced.

Embodiment is also, a little surprisingly, the most plausible route to cognitive enhancement rather more speculative proposals such as brain implants. This is not just technology as a tool or just as a means to an end, but a way of thinking and experiencing the world through literally quite (on occasions) different eyes. Faced with this is complexity, Chemero (2009), in his *Radical Embodied Cognitive Science*, has questioned the need for only one account of embodiment, arguing that specific accounts are better able to explain specific behaviours. We agree.

A final consequence of our embodiment is that we may be unable to communicate with aliens. If we ever do make contact with extra-terrestrials it is unlikely that they will appear over our cities in vast spacecraft, instead, the current thinking is that we are more likely to exchange mathematical formulae by radio. Mathematics is believed to be universal, and as such, would serve as a common language. For example, Newton's laws of motion, which are expressed as mathematic formulae, are equally true on Earth, Mars and 51 Pegasi b (the first extrasolar planet to be discovered). Unlike cricket. Cricket is an arcane sport and because of its complexity, it was recently proposed that the rules of cricket should be broadcast into space as part of active SETI – the Search for Extra-Terrestrial Intelligence as proof of our undoubted intelligence (Telegraph newspaper, 2015). This may not have been an entirely serious suggestion but it does serve to highlight the role of our bodies in cognition. While an intelligent alien might understand the equation $F = ma$ (Newton's second law), it is unlikely they will ever appreciate the elegance of a cover drive (a cricket stroke), or ever be able to play such a stroke because, unlike mathematics, such practical, embodied knowledge and skills are intimately related to the size, shape and capabilities of the body of the player. A cricket player needs to be able to hold a bat just so, and to track the trajectory of the ball after it leaves the bowler's hand and to strike the ball with a straight bat and so on. It is a game which, arguably, only humans can play – humans here being defined by in terms of the dimensions, dynamics and capabilities of our bodies. This also illustrates Ryle's observation that there are two forms of knowledge, namely, "knowing-how" and "knowing-that" (Ryle 1945). Knowing-that can be reduced to a set of statements, such as, Paris is the capital of France; Paris experiences more rainfall than London; more Scots live in London than do in Edinburgh. In contrast, knowing-how is likely to reflect our embodiment – an example of which is whether one can play cricket.

References

Anderson ML (2003) Embodied cognition: a field guide. Artif Intell 149:91–130

Bongard JC, Zykov V, Lipson H (2006) Automated synthesis of body schema using multiple sensor modalities. In: Proceedings of the international conference on the simulation and synthesis of living systems (ALIFEX)

Botvinick M, Cohen J (1998) Rubber hands' feel' touch that eyes see. Nature 391(6669):756–756

Brugger P, Kollias SS, Muri RM, Crelier G, Hepp-Reymond MC, Regard M (2000) Beyond remembering: phantom sensations of congenitally absent limbs. PNAS 97(11):6167–6172

Chemero A (2009) Radical embodied cognitive science. MIT Press, Cambridge, MA

Clark A (1997) Being there: putting brain, body, and world together again. MIT Press, Cambridge, MA

Clark A (2003) Natural born cyborgs? Springer, Berlin/Heidelberg

Damasio A (1994) Descartes' error: emotion, reason, and the human brain. Putnam, New York

Damasio A (1999) The feeling of what happens: body and emotion in the making of consciousness. Harcourt Brace and Co., New York

Edelman GM (2003) Naturalizing consciousness: a theoretical framework. Proc Natl Acad Sci 100(9):5520–5524

Ehrsson HH, Wiech K, Weiskopf N, Dolan RJ, Passingham RE (2007) Threatening a rubber hand that you feel is yours elicits a cortical anxiety response. Proc Natl Acad Sci 104(23):9828–9833

Fishkin KP, Gujar A, Harrison BL, Moran TP, Want R (2009) Embodied user interfaces for really direct manipulation. Commun ACM 43(9):74–80

Fitzmaurice GW, Ishii H, Buxton W (1995) Bricks: laying the foundations for graspable user interfaces. In: Katz IR, Mack RL, Rosson MB, Nielsen J (eds) Proceedings of the ACM CHI 95 human factors in computing systems conference. Denver, Colorado, pp 442–449

Freeman WJ (1999) Societies of brain. LEA, Hillsdale

Gallagher S (1986) Body image and body schema: a conceptual clarification. J Mind Behav 7(4):541–554

Gallagher S (2005) How the body shapes the mind. Oxford University Press, Oxford

Gallagher S, Zahavi D (2008) The phenomenological mind. Routledge, London

Gallup GG (1970) Chimpanzees: self-recognition. Science 167(3914):86–87

Head H, Holmes G (1911) Sensory disturbances from cerebral lesions. Brain 34(2–3):102

Hurtienne J (2009) Cognition in HCI: an ongoing story. Hum Technol 5(1):12–28

Iacoboni M, Woods RP, Brass M, Bekkering H, Mazziotta JC, Rizzolatti G (1999) Cortical mechanisms of human imitation. Science 286:2526–2528

Iacoboni M, Molnar-Szakacs I, Gallese V, Buccino G, Mazziotta JC, Rizzolatti G (2005) Grasping the intentions of others with one's own mirror neuron system. PLoS Biol 3(3):e79

IJsselsteijn WA, De Kort YA, Haans A (2006) Is this my hand I see before me? The rubber hand illusion in reality, virtual reality, and mixed reality. Presence 15(4):455–464

Kirsh D (2013) Embodied cognition and the magical future of interaction design. Trans Comput Hum Interact 20(1):3

Klemmer SR, Hartmann B, Takayama L (2006) How bodies matter: five themes for interaction design. In: Proceedings of the 6th conference on designing interactive systems. ACM Press, New York, pp 140–149

Lakoff G, Johnson M (1999) Philosophy in the flesh. Basic Books, New York

Lenggenhager B, Tadi T, Metzinger T, Blanke O (2007) Video ergo sum: manipulating bodily self-consciousness. Science 317(5841):1096–1099

Limanowski J (2014) What can body ownership illusions tell us about minimal phenomenal selfhood? Front Hum Neurosci 8:946

Maselli A, Slater M (2013) The building blocks of the full body ownership illusion. Front Hum Neurosci 7:83

Merleau-Ponty M (1945/1962) Phenomenology of perception (trans: Smith C). Routledge Classics, London

Metzinger T (2004) Being no one: the self-model theory of subjectivity. MIT Press, Cambridge, MA

Oatley K, Johnson-Laird PN (1996) The communicative theory of emotions: empirical tests, mental models, and implications for social interaction

Piper B, Ratti C, Ishii H (2002) Illuminating clay: a 3-D tangible interface for landscape analysis. In: Proceedings CHI'02. ACM Press, New York, pp 355–362

Ramachandran VS, Oberman LM (2006) Broken mirrors: a theory of autism. Sci Am 295:62–69

Rizzolatti G, Craighero L (2004) The mirror neuron system. Annu Rev Neurosci 27:169–192

Rizzolatti G, Sinigaglia C (2006) Mirrors in the brain. Oxford University Press, Oxford

Ryle G (1945) Knowing how and knowing that: the presidential address. Proc Aristot Soc 46:1–16

Shaer O, Hornecker E (2010) Tangible user interfaces: past, present, and future directions. Foundations Trends Hum Comput Interact 3(1–2):1–137

Sheets-Johnstone M (2009) The corporeal turn: an interdisciplinary reader. Imprint-Academic, Exeter

Simon HA (1957) Models of man: social and rational. Wiley, Inc., New York

Ullmer B, Ishii H (1997) The metaDESK: models and prototypes for tangible user interfaces. In: Proceedings. UIST'97. ACM Press, New York, pp 223–232

Valera FJ, Thompson E, Rosch E (1991) The embodied mind: cognitive science and human experience. MIT Press, Cambridge, MA

Whitehead AN (1925/1997) Science and the modern world. Free Press, New York

Wicker B, Keysers C, Plailly J, Royet JP, Gallese V, Rizzolatti G (2003) Both of us disgusted in my insula: the common neural basis of seeing and feeling disgust. Neuron 40:655–664

Wilson M (2002) Six views of embodied cognition. Psychon Bull Rev 9(4):625–636

Wilson AD, Golonka S (2013) Embodied cognition is not what you think it is. Front Psychol 4:58. No page numbers (published on line)

Web Resources

Ramachandran VS (2000) Mirror neurons and imitation as the driving force behind "the great leap forward" in human evolution. Retrieved from EDGE: The third culture. http://www.edge.org/3rd_culture/ramachandran/ramachandran_p1.html

Self-models (2007) http://www.scholarpedia.org/article/Self_models

Telegraph (2015) http://www.telegraph.co.uk/news/11408986/Why-we-should-bowl-the-little-green-men-a-googly.html. Last retrieved 15 February 2016

Chapter 5
Distributed, External and Extended Cognition

Anyone who has closely observed the practices of cognition is struck with the fact that the "mind" never works alone. The intelligences revealed through these practices are distributed across minds, persons, and the symbolic and physical environments, both natural and artificial. (Pea 1993, p. 47)

5.1 Introduction

One reason why classical cognition may have failed to maintain traction within HCI is its mismatch with the very thing it is trying to explain. Classical cognition take place exclusively inside the head of an individual, while HCI is about using and interacting with technology. Any account of the psychology of interaction must recognise that the effective use of technology is a result of these two quite different domains working together. This being said, there have been a number of proposals regarding the role of the external in cognition. In Chap. 2 we discussed the pivotal role artefacts play in mediating cognition and in this chapter we consider three other proposals which significantly extend this position.

The first of these is *distributed cognition*. The argument in favour of cognition being distributed can be traced back to the work of one of the founding fathers of psychology, Wilhelm Wundt working in the 1870s. Wundt is probably best known for his pioneering work in the laboratory-based study of such things as our ability to judge and distinguish between levels of brightness or loudness. However, this comprised only one half of his work, the other being devoted to *Volkerpsychologie* or "folk psychology". Folk psychology is concerned with what he described as the "higher psychological functions". In essence he was an advocate of a two component approach in which he distinguished the low level laboratory from the more qualitative approaches he adopted to understand the higher level functions. Cole and Engeström (1993), in reviewing Wundt's work, note that he proposed the use of ethnography, folklore and linguistics to study folk psychology and the use of these

© Springer International Publishing Switzerland 2016
P. Turner, *HCI Redux*, Human–Computer Interaction Series,
DOI 10.1007/978-3-319-42235-0_5

techniques was to provide a description rather than an explanation of what was at work. They summarise his position by stating that, "while elementary psychological functions may be considered to occur 'in the head', higher psychological functions required additional cognitive resources that are to be found in the sociocultural milieu" (*ibid*, p. 3). In short, the higher psychological functions required resources lying outside an individual's own cognition.

A more contemporary and familiar treatment of distributed cognition lies with the work of Hutchins (Hutchins 1995a, b) who is usually credited with the concept itself. His primary claim is that cognitive processes are distributed among multiple human actors, external artefacts and representations and the relationships between these elements which work together to achieve the system's goal.

Next we consider the *external cognition* proposal (Scaife and Rogers 1996). This is quite Vygotskian in character in that it is proposed that we offload some of the demands of cognition on to artefacts, bringing together "knowledge in the head" with "knowledge in the world". Scaife and Rogers (1996) developed this treatment to account for how graphical representations are used during learning, problem-solving and human-computer interaction itself. Their intention was to show how a range of graphical representations, including diagrams, animations and virtual reality, are used when carrying out tasks. Their framework is intended to help designers determine which kinds and combinations of graphical representations could be used to support different kinds of activities. Despite this diversity, the central theme remains one of computational offloading, that is, the extent to which the use of these external representations can reduce the cognitive effort required to complete a task. It should be said that external cognition portrays the contribution of the external world in a fairly passive light.

Finally we consider Clark's *extended cognition* proposal which promotes the position that all manner of things can play an active role in of our cognition. This shares some of the properties of external cognition but at heart it is much more radical. We think with our brains, our bodies and with all of those things which make up the world as and when we need to do so. Consider the task of calculating two numbers, say, 978 * 965. This is likely to beyond most people's powers of mental arithmetic and let us imagine that the battery in our phone is dead too. We have to reach for pencil and paper and recall the method we were taught to multiply two large numbers ("long multiplication"). The extended cognition proposal invites us to recognise the pencil, paper, and decimal notation, the know-how of to use a pencil and how to multiple two numbers and let us not forget the *sotte voce* "five times eight are forty" work together to achieve the task. Here the pen and paper (and so forth) are not merely adjuncts to our thinking but are fully part of it.

Applying any of these three perspectives is quite straightforward as there are any number of methods and areas of study within HCI to which these accounts are immediately applicable. For example, the practices of user centred design (UCD) and task analysis (TA), which are a family of methods and approaches to the design of interactive systems, seem obvious choices. A central aim of both is to understand how people do their jobs, how they are organised and, of course, the range and characteristics of the artefacts employed and how they are used – in short, how people think with things. Another self-evident application area for this "thinking and behaving with things" approach to cognition is tangible interaction.

Artefacts in UCD and Task Analysis

The classic text on UCD is Norman and Draper's *User Centered System Design* (1986). The authors make it clear that UCD is multidisciplinary and involves elements from "computer science, psychology, artificial intelligence, linguistics, anthropology, and sociology – the cognitive sciences" (p. 2) and that UCD is "about the design of computers, [...] from the user's point of view" (ibid). In UCD, the analyst aims to document and understand the variety of artefacts used by people as part of their jobs. These can include interactive technologies and the ordinary everyday paraphernalia which fill the workplace ranging from standard forms, date stamps, barcode readers, different coloured pens, staplers, folders, Post-It® notes, checklists, telephones, in and out trays, wall charts, manuals and, so course, the language used between co-workers are of interest too. As we can see, in a typical office, this can be a long list. At the risk of doing task analysts an injustice we can regard the initial analysis and scoping phases of UCD as sharing many of the same objectives, methods and thinking as task analysis proper. So we may regard UCD and TA in the same (conceptual) breath with respect to their treatment of artefacts.

CSCW: Artefacts and Articulation

Again, as we have already noted, the study of computer supported cooperative work (CSCW) in the 1990s brought with it a number of lasting changes to how HCI was conducted both theoretically and methodologically (e.g. Grudin 1988; Schmidt and Simone 1996; Heath and Luff 2000). Of the methodological changes, the widespread adoption of ethnography is the most important and of this, the most noteworthy examples include the studies of the London Underground control centre, Reuters and an air traffic control centre.

Bowers (1994) introduces the idea of articulation work (in the context of getting a computer network to function) as, "the work to make the network work", is not to be dismissed as infrastructural or as merely "oiling the wheels". Indeed Bowers had identified a class of endeavour which was required to ensure that the main focus of work was both achievable and achieved. Subsequent research found widespread examples of this kind of articulation work, the characteristics of which has been most fully described by Schmidt and Simone (1996). They begin by describing cooperative work as the interplay between multiple people working individually but through their interaction changing the state of a common body of work. However as this work is inherently distributed, other kinds of work must be undertaken to ensure that this cooperative work, works. They write, "To deal with this [...] individual and yet interdependent activities must be coordinated, scheduled, aligned, meshed, integrated, etc. – in short, articulated". Articulation work can then be seen as comprising those epistemic actions which ensure that the focus of the cooperative work is made easier (i.e. "scheduled, aligned, and so forth") and all of this relies on things. Articulation work employs a whole host of things to scaffold pragmatic work and it make it less demanding.

Other examples of articulation work can be found in studies of air traffic controllers. Among these studies, Bentley et al. (1992) were among those who have reported on the use of *flight strips*. A flight strip is a strip of paper (or card) annotated with key details of a particular aircraft such as destination, heading, speed and so forth. This external representation is physically organised on a flight progress board where they are aligned and organised according to the reporting points over which a flight will pass. These strips allow the experienced controller to become aware "at a glance" of the disposition of the airspace. While flight strips are not directly involved controlling or directing aircraft, they do make it significantly less difficult.

A final example of articulation work is provided by Heath and Luff (1992, 2000) who have reported on the importance of language in their studies of complex real time working environments. They found that staff in situations as diverse as a London underground control room and a Reuters newsroom, monitored the spoken "out louds" and other verbal asides of the room's controller and fellow workers as a routine part of their work. In the case of the London underground, the overall controller shared his work (including his reasoning and individual actions) by talking "out loud". This talk is not directed at a particular colleague within the control room – which might entail a subsequent conversation, and would necessarily divert attention away from individual tasks – instead this is a form of "self-talk". This is not language as "communication" but as articulation. This monitoring alerted staff to changes to the system without interrupting their own work. Here language serves both to provide coordination and mutual awareness and simplify the tasks of the staff in controlling their track and trains.

In these examples we see, time and again, that articulation relies on thinking with things be it a flight strip, train timetable or overhead "self-talk". This is not simple Vygostskian artefact mediation where a task is completed by means of this mediation but it has a degree of indirectness – it is the work which is needed to make the work, work.

5.2   Distributed Cognition

Hutchins has proposed that cognition can be viewed as computation which takes place via the "… propagation of representational states across media" within a system, whereby the "presentational media may be inside as well as outside the individuals involved". (Hutchins 1995a, p. 373). So, we are no longer focussed on individual "cognition" but on a much broader "cognitive system" reflecting the dynamics and complexity of real time systems such as those found in navigation and air traffic control or accident and emergency rooms. For these reasons, distributed cognition has been seen to be an appropriate way to describe the pedogagy of the classroom, the works of a busy office, and every time we travel by air or train or ship. All of these quite ordinary situations can easily be seen as a system of intelligent actors interacting with each other by way of a range of artefacts, technology and representations to achieve their goals (e.g. learning, working, travelling). In these instances, cognition, in some sense, is spread or distributed across these arrays. Part of the appeal of Hutchins' account of cognition is that it readily incorporates a variety of social and organisational perspectives which are conspicuously absent in classical accounts. In short, distributed cognition offers the potential means to describe how socially shared and technologically mediated activities achieve their goals.

In his principal case study, Hutchins demonstrates that the successful navigation of a ship requires a complex system of people working together using an array of technologies. Having decided to study navigation, he identifies the unit of analysis as the "team on the bridge of a ship" (1995a, p. *xv*). This team is hierarchically organised, with duties being precisely delegated among crew members, a feature which is important to its successful operation. In addition to the organisation of the team, they rely on a number of technologies and charts, onto which much of their cognitive work is offloaded. Not everything is push-button digital and the system includes devices such as a "hoey", which is a one-arm protractor used to convert the digitally represented bearing as an angle (ibid, p. 124). In describing a distributed cognitive system he tells us that we must not forget the skill and experiences the crewmembers have in using these technologies. In all, humans are components in a complex cognitive system, where parts of the cognitive process take "place not in anyone's head but in an instrument or on a chart" (Giere 2006 p. 99). (*There are echoes of Clark's radical extended cognition here which we consider at the end of this chapter.*)

Other examples of distributed cognition are readily available and the following is well known. On July 20th 1969, astronauts Neil Armstrong and Buzz Aldrin landed on the Moon. At mission control, Charlie Duke – as the voice of mission control – followed the process closely. What follows is a transcript of the last few seconds of the landing of the Lunar Module (Edited from the Apollo 11 Flight Journal).

Aldrin: 4 forward. 4 forward. Drifting to the right a little. 20 feet, down a half.
Duke: 30 seconds
Aldrin: Drifting forward just a little bit; that's good.
Aldrin: Contact light
Armstrong: Shutdown
Aldrin: Okay. Engine Stop
Aldrin: ACA out of Detent.
Armstrong: Out of Detent. Auto.
Aldrin: Mode Control, both Auto. Descent Engine Command Override, Off. Engine Arm, Off. 413 is in.

Duke: We copy you down, Eagle.
Armstrong: Engine arm is off. Houston, Tranquility Base here. The Eagle has
    landed.
Duke: Roger, Twan ... (correcting himself) Tranquility. We copy you on the ground.
    You got a bunch of guys about to turn blue. We're breathing again. Thanks a lot.

A question which we might then ask is, who landed the lunar module? Despite
the historic importance of this transcript it is, nonetheless, typical of the data col-
lected as part of distributed cognition research, as it consists of people talking to
each other, using a variety of instruments and controls, as they work together to
complete a task. We know that Armstrong as lunar module commander was operating the controls with Aldrin (the lunar module pilot) feeding him a constant stream
of information regarding the spacecraft's disposition including altitude ("20 feet")
and lateral motion ("Drifting forward just a little bit"). So, reasonably, they both
landed the lunar module. And, of course, Duke contributed fuel information "30
seconds" which he relayed from Earth as he monitored its status. This also introduces an undisputed measure of distribution. The astronauts were also relying on
the computer built at MIT which contained software to control the lunar module's
powered descent. And the landing radar. And the images of the moon's surface
taken by earlier lunar orbiter missions. And the checklists and step-by-step procedures developed by NASA. And the countless hours of training the astronauts
received prior to their flight. And the estimated 400,000 people working on the
design and development of the Apollo programme. And we could go on. In landing
on the moon, Armstrong and Aldrin relied on this wide range of representational
artefacts and the changing states of the system which they shared with each other
providing mutual awareness and coordination.

Thus, an answer to the question as seemingly straightforward as who landed the
lunar module, from the perspective of distributed cognition we need to consider the
"cognitive" system as a whole rather than identifying the behaviour of a single individual. While this is a striking example, the basic question and form of analysis are
easily generalised to "who landed my holiday flight?" or "who was responsible for
setting my broken leg?" or "who awards a degree?". Unless we are living in a cave
on a remote island (and did we get there unaided?), cognition involves others.

Complexity

The potential complexity of distributed cognitive systems necessarily raises the
issue of redundancy. As potentially multiple individuals and multiple forms of representation are in play in a distributed cognitive system, we should recognise that
the "same" information may appear more than once. This information is also likely
to be more or less complete, and in a different format, and more or less well understood. We can, of course, make this even more complex by recognising that the
agents in any distributed system will have different levels of skills, and have tasks
differently assigned to them. They are also likely to interpret information against to
this heterogeneous background as evidenced by Leigh-Starr and Griesemer's (1989)

work on boundary objects. A boundary object (which is a sociological term) is in this context a representational artefact, such as an instruction manual or the reading from an instrument or, a documented procedure, which is necessarily used in different ways by different people depending upon their needs, motivations, tasks – in short, their situation. Cognition may be distributed but this only serves to underline that it is also situated. These observations serve to indicate that there must be significant (but largely unspoken) levels of inter-subjectivity at work to ensure mutual awareness and coordination in any distributed system.

To date most attention has focused on the cognitive systems associated with working practice as found in an aircraft cockpit (e.g. Hutchins and Klausen 1996), or examples of explicit team working such as in air traffic control (e.g. Halverson 1995; Wright et al. 2000). As we saw in the lunar landing example, methodologically, distributed cognition research is often interested in capturing the ways in which language is used, and the representational states of media. But it also recognises that there is necessarily more than one point of view or level of analysis which can be adopted. Hutchins (1995a, b) has presented a distributed cognition analysis of what he claims is the cognitive system required to steer a ship into harbour. He offers two levels of analysis. At the micro-level, Hutchins describes the coordination of representational states across a variety of media which are involved in plotting a fix. This involves the navigation team regularly taking and plotting bearings of the ship as it enters the harbour. This is a routine activity requiring the coordination of people and artefacts. At the macro level, however, Hutchins also describes how plotting a fix provides an opportunity for the members of the team to be immersed in how things are done in the navy, he writes that "… most learning in this setting happens in the doing". Similarly, Hutchins and Klausen (1996) present a study of cognition in the cockpit. The study examines the interactions among the internal and external representations and the distribution of activity among members of a cockpit flight crew. One level of analysis revealed a pattern of cooperation and coordination among the crew which provided a structure for propagating and processing information, while at another level of analysis it showed shared cognition emerges.

While distributed cognition has the potential to describe the everyday use of interactive technology it tends only to be applied to largely real time systems. It has not, in the main, been adopted as a means of describing the unremarkable but this may change, for as soon as it is recognised that cognition can be thought of as computation stretched over people and artefacts and acting as some kind of dynamic information wave-front we might find a theoretical basis for the Internet of Things.

Other People

If people are working together and exchanging information just how is this distribution and coordination managed? Fortunately we can again draw upon reported CSCW findings. CSCW has a strong technology focus and favours sociology over psychology but it has also identified many of the "psychological" factors relevant to successful cooperative working. These include, mutual awareness, cooperation and articulation. While these are not purely cognitive phenomena (and do not appeared in mainstream psychology) they nonetheless retain a significant psychological component. By way of illustration, we will briefly consider mutual awareness.

Distributed cognition should not been taken as primarily information-centric description which ignores the social dimensions of distribution. Indeed, participants in a distributed cognitive system need to be mutually aware and, have an understanding of the state of their joint work (or play or whatever it is that is being shared) at any particular time. Dourish and Bellotti agree "Awareness is an understanding of the activities of others, which provides a context for your own activity." (Dourish and Bellotti 1992, p. 107) but moving beyond this truism has proved to be nontrivial. Moran and Anderson (1990, p. 386) write, "Most computer interfaces are designed for people to pay attention to them. But people deal with complex situations by not attending to most of it, most of the time ... [despite] ... The environment [being] rich with many things (including other people) that could be attended to." The quotation goes on to highlight the need of the environment to be able to signal the availability of things without distracting people or redirecting their attention from their primary purpose. For example, an airline pilot should be made aware of number 1 engine has just suffered a bird strike ahead of the fact that the inflight movie is not working. Mutual attention has proved reliably difficult to quantify (much less to design for) however, a particularly interesting ethnographic study of it has been reported by Olson and Olson (2000) who observed the people working in nine different corporate contexts. The researchers posed the question – "what did these teams have by way of awareness mechanisms that (physically) distant teams do not?". Table 5.1 (which is adapted from Olson and Olson, figure 3, p. 148) holds a summary of their findings. What the Olsons found was that there is a significant volume of awareness information to be had from simple physical proximity (working in the same room) which technological mediation would struggle to match.

Shared Mental Models

Another approach to modelling awareness is by way of shared mental models, for example, Mohammed and Dumville (2001) have proposed a direct extension to the concept of individual mental models (see Chap. 1). The key idea is to isolate task-relevant knowledge shared by all team members – knowledge about task relevant objects, knowledge of how to carry out domain procedures, knowledge about domain goals and constraints. Carroll et al. (2006) have also proposed their own major extension to mental models based on this work. They propose a shift from static knowledge ("knowledge in common") to something more dynamic and constructive. They note that the knowledge in common approach to awareness has been limited to relatively simple tasks. In their formulation they suggest that mutual awareness comprises sharing *common ground*, belonging to a *community of*

Table 5.1 How distance matters

Characteristic	Description	(psychological) Implications
Rapid feedback	As interaction flows, feedback is rapid	Quick corrections possible
Multiple channels	Information from voice, facial expression, gesture, body posture etc. flows among participants	There are many ways to convey a subtle or complex message (provides redundancy)
Personal information	The identity of the contributors to conversation is usually known	The characteristics of the person can help the interpretation of meaning
Nuanced information	The kind of information that flows is often analogue (continuous) with many subtle dimensions (e.g. gesture).	Very small differences in meaning can be conveyed; information can easily be modulated.
Shared local context	Participants have a similar situation (time of day, local events)	Allows for easy socialising as well as mutual understanding about what is on each others' mind. We know when people are going for lunch, or going home – and hence the time of day.
Information "Hall" Time Before & After	Impromptu interactions take place among participants upon arrival and departure	Opportunistic information exchanges and social bonding
Co-reference	Ease of joint reference to objects	Gaze and gesture can easily identify the referent deictic terms
Individual Control	Each participant can freely choose what to attend to.	Rich, flexible monitoring of how the participants are reacting.
Implicit Cues	A variety of cues as to what is going on are available in the periphery	Natural operations of human attention provide access to important contextual information.
Spatiality of reference	People and work objects are located in space	Both people and ideas can be referred to spatiality, for example the use of "air boards" (that is drawing shapes in the air with our figures).

practice, exchange of *social capital*, and participate in *human development*. Elaborating on these, they write that: common ground is essentially the shared knowledge and beliefs which allows members to communicate and cooperate easily. This is complemented by membership of a community of practice which relies on shared goals, values, and practices. Against this background, social capital is formed when "mutually satisfying interactions among members creates a persistent social good" this, in turn, provides the social glue to hold the group together at difficult times Finally, participants are expected to learn from these real-world cooperative working episodes.

As we can see, these components of shared mental models are loosely psychological in character but include sociological elements too. As interesting as distributed cognition, it remains very much a case of work in progress.

5.3 External Cognition

Scaife and Rogers (1996) introduced the term *external cognition* which refers to the "interaction between internal and external representations when performing cognitive tasks" (p. 188). This idea has taken a number of different forms beyond this definition, and this section will try to give an impression of the similar but diverse thinking in this area.

Scaife and Rogers begin by describing external cognition as a form of computational offloading, i.e. the extent to which external representations can reduce the amount of cognitive effort required to solve a problem or complete a task. Thus external cognition involves the use of external artefacts and representations, such as writing, signage, visualizations and a wide variety of physical and computational objects to augment, redefine and otherwise offload some of the computation burden encountered in using interactive and digital technology.

Donald (1991) offers the term *exogram*, paralleling a memory engram, to refer to such external symbols. He notes that an exogram last longer than human memories and have (potentially) a much greater capacity, and that they are easily transmitted, retrieved and manipulated by means of digital technology than their biological equivalents (1991, pp. 315–316). The use of exograms is important because they extend and support our cognitive abilities unlike any other creature which is restricted to engrams alone.

Further perspectives are offered by Kirsh and his observation that "people make mental tools of things in the environment" (Kirsh 1995a, p. 34) while Lave writes of, "environmental calculating devices" to capture the same idea. And, of course, a familiar example is the way in which a blind man uses a white cane. When first used, the cane is experienced as an awkward, unfamiliar external object. As it is mastered, there is a shift in the locus of the experience, it ceases to be something which exerts a pressure in the hand to the means by which an appreciation of the local environment is afforded. As Merleau-Ponty writes, "the blind man's stick has ceased to be an object for him, and is no longer perceived for itself, its point has become an area of sensitivity, extending the scope and active radius of touch, and providing a parallel to sight" (Merleau-Ponty 1962, p. 143). It can also be seen as a means of extending our reach, as Verbeek (2005, p. 125) writes, "the intentional relation between human beings and the world is thus, as it were, extended or stretched out through artifacts". It is the way in which the blind man "sees" the world. The white cane has become part of the blind man's cognitive apparatus by scaffolding his perception of the world.

Changing the Cognitive Landscape

Kirsh (2010) poses and then answers a question central to this chapter, "Why do people create extra representations to help them make sense of situations, diagrams, illustrations, instructions and problems?". He answers that external representations save on cognitive resources but suggests that this explanation is not enough in itself. He goes on to argue that external representations enhance cognitive power and permit us to think the "unthinkable". His position rests on a novel treatment of the usefulness of the external. He begins by reminding us that people interact with and create external structures when thinking because through such interaction it is easier, more efficient and more effective than by working inside the head alone. He defines efficiency and effectiveness as follows: efficiency usually translates as speed and accuracy. Interactive cognition enhances efficiency because it regularly leads to fewer errors or to greater speed. While effectiveness means coping with more demanding problems.

He continues, "why bother to mark, gesture, point, mutter, manipulate inert representation, write notes, annotate, rearrange things, and so on? Why not just sit still and 'think'?" His answer begins with the common observation that as we are so tightly coupled with the world we necessary drift into using it but to this he adds that we also change "the terrain of cognition" and this can do more than simply reduce the computational cost. These changes to the terrain of cognition may involve:

- Having access to new operators, that is, we can do some things from the "outside" that we cannot from the "inside";
- it also may be possible to encode structures of greater complexity from the "outside", than from the "inside";
- processes can be run with greater precision/accuracy "outside" than "inside". In this instance we may make use of the world itself to simulate processes that are difficult to carry out "inside";
- simulating actions difficult or impossible to perform internally, say, involving other people.

In short, these other ways of thinking about external cognition change the domain and available range of cognitive operators. Kirsh writes that "as our environments and technology change, we will be able to think about things that today are unthinkable". There is a further reason why people interact with external representations: to prepare themselves to coordinate the internal and external components of cognition. We recall that Scaife and Rogers spoke of these processes as being interwoven and here the idea is developed further. This is both interesting and surprisingly commonplace, for example, before people use a map to way-find, they typically orient the map with their surroundings; they line the maps up with the world. Interestingly, mobile phones and tablet computers now come equipped with digital compasses and gyroscopes to help with this registration. He also notes from a series of pilot studies that people were found to engage in "interpreting" actions when they follow, say, origami instructions. People were found to re-orient or register the origami paper with the instruction sheet; they were observed to self-talk, gesture, and move the paper about. These activities are part of making sense of the instructions. The same is true of making sense of self-assembly furniture instructions.

Kirsh concludes that these acts of registration anchor our mental processes in the external world and serves to restrict the focus of our attention. Thus we have altered the cognitive terrain (rather than the pattern of interaction) and have prepared ourselves to work on this proximal project alone scaffolded by these acts of anchoring and registration.

Three Characteristics of External Cognition

Returning to Scaife and Rogers we find that they identify the three central characteristics of external cognition as follows: computational off-loading, representation and graphical constraining.

Computational offloading, as we have already seen, refers to the extent to which our use of external representations can reduce the amount of cognitive effort required to solve a range of problems. Recalling their interest in the use of graphics, they write that "explicitly representing the problem state in diagrams in this way enables solutions to be more readily "read-off"" (ibid, 189).

Re-presentation (their use of the hyphen is deliberate) involves the use of different external representations which have the same underlying structure, but which make comprehension, problem solving and so forth easier. The use of graphs is an obvious example, as are other forms of representations which might also include a scientist's use of a specialised notation to capture complex ideas in a few characters. An often cited example of this is the use of pie-charts by Florence Nightingale, a reforming nurse working during the Crimean Wars of the nineteenth century. She used graphs to communicate more clearly the extent of casualty figures to British members of parliament. At that time the British were incurring significantly more casualties from disease and poor medical treatment than from enemy action. Although these data were readily available they were not easily understood particularly by the decision-making classes of that time. Pie-charts changed that.

Cocktails with Shakespeare

We begin our final set of examples with a cocktail. Consider how a cocktail recipe might be re-presented. A cocktail typically has a recipe of different spirits, fruit juices and so forth which a waiter is required to mix in the correct proportions, shake with ice and serve with a flourish. Clark (2001) has reported on how skilled cocktail waiters organise the layout of the bottles of spirits and other ingredients they require to make a cocktail to match the sequence of their use (e.g. begin by adding crushed ice, then add a measure of rum followed by ... and so on). This representation as a spatial ordering of the bottles and other ingredients helps the waiter to remember the sequence of the recipe. This example also illustrates evidence of the interleaving of the internal and external, and in this instance by effectively anchoring internal processes in line of external bottles.

Kirsh has also written of the "intelligent use of space" (Kirsh 1995a). Here he reports data he gathered from a variety of sources including "videos of cooking, assembly and packing [and] everyday observations in supermarkets, workshops and playrooms" (p. 34). One example of this is the description of someone preparing a salad. The chef begins by cutting each of the fruits and vegetables into thin slices and placing them in separate piles. These were then arranged on large platter. This

Table 5.2 Based on Kirsh (1995a, p. 66)

Capacity improved	What has been reduced	Mechanism
Recall	Probability of an error in prospective memory	Reminders
Visual search	Time complexity of search	Use known ordering such as chunks or alphabets
	Descriptive complexity of environment	
Perceptual activity	Granularity of perception	Vernier effect (Kirsh's term for being able to make fine distinctions in groupings)
	Micro-categorisation	
Reasoning	Time complexity of planning	Cue next action though a known ordering
Execution	Probability of capture error	Maximise cue separation

was done to ensure that the fruits and vegetables were presented in a "uniform and aesthetic manner" and without running out of any one ingredient until they were all used up. We all do much the same when confronted with a jigsaw puzzle, people typically group the pieces with a straight edge into a single pile, or all examples of the blue pieces as they represent the sky or the sea. The assembly of flat-pack furniture is often approached in a similar fashion, screws and bolts are grouped by size and arms and legs are distinguished from seats and backs. Table 5.2 identifies a number of different strategies which people adopt to simplify the problems we face and to and offload the burden, into the environment and from our overtaxed cognition.

More mundane examples of temporal and spatial constraining are all about us. Malone (1983), for example, writes of his interest in creating an automated means to a tidy desk. As part of this he has reported a study of how people organise their office desks. What he found was that the state of the desk itself provided reminders of the things which the owner of the desk had to do. For example, Malone's interview with the "Kenneth" revealed that, "Beside my terminal [...] are basically piles of stuff about what I need in hacking in the recent past. The deeper you go, the further back it is. Off to the right is stuff that I've shoved to the right when the pile beside my terminal got too high. But I've periodically pruned it so it's no longer useful; it's just a pile of junk ..." (p. 103). Malone observes that "Kenneth" is using the spatial organisation of the different piles of paperwork to remind him of where he was with different aspects of his work. There is also an implicit date and time 'stamp' here too with older paperwork lying beneath the newer.

From quite a different perspective comes the work of Tribble (2011) concerning the ways in which set (stage) design in Elizabethan plays supports the actors' memories of the plot of a play. Tribble (2011) tells us that a repertory company of players of that time (c.1600) would typically be expected to perform six plays every week with very few repeat performances. She has observed that the availability of the doors – opening onto and affording egress from the stage – helped the actors to remember what to do next (enter stage left, proclaim "the Scots are routed" and then exit stage right – all other doors being locked). Thus the stage and its players, props and so forth comprise what she and Sutton describe as a "cognitive ecology" in which, "we remember, feel, think, sense, communicate, imagine, and act, often collaboratively, on the fly, and in rich on going interaction with our environments" (Tribble and Sutton 2011).

Thinking with Our Hands

Arguably, thinking with our hands might seem to be a feature of our embodiment but here we shall treat gesture as an external artefact. Hostetter and Alibali (2008) have distinguished among three forms of gesture, as follows:

- representational gestures – that is, movements that represent the content of speech by pointing to a referent in the physical environment (deictic gestures), depicting a referent with the motion or shape of the hands (iconic gestures), or depicting a concrete referent or indicating a spatial location for an abstract idea (metaphoric gestures).
- beat gestures (movements that emphasize the prosody or structure of speech without conveying semantic information) and
- interactive gestures (that is, movements used to manage turn taking and other aspects of an interaction between multiple speakers)

Their argument is that gesture arises from simulated action which they claim underpins language and mental imagery. In essence, gesture reflects what is possible, given that familiar mix of our bodies and the physical environment.

"Thinking with our hands" is the subtitle of Goldin-Meadow's book on gesture. She asks, "is gesture just a prop for intra-agent communication?", that is, do listeners actually appreciate meaning through others' gesture? Or might gesture actually have a process in thinking (cognition) itself? The initial presenting evidence is intriguing, as she tells us that, we gesture when talking on the phone; we gesture when we talk to ourselves and we gesture in the dark when no one can see us. It has also been observed that people who have been blind from birth spontaneously gesture (Goldin-Meadow 2003, pp. 136–149). On the face of it, to treat gesture as a simple adjunct to communication does seem a little unfair. Rauscher et al. (1996) also found that when people are prevented from gesturing when describing a spatial scene they showed significantly poorer fluency in their descriptions and those who were. Similarly Goldin-Meadow (2011) reported an experiment in which she has contrasted the abilities of two matched groups of children to memorise a list and then carry out some mathematical problem solving before recalling the list. The children were assigned to either free-to-gesture and no-gesture condition. The free-to-gesture group recalled noticeably more in the memory test. Furthermore, Goldin-Meadow tells us that there is evidence which indicates that the level of gesturing increases with task difficulty; and that gesturing is seen to increase when speakers must choose between options; and that gesturing increases when reasoning about a problem rather than merely describing the problem or known solution. Goldin-Meadow accounts for these data by suggesting that gesturing shifts or reduces the cognitive load, that is, it acts to scaffold our cognition. She writes, "gesture ... expands the set of representational tools available to speakers and listeners. It can redundantly reflect information represented through verbal formats or it can augment that information, adding nuances possible though visual and motor formats" (2003, p. 186). Similarly, Rauscher et al. (1996) also found that when people are prevented from gesturing when describing a scene they showed significantly poorer fluency than those who were free to do so. These findings neatly making a lie of the old admonition (typically directed at children in toy stores) that, "look with your eyes not with your hands".

Finally, for Kirsh (1995b) a *complementary strategy* is one is able to recruit external elements to reduce cognitive load and he includes examples of gesturing and thinking with our hands in this. He suggests that pointing, arranging the position and orientation of artefacts so as to simplify perception. He found that, for example, when people were asked to determine the dollar value of collections of coins placed before them they were slower and more error prone when they were not allowed to touch the coins or to move their hands.

Thinking with Language

For Clark (1997a, b), the most important artefact is language, describing it as, "a tool that alters the nature of the computational tasks involved in various kinds of problem solving" and, "in many ways the ultimate artefact" (*ibid* p. 193 and p. 218). He writes that we use language to redefine problems thus simplifying our dealings with the world and identifies a number of different ways in which it scaffolds our cognition. He suggests that language helps us to remember (by way of diaries and notebooks) and it makes things simpler through the use of signage.

Consider the task of entering data into a spread sheet. As the data are complex and important, many of us in performing this task verbalise the data aloud. The act of speaking aloud helps, for example, to cross check what we are reading, with what we are saying with what we are typing. Indeed. prior to smart phones, telephone numbers were typically remembered by repeating aloud 123-456-789 as we dialled. While this might be described as rehearsal (i.e. maintaining the contents of our short term/working memories), it can equally be regarded as scaffolding the task in hand.

Sutton et al. (2011) calls this "self-talk" and has identified it in a number of different contexts ranging from sports to jazz music. He has reported evidence of self-talk in cricketers. He and his colleagues found that these sportsmen talked to themselves before playing a shot. In a series of interviews, these cricketers report that they tell themselves to "watch the ball" and to "play straight" while facing the balls being bowled at them. This should not be regarded as a preparatory tactic as the cricketer themselves tells us, "I usually say that just as the bowler's heading up into his delivery stride. So that's at the point of delivery." (quoted by Sutton et al. 2011, p. 92). Sutton concluded that these verbal nudges are, "a material symbol, an iterated and interactive self-stimulatory loop". Wheeler (2005) agrees and adds that the role of these "nudges" is to distribute "intelligence, coordinating or often re-setting and re-chunking patterns of movement or affect or mood, as one among many forms of scaffolding". In short, self-talk shows the interleaving of the internal and the external.

Thinking with Things That Make Us Smart

In Norman's *Things that Make Us Smart* (1993a, b) he describes a study conducted by Zhang and Norman (1994) which was a variant on the "Tower's of Hanoi" puzzle. In this study there are three congruent puzzles with identical rules but each makes use of different set of artefacts. The first comprises three pegs and three rings. The goal is to reach a final state in which there is one ring per peg and the rings are in descending order by size. Puzzles 2 and 3 were very similar except they relied on a different set of artefacts. The rings-on-pegs being replaced by oranges with bowls and coffee cups with plates. Zhang asked whether the characteristics of the artefacts affect how the puzzle is completed. All three puzzles are logically identical but individual examples prove to be significantly more difficult than others to solve. He found that when people were asked to solve the problem using the oranges that it took almost two and a half times longer to complete than when they were solving the same problem with the coffee cups. Not only did it take longer but it required many moves and they made very many more errors. Norman argued that the oranges and the cups offered fewer physical constraints (than the rings) to force compliance with the rules, writing "the more information present in the environment, the less information needs to be maintained within the mind." Norman also claims that many participants in the study did not realize that the three puzzles were different examples of the same problem.

Thinking with a Tea-Trolley

Finally, we report on the work of the EU-funded DISCOVER project which was concerned with creating a collaborative virtual environment (CVE) which could deliver effective maritime and off-shore (oil) emergency training. Preliminary work involved scoping the nature of the existing training provision which took the project team to the *Centre* – a well respected UK based organisation. This description of the work of the Centre is based on observing their patterns of training over a number of days. At *The Centre*, training scenarios are played out in a room adapted from a conventional lecture room. The 'bridge' can be found behind a screen in one corner of the room, and contains the ship's blueprints laid out on a table, alarm and control panels, communication devices and various reference manuals and a crew list. The other piece of simulation equipment is in the main body of the room. This comprises a set of four shelves rather resembling a large domestic tea-trolley each bearing the relevant blueprint plan for a four-deck section through the ship. Both these plans and those on the 'bridge' can be annotated with schematic depictions of hazard such as smoke, and are populated by miniature models of crew members who can be moved around, knocked over to simulate injury or death and so on. The simulation is completed by an 'engine room', located in one of the tutor's offices down the corridor from the lecture room, and simply equipped with a pair of walkie-talkies and more blueprints. A typical scenario at *The Centre* concerns a badly maintained ship taken over by the current crew at short notice, and carrying a hazardous cargo which subsequently catches fire. A fire team is sent to investigate, and the situation is exacerbated by crew members being overcome by smoke, power failures, engine stoppages and sundry other hazards. Trainees form teams of the bridge party, the party dealing with at first hand (working around the trolley) and the engine room. Although we would describe this as make-believe, each training session is conducted in the utmost seriousness and attracts captains and crews from all of the world's major maritime companies.

It could be observed that the simple external, concrete props of the miniature figures, the deck plans and so forth were sufficient to scaffold reasoning about the best course of action in a manner that a purely text scenario or discussion would not.

5.4 Extended Cognition

Finally, the origins of the more radical *extended cognition* proposal lies with Clark and Chalmers' paper entitled *The Extended Mind* (1998) in which they consider the boundaries of our cognition and our minds. They argue that to say that the mind is limited to the boundaries of the skull is essentially arbitrary and that any distinction drawn among brain, body and the environment is equally arbitrary. Instead we should recognise that these three components can act as a coupled system. This coupled system is what advocates of extended cognition mean by cognition. Their criterion (or justification) for this grouping is that all three elements share the same purpose. Specifically, the coupling with the external entity is in a two-way interaction with every element of the system playing an active causal role, as they collectively direct behaviour. They argue that if we were to excise the external from this cognitive system, it would be equivalent to removing part of the system's brain. The Clark and Chalmers' proposal then, is "that this sort of coupled process counts equally well as a cognitive process, whether or not it is wholly in the head" (ibid, p. 10). The extended cognition proposal has grown in popularity, for example, Rowlands (1999, p. 22) writes that "cognitive processes are not located exclusively inside the skin of cognizing organisms" and Gibbs (2006, p. 12) tell us that "cognitive processes are partly constituted by physical and bodily movements and manipulations of objects in real world environments".

In the *Extended Mind* (1998) in which Clark and Chalmers posed the question, "Where does the mind stop and the rest of the world begin?" (We should note that their use of "mind" is deliberate and is taken to be quite different from "cognition" in that it involves intentional states such as believing). In answering their own question, they note that it invites two replies. The first is that some accept the boundaries of "skin and skull", and argue that what is outside the body is also outside the mind. The other reply is that the meaning of the question itself suggests it "just ain't (all) in the head". From this position they argue that this form externalism carries over into the mind which must necessarily have an external aspect too. However, Clark and Chalmers suggest a third position. They propose a different form of externalism, one which is based on the active role of the environment in driving cognitive processes. They further illustrate this position with an example based on playing Tetris™. They ask us to consider the following:

1. A person sits in front of a computer screen which displays a pattern of the falling zoids and is asked to assess whether the shapes match the gaps awaiting their embrace below. To assess this, the person must mentally rotate the zoids to align them with the gaps.
2. A person sits in front of a similar computer screen, but this time can choose either to physically rotate the falling zoids, using a rotate button, or to rotate mentally the zoids as before.
3. Sometime in the near future, a person sits in front of a similar computer screen. This individual has "a neural implant" which can perform the rotation as effectively as though they were using the "rotate button". This "extended" person is able to choose between the implant or the external button but there is a computation cost to each.

Clark and Chalmers then ask, "how much cognition is present in these cases?" They suggest that all three cases are similar, arguing that in case (3) with the neural implant seems clearly to be on a par with case (1). And case (2) with the rotation button displays the same sort of computational structure as case (3), although it is distributed across agent and computer instead of internalized within the agent. So, if the rotation in case (3) is cognitive, on what basis do we count case (2) as different? One might conclude that we cannot regard to the skin/skull boundary as justification, since the legitimacy of that boundary is the very thing that is at issue. This then is the position of many who advocate the extended cognition position. So far we have discussed "cognitive processing" – problem solving, remembering things and so forth but can this be said to extend to the mind? Clark and Chalmers distinguish minds from cognition in a number of different ways not least of which being that our minds are intentional, that is, they are given to believe things. Clark and Chalmers explore these ideas in their now famous thought experiment – *Inga and Otto*.

Inga and Otto

Inga hears from a friend that there is an exhibition at the Museum of Modern Art, and decides to go and see it. She thinks for a moment and recalls that the museum is on 53rd Street, so she walks to 53rd Street and goes into the museum. It seems clear that Inga believes that the museum is on 53rd Street, and that she believed this even before she consulted her memory. It was not previously an occurrent (that is, actual rather than hypothetical) belief, but then neither are most of our beliefs. The belief was sitting somewhere in memory, waiting to be accessed. Now consider Otto. Otto suffers from Alzheimer's disease, and like many people with Alzheimer's, he relies on information in the environment to help structure his life. Otto carries a notebook around with him everywhere he goes. When he learns new information, he writes it down. When he needs some old information, he looks it up. For Otto, his notebook plays the role usually played by a biological memory. Today, Otto hears about the exhibition at the Museum of Modern Art, and decides to go see it. He consults the notebook, which says that the museum is on 53rd Street, so he walks to 53rd Street and goes into the museum. Clearly, Otto walked to 53rd Street because he wanted to go to the museum and he believed the museum was on 53rd Street. And just as Inga had her belief even before she consulted her memory, it seems reasonable to say that Otto believed the museum was on 53rd Street even before consulting his notebook.

For in relevant respects the cases are entirely analogous: the notebook plays for ordinary non-occurrent belief; it just happens that this information lies beyond the skin. The alternative is to say that Otto has no belief about the matter until he consults his notebook; at best, he believes that the museum is located at the address in the notebook. But if we follow Otto around for a while, we will see how unnatural this way of speaking is. Otto is constantly using his notebook as a matter of course. It is central to his actions in all sorts of contexts, in the way that an ordinary memory is central in an ordinary life. The same information might come up again and again, perhaps being slightly modified on occasion, before retreating into the recesses of his artificial memory. To say that the beliefs disappear when the notebook is filed away seems to miss the big picture in just the same way as saying that Inga's beliefs disappear as soon as she is no longer conscious of them. In both cases the information is reliably there when needed, available to consciousness and available to guide action, in just the way that we expect a belief to be.

The Bounds of Cognition

As we have seen, Clark places cognition in the brain, body and those aspects of the environment which might serve to solve the problems facing us. His, "whatever mix of problem-solving resources will yield an acceptable result with minimum effort" (Clark 2008, p. 13) tells us that this is effectively an economic model, that is, how can, I deal with this task at the least cost with respect to required effort, engagement, efficiency and so forth. Most importantly, Clark argues that the external is an active and equal (strictly, an equivalent) partner in this system. This is not just cognitive off-loading as it is more closer to a partnership. Ludwig (2014) has noted, that a consequence of the external cognition proposal is that we cannot exclude resources such as Wikipedia or Google from treatment as an active and equal component in our cognitive processes. This for many people might be a step too far; just because I have access to knowledge does mean that I can use it or treat it as though it were a part of my cognition? In conclusion, from a practical perspective there is an overlap between distributed cognition, external cognition and embodied cognition but conceptually they are quite distinct. However, irrespective of the position we adopt it is easy to agree with Clark (2003) when he writes, "The human mind has never been bound and restricted by the biological skin-bag ... the ancient fortress of skin and skull".

Extended cognition is therefore an attractive proposal which has a good measure of intuitive appeal but it is not without its critics. A robust challenge comes from Adams and Aizawa's *The Bounds of Cognition* (2008) which offers a well-reasoned critique and a number of interesting objections. For example, and in no particular order, if cognition does extend into the environment just what it is that is doing this extending? And does this apply to all forms of cognition, or only those which are technologically mediated? And where is the demarcation line drawn, between this side "cognitive" – that side "not cognitive" – in short, what are the limits of cognition?

5.5   In Conclusion

In this chapter we have considered the theory and evidence for "thinking with things". Distributed cognition argues that technology is shared across other people and the technology they used when they are engaged in a common task. This is pervasive but while things are undoubtedly involved in these cognitive systems, the strongest sense one gains from reading this accounts is one of social distribution. Cognition spread across people which, of course, reminds us of Activity Theory though the term "stretched across" is more often used. At the other extreme is Clark and Chalmers' proposal of extended cognition. Here cognition is whatever works – any workable and computationally inexpensive combination of brain, body and environment which allows us to achieve our goals. A problem for some researchers in this account is in ascribing equally agency and functional equivalence to the biological and non-biological components of cognition. Suddenly a "memory" perhaps stored as a particular pattern of connections in the hippocampus is no more privileged than a note in a piece of paper or a pattern of bits on a USB stick holding the same information (though episodic memory, as we shall see in the next chapte, may present a problem here). If Clark and Chalmers are right then we have opened a door to the theoretical basis of the technological enhancement of our cognition.

As ever, the middle ground is the more palatable. Vygotski argued that all cognition is mediated by tools of any stripe and external cognition could be seen as an extension and elaboration of this. External cognition is an everyday fact of the daily appropriation of digital technology we all engage in.

Coda: Is HCI Making Us Stupid?

The title of this coda is, of course, borrowed from Nicholas Carr's essay in the Atlantic magazine (Carr 2008) in which he asks, "Is Google making Us Stupid?", subtitled *what the internet is doing to our brains*. He introduces his piece by quoting from the scene in Kubrick's 2001: A Space Odyssey where HAL's memory circuits are being disconnected by the surviving astronaut. Carr writes, "My mind isn't going—so far as I can tell—but it's changing. I'm not thinking the way I used to think. I can feel it most strongly when I'm reading.[...] my concentration often starts to drift after two or three pages. I get fidgety, lose the thread, begin looking for something else to do. I feel as if I'm always dragging my wayward brain back to the text. The deep reading that used to come naturally has become a struggle". Carr's intuitions have been confirmed in a number of studies which we now briefly consider. Sparrow et al. (2011) tested whether people remembered information that they expected to have later access to – as they might with information they could access online. Participants were given 40 trivia statements to read typical of those which might be look up online (e.g. An ostrich's eye is bigger than its brain and the space shuttle Columbia disintegrated during re-entry over Texas in February 2003). They then typed these statements into a computer. Half the participants believed what they had typed would be saved by the computer, the other half were told that the information would be erased but they were explicitly asked to try to remember the information. After the reading and typing task, participants were asked to write down as many of the statements as they could remember. The erased/explicitly remember group showed significantly better recall. Sparrow and her colleagues concluded that "participants apparently did not make the effort to remember when they thought they could later look up the trivia statements they had read" (ibid, p. 777). Complementing this, Barr et al. (2015) have reported a series of experiments in which they found that when people are presented with problems those who were more likely to think intuitively or automatically tended to rely on their smartphones for information. The researchers did not find similar effects with the time spent using their phones to access social media or for fun nor did the propensity to boredom affect their findings. The authors claim that these findings demonstrate that people may be engaged in offloading cognitively demanding tasks to technology.

The appeal of this kind of memory augmentation using technology is not new. Bush (1945) proposed the 'memex' system which is a little like a cross between a personal computer, the Web and a rather dated piece of furniture. Let us consider an extended quotation from this famous paper for a moment. *"Consider a future device for individual use, which is a sort of mechanized private file and library. It needs a name, and, to coin one at random, "memex" will do. A memex is a device in which an individual stores all his books, records, and communications, and which is mechanized so that it may be consulted with exceeding speed and flexibility. It is an enlarged intimate supplement to his memory. [...] Only a small part of the interior of the memex is devoted to storage, the rest to mechanism. Yet if the user inserted 5000 pages of material a day it would take him hundreds of years to fill the repository, so he can be profligate and enter material freely."* We now rely on our phones or tablets to access the Web for this kind of augmentation.

Sixty years later and Wegner and Ward (2013) report that using Google gives people the sense that the Internet has become part of their own cognition. They note that we "off-load memories to 'the cloud' just as readily as we would to a family member, friend or lover." They also asked a number of people a series of trivia questions, with one group being given access to a search engine and the others having to rely on their own knowledge. The group that were able to search for the answers reported a higher opinion of their own intelligence after the tests than the other set of participants, suggesting that they had come to think of Google as an extension of their own cognition. Their results suggest that when faced with difficult questions, people are primed to think about computers and they have the expectation that they would have future access to that information, as a result they showed lower levels of recall of the information itself but enhanced recall for where to access it. They authors note that the Internet has become a primary form of external or "transactive" memory, where information is stored collectively outside ourselves. They also point out an irony of this "information age": we have a generation of people now who think they know more than previous generations, although their habitual use of the Internet for searching for information actually indicates that they may know even less about the world around them than their forebears.

Fisher et al. (2015) have also reported in a series of experiments which involved that searching the Internet for explanatory knowledge creates an illusion whereby people mistake access to information for their own personal knowledge. Evidence from a series of nine experiments shows that searching for information online leads to an "illusion such that externally accessible information is conflated with knowledge "in the head" (p. 682). they conclude that our minds treat the Internet as a transactive partner, which broadens the scope of knowledge to which we have access.

Finally, in a large commercial survey conducted by Kaspersky Lab (Kaspersky 2015) across the United States, the results of which have been widely reported in the popular press, they found a large number of people who claimed to be dependent on the Internet and their smartphones and so forth as their means for remembering. Of those surveyed 91 % agreed that they use the Internet as an "online extension of their brain" and 44 % also admitted to using their smartphone as their memory. It was reported that many respondents are happy to forget, or risk forgetting information as they can easily find online, while about 50 % said that they would use the Internet rather than trying to remember. Almost 30 % said that they would forget a fact which they had retrieved online as soon as they had used it. This study also found that this *digital amnesia* was even more prevalent in the older age groups.

It is too early to tell whether this reliance on technology is to our benefit, is causing harm or is simply a symptom of laziness (or stupidity). I suspect that by the time that we have sufficient evidence of harm we will probably to be unable to communicate with its victims except by emoji.

References

Adams F, Aizawa K (2008) The bounds of cognition. Wiley-Blackwell, Oxford
Barr N, Pennycook G, Stolz JA, Fugelsang JA (2015) The brain in your pocket: evidence that smartphones are used to supplant thinking. Comput Hum Behav 48:473–480

Bentley R, Hughes JA, Randall D, Rodden T, Sawyer P, Shapiro D, Sommerville I (1992) Ethnographically-informed systems design for air traffic control. In: Proceedings of the ACM conference on computer supported cooperative work, Toronto, Ontario. ACM Press, New York, pp 123–129

Bowers J (1994) The work to make a network work: studying CSCW in action. In: Proceedings of the 1994 ACM conference on Computer supported cooperative work, pp 287–298

Bush V (1945) As we may think. Atlantic Mon 176(1):101–108

Carroll JM, Rosson MB, Convertino G, Ganoe CH (2006) Awareness and teamwork in computer-supported collaborations. Interact Comput 18:21–46

Clark A (1997a) The dynamical challenge. Cogn Sci 21(4):461–481

Clark A (1997b) Being there: putting brain, body, and world together again. MIT Press, Cambridge, MA

Clark A (2001) Mindware: an introduction to the philosophy of cognitive science. Oxford University Press, New York

Clark A (2003) Natural-born cyborgs: minds, technologies, and the future of human intelligence. Oxford University Press, Oxford

Clark A (2008) Supersizing the mind. Oxford University Press, Oxford

Clark A, Chalmers DJ (1998) The extended mind. Analysis 58:10–23

Cole M, Engeström Y (1993) A cultural-historical approach to distributed cognition. In: Salomon G (ed) Distributed cognitions – psychological and educational considerations. Cambridge University Press, Cambridge, pp 3–45

Donald M (1991) Origins of the modern mind. Harvard University Press, Cambridge, MA

Dourish P, Bellotti V (1992) Awareness and coordination in shared workspaces. In: Proceedings of the 1992 ACM conference on Computer-supported cooperative work. ACM, New York, pp 107–114

Fisher M, Goddu MK, Keil FC (2015) Searching for explanations: how the internet inflates estimates of internal knowledge. J Exp Psychol Gen 144(3):674–687

Gibbs RW (2006) Embodiment and cognitive science. Cambridge University Press, Cambridge

Giere RN (2006) The role of agency in distributed cognitive systems. Philos Sci 73(5):710–719

Goldin-Meadow S (2003) Hearing gesture: how our hands help us think. Harvard University Press, Cambridge, MA

Goldin-Meadow S (2011) Learning through gesture. Wiley Interdiscip Rev Cogn Sci 2(6):595–607

Grudin J (1988) Why CSCW applications fail: problems in the design and evaluation of organization interfaces. In: Proceedings of CSCW '88, ACM Press, New York

Halverson CA (1995) Inside the cognitive workplace: new technology and air traffic control. Cognitive Science Department. University of California, San Diego

Heath C, Luff P (1992) Collaboration and control: crisis management and multimedia technology in London Underground Line Control Rooms. Comput Supported Coop Work 1(1-2):69–94

Heath C, Luff P (2000) Technology in action. Cambridge University Press, Cambridge

Hostetter AB, Alibali MW (2008) Visible embodiment: gestures as simulated action. Psychon Bull Rev 15(3):495–514

Hutchins E (1995a) Cognition in the wild. MIT Press, Cambridge, MA

Hutchins E (1995b) How a cockpit remembers its speed. Cogn Sci 19:265–288

Hutchins E, Klausen T (1996) Distributed cognition in an airline cockpit. In: Engeström Y, Middleton D (eds) Cognition and communication at work. Cambridge University Press, Cambridge, pp 15–34

Kirsh D (1995a) The intelligent use of space. Artif Intell 73:31–68

Kirsh D (1995b) Complementary strategies: why we use our hands when we think. In: Proceedings of the seventeenth annual conference of the Cognitive Science Society, pp 212–217

Kirsh D (2010) Thinking with external representations. AI & Soc 25:441–454

Leigh-Starr S, Griesemer J (1989) Institutional ecology, 'translations' and boundary objects: amateurs and professionals in Berkeley's Museum of Vertebrate Zoology, 1907–39. Soc Stud Sci 19(3):387–420

Ludwig D (2014) Extended cognition and the explosion of knowledge. Philos Psychol 3:1–14

Malone TW (1983) How do people organize their desks? Implications for the design of office automation systems. ACM Trans Off Syst 11:99–112

Merleau-Ponty M (1945/1962) Phenomenology of perception (trans: Smith C). Routledge Classics, London

Mohammed S, Dumville BC (2001) Team mental models in a team knowledge framework: expanding theory and measurement across disciplinary boundaries. J Organ Behav 22:89–106

Moran TP, Anderson RJ (1990) The workaday world as a paradigm for CSCW design. In: Proceedings of the conference on Computer supported collaborative work. Los Angeles, California

Norman DA (1993a) Cognition in the head and in the world: an introduction to the special issue on situated action. Cogn Sci 17:1–6

Norman DA (1993b) Things that make us smart. Perseus Books, Cambridge, MA

Norman DA, Draper SW (1986) User centered system design. Erlbaum Associates, Hillsdale

Olson GM, Olson JS (2000) Distance matters. Hum Comput Interact 15:139–178

Pea RD (1993) Practices of distributed intelligence and designs for education. In: Salomon G (ed) Distributed cognitions: psychological and educational considerations. Cambridge University Press, New York, pp 47–87

Rauscher FH, Krauss RM, Chen Y (1996) Gesture, speech, and lexical access: the role of lexical movements in speech production. Psychol Sci 7(4):226–231

Rowlands M (1999) The body in mind: understanding cognitive processes. Cambridge University Press, Cambridge

Scaife M, Rogers Y (1996) External cognition: how do graphical representations work? Int J Hum Comput Stud 45(2):185–213

Schmidt K, Simone C (1996) Coordination mechanisms: towards a conceptual foundation of CSCW systems design. Computer Supported Cooperative Work. J Collaborat Comput 5(2–3):155–200

Sparrow B, Liu J, Wegner DM (2011) Google effects on memory: cognitive consequences of having information at our fingertips. Science 333:776–778

Sutton J, Mcilwain D, Christensen W, Geeves A (2011) Applying intelligence to the reflexes: embodied skills and habits between Dreyfus and Descartes. J Br Soc Phenomenol 42(1):78–103

Tribble EB (2011) Cognition in the Globe: attention and memory in Shakespeare's theatre. Palgrave MacMillan, New York

Tribble EB, Sutton J (2011) Cognitive ecology as a framework for Shakespearean studies. Shakespear Stud 39:94–103

Verbeek P-P (2005) What things do. Penn State Press, Pennsylvania

Wegner DM, Ward AF (2013) The internet has become the external hard drive for our memories. Scientific American

Wheeler M (2005) Reconstructing the cognitive world. MIT Press, Cambridge, MA

Wright P, Fields R, Harrison M (2000) Analysing human-computer interaction as distributed cognition: the resources model. Hum Comput Interact 51:1–41

Zhang J, Norman DA (1994) Representations in distributed cognitive tasks. Cogn Sci 18:87–122

Web Resources

Carr N (2008) Is Google making us stupid. The Atlantic magazine. Available from http://www.theatlantic.com/magazine/archive/2008/07/is-google-making-us-stupid/306868/.   Last retrieved 3 March 2016

Kaspersky (2015) https://kasperskycontenthub.com/usa/files/2015/06/Digital-Amnesia-Report.pdf

Chapter 6
Enactive Cognition

the mind is not in the head (Varela 1999, p. 72)

6.1 Introduction

The first five chapters of this book have seen an argument that cognition relies on contributions from the brain, the body, (possibly) other people and aspects of the environment. This chapter offers a perspective which is distinct from what we have seen so far, and this is enactive cognition.

Varela, Thompson and Rosch introduced the concept of enactive cognition in their *Embodied Mind* (1991). Enaction places a strong emphasis on the idea that the experienced world is the product of the mutual interactions among the physical make-up of the organism, its sensorimotor capabilities and the environment itself. This triadic coupling of brain-body-world, which superficially is not very different to what we have seen already, lies at the heart of their account and establishes the basis of the phenomenological perspective that cognition "*brings forth a world*" as a consequence of their interaction. Further, we organisms are not merely the passive recipients of cognition but we should recognise that our cognitive abilities are enacted. So, what does it mean to enact? Here Di Paolo et al. (2014, p. 39) helpfully tell us that, "Organisms do not passively receive information from their environments, which they then translate into internal representations. Natural cognitive systems are simply not in the business of accessing their world in order to build accurate pictures of it. They participate in the generation of meaning through their bodies and actions often engaging in transformational and not merely informational interactions; *they enact a world*." (italics in the original). From this reading, it becomes clear that enactive accounts do not treat the world as a given. There is no objective world to be experienced. Instead, it is, "something we engage in by moving, touching, breathing, and eating" (Valera 1999 p. 8). From this position it follows, for example, that knowing-how to do something is dependent upon those experiences

© Springer International Publishing Switzerland 2016   99
P. Turner, *HCI Redux*, Human–Computer Interaction Series,
DOI 10.1007/978-3-319-42235-0_6

we have in our own *particular* bodies with their *particular* sensorimotor capacities embedded in the *particularities* of the body's own biological being and cultural setting. Thus our know-how is personal. So too our perception, sense-making and our memories. Consequently, and unlike the treatments of cognition we have considered so far, enaction offers its own positions on these cognitive faculties too. This, from the point-of-view of HCI, is perhaps, the biggest difference between enaction and the other accounts of cognition.

Enaction argues that cognition arises through the interaction between an organism and its environment: any organism and any environment. This suggests that cognition is not exclusively the preserve of the most advanced of species but is more or less synonymous with life itself. Indeed Maturana and Varela (1980) tell us very clearly that cognition is "a biological phenomenon and can only be understood as such". They define a cognitive system as one "whose organization defines a domain of interactions in which it can act with relevance to the maintenance of itself". This emphasis on self-maintenance also distinguishes enaction from the other accounts.

Inevitably, any discussion of enaction must recognise that it is a spectrum of theoretical positions, at one end is the observation that enactive knowledge is acquired by doing, such as, by riding a bicycle, playing sports or working in the garden. At the other extreme, it has been proposed that our cognition relies on both basic and encultured minds, the former have no content (sic) despite being responsible for the "vast sea of what humans do and experience", whereas our encultured, scaffolded minds are capable of language, and more speculative thinking and planning (Hutto and Myin 2013).

Given all of this, enaction has been proposed as the basis of a whole new paradigm for cognitive science itself, claiming that it solves core issues in cognitive science such as the mind-body problem. Its advocates also claim that enaction provide a genuine articulation of the many disciplines contributing to cognitive science, thus enactive cognition was come to be regarded as the fourth "E" of cognition, joining "embedded", "embodied" and "extended" (Stewart et al. 2010).

Of course, what is missing from this introduction is any mention of interactive technology. While there is the occasional reference to the occasional development, there is no apparent body of technology which has been designed and constructed along enactive principles. Those references which do pop up from time to time tend to be isolates. So why, given the paucity of technological examples and the comparative unfamiliarity of aspects of the conceptual framework, have we included enaction in this volume? Firstly, I am personally drawn to radical theory but more seriously, enaction emerges as a means of providing a fascinating and potentially invaluable extension to existing accounts. For example, the discussion of situatedness (*cf.* Suchman, Dourish, Clancey) and the treatments of embodiment (*cf.* Gallagher and Metzinger) and understanding of cognitive scaffolding (*cf.* Vygostki, Rogers and Kirsh) are enriched by this fresh perspective in the hands of the Enactionists. Then if we add what enaction brings to the specifics of memory, and perception-affordance, we can only conclude that engagement with it offers real returns.

6.2   Enactive Cognition

Predating Valera, the term *enaction* was used by Bruner (1966) to describe a child's initial understanding of the world. Enactive knowledge or the formation of an enactive representation (a concept of extreme anathema to contemporary thinking), might be treated as though it were roughly equivalent to that which is acquired during Piaget's sensorimotor period of development. It comprises knowledge about the world which the child has acquired from her actions (e.g. shaking a rattle or, perhaps, swiping the screen of a tablet computer). Bruner tells us that it is the first of the three mode of representation and he likens this kind of "intelligence" to a fixed succession of static images each of which is connected to an action. He writes that the child seems able to "hold an object in mind by less and less direct manual prehension of it". During the enactive stage, small children can perform actions without knowing how. (*We should note, however, that Bruner's work and the treatment of enaction discussed here, were developed independently of each other*).

Varela and his colleagues define enactive cognition as self-regulating, self-generating and embodied which we now consider in turn (Varela et al. 1991).

Autopoiesis

Autopoiesis refers to a system being self-regulating or self-organising. The term was originally coined by Maturana (1970) to describe the self-regulation of biological systems and refers to a system's organisation and complexity rather than, say, its physical make-up. It was subsequently adopted by Varela and applied to cognition. Within enactive thinking, a system is cognitive, if and only if, it generates its own actions and then uses the feedback from these actions to guide further actions and so forth – this is the means by which cognition maintains its autopoiesis. In quite a nice illustration of this, Valera describes the difference between this kind of immediate actions one might take and those which are the result of detached deliberation. He considers this with respect to Piaget's treatment of morality in children (this may seem a odd choice but Valera was writing about ethical know-how at the time). Piaget has argued that "pure reason" is "the arbiter both of theoretical reflection and daily practice" and that to understand judgment and behaviour one must understand these underlying cognitive processes. Valera, of course, has disagreed with this "reason-first" approach arguing that the focus should be understanding the skilled behaviour itself and not the inferred context-free judgments ("pure reason") upon which it is said to depend.

Bring Forth Worlds

McGann (2007) writes that enaction is "the exercise of skilful know-how in situated and embodied action". Enactive behaviour is skilful, situated and embodied and it is this which "brings forth" the world through its dynamic coupling with the environment. More recently Kirsh (2013) has introduced the term "enactive land-scape" to describe the structure that an agent co-creates with the world when he or she acts in a goal-oriented manner. So described, an enactive landscape captures the goal- or activity-dependent nature of the world. Bruner would agree as he made it abundantly clear that he believed that we all actively construct our own reality. He wrote, "Contrary to common sense, there is no unique 'real world' that pre-exists and is independent of human mental activity and human symbolic language; that which we call the world is a product of some mind whose symbolic procedures construct the world" (Bruner 1986 p. 95).

We can return to Brooks (*cf.* Chap. 4) for a concrete example of this. Brooks, in developing robots that can perform real world tasks, has found that doing so, that the use of a "stored description" approach to navigating the environment (e.g. the use of a map) was simply too inflexible to enable that the robot could cope with a dynamic environment. One of these robots was called Herbert (Brooks et al. 1988; Brooks 1999). Herbert was designed to wander around the MIT lab disposing of empty drinks cans. This fairly task was realised by a number of sub-tasks including distinguishing between empty and full drinks can, avoiding the furniture in its path, and manoeuvring around the mobile residents of the lab. Herbert was able to accom-plish its tasks by way of what Brook's calls a "subsumption architecture" which consisted of a number of connected layers, each responsible for performing a spe-cific tasks. As Herbert moved through its environment, it encountered things which activate particular layers. Thus the various connected layers together with these environmental features it encounters determine the robot's response. The lowest-level layer implemented a behaviour that ensured that the robot would avoid hitting objects. The next layer enabled the robot to wander about while not busy avoid objects. The third layer allowed the robot try to explore and did so by suppressing the activity of the layer beneath it. Brooks notes that this architecture is not an example of connectionism (artificial neural networks); not does it rely on produc-tion rules or German philosophy for that matter. Brooks tells us that Herbert "use[s] the world as its own best representation". (A quote which was to be widely repeated.) Herbert does not rely on a central planning facility as this has been superseded by an interface which is continuously being constructed between the system and the world. In short, Herbert illustrates the rather mysterious ability to bring forth its own world rather than relying on a ready-made representation of it.

One final thought, Moravec (1988) has observed that there is effectively an inverse relationship between computers and humans: what we find easy, computers find difficult. He writes, "it is comparatively easy to make computers exhibit adult level performance on intelligence tests or playing checkers, and difficult or impos-sible to give them the skills of a 1-year-old when it comes to perception and mobility". In short, what we find comparatively easy such as walking across an obstacle filled room has proved to be demanding for artificial intelligences and robots whereas tasks most people would find to be difficult such as playing chess well have proved to (fairly) simple to implement. His explanation for this is an appeal to evolution. We have been very effective animals for millions of years – able to walk, find our way about, reproduce, and a dozen other things common to other animals but which rely on sensorimotor skills and these skills are "encoded" into the brain. In contrast, being able to solve quadratic equations requires abstract thought which has only developed relatively recently (perhaps only in the last 50,000 years), and we are still learning how to use it. Quadratic equations have to be taught in schools to reluctant teenagers who find them boring and irrelevant whereas these self-same students taught themselves to walk largely by themselves.

Embodied

"By using the term embodied we mean to highlight: first, that cognition depends upon the kinds of experience that come from having a body with various sensorimotor capacities, and second, that these individual sensorimotor capacities are themselves embedded in a more encompassing biological, psychological and cultural context. By using the term "enaction" we mean to emphasize once again that sensory and motor processes, perception and action, are fundamentally inseparable in lived cognition" (Varela et al. 1991, p. 173). For Valera, this lived cognition is a dynamic sensorimotor activity that emerges from the bodily activities of the organism which act upon a world. This may sound a little circular but here the claim is that cognition comprises multiple sensorimotor feedback loops. Hutto and Myin (2013, p. 7) also describe cognition as loopy, not linear, while Clark (2009) invites us to think of it as "Escher Spaghetti" – "not just multiple criss-crossing strands (like ordinary spaghetti), but strands whose ends feed back into their own (and others) beginnings, making 'input' and 'output', and 'early' and 'late' into imprecise and misleading visions of complex recurrent and re-entrant dynamics". The power of these sensorimotor loops can be readily seen in a Braitenberg vehicle.

These vehicles are simple machines that use basic sensorimotor connections to produce apparently intelligent behaviour. They were originally developed as a thought experiment by cyberneticist Valentino Braitenberg to illustrate the behaviour of simple intelligent agents (Braitenberg 1984). A Braitenberg vehicle embodies the simplest form of behaviour based on what might be described as a form of embodied cognition. What we witness when we build these simple machines is "intelligent" behaviour that emerges from the sensorimotor interaction between the robot and its environment. There is no need for an internal memory, or a representation of the environment, or the power of inference. A Braitenberg vehicle is an agent that can autonomously move around by means of its sensors and wheels (each driven by its own motor). A typical Braitenberg vehicle might have two light detectors (left and right) each stimulating a wheel on the same side of the vehicle's body. It obeys simple rules such as: more light right => right wheel turns faster => turns towards the left, away from the light. By cross connecting the sensors and motors (the key components making up a sensorimotor loop) a range of apparently intelligent behaviour emerges such as fear of light, aggressive behaviour and combinations such as when close to light => act fearful and when far from light => act aggressive.[1] In a very similar fashion, infants, through their sensorimotor dealings with objects and other people, learn to distinguish between themselves and the environment by establishing body specific sensorimotor contingencies. For example, every event the infant perceives (e.g., the clapping of hands), whether self-initiated or not, consists of correlated multisensory impressions. In time, the infant learns that some of these patterns of sensorimotor contingencies are exclusively associated with the body, and hence are self-specifying. When the visual image of clapping hands is accompanied immediately by a tactile sensation in the hands, then it must be your hands that is doing the clapping.

As we mentioned in the introduction to this chapter, we will now the lower level elements of cognition, specifically, memory, scaffolding and perception as applied to HCI from an enactive perspective. We begin with episodic memory.

6.3   Episodic Memory

For many, memory is the foundation upon which the cognitive life of the individual rests. Blakemore (1988) observes that "… without the capacity to remember and to learn, it is difficult to imagine what life would be like, whether it could be called living at all. Without memory, we would be servants of the moment, with nothing but our innate reflexes to help us deal with the world. There could be no language, no art, no science, no culture." While this may be regarded as an overstatement, memory is important yet despite this, HCI has chosen to treat it as mere design guidelines, e.g. design for recognition rather than recall; chunk information because short term memory is limited. Memory in HCI is treated as though it has nothing to do with us. It is neither personal nor meaningful. It is a store of disembodied facts. So, instead of the usual impersonal treatment of memory, typified by the venerable multi-store model of Atkinson and Shiffrin (1968) we consider the role of episodic memory.

Tulving (1972) coined the term *episodic memory* to refer to our ability to not just recall but to re-experience specific events where and when they happened. This is distinct from other kinds of memory in being explicitly concerned with our past and accompanied by the feeling of remembering, whereas other knowledge that we acquire is purely factual, without any personalised "past-ness" attached to it as Clayton et al. (2007) put it. Indeed, William James tells us, "Memory requires more than the mere dating of a fact in the past. It must be dated in my past." (James 1890, p. 650). It is for this reason that Tulving makes the distinction between remembering and knowing. Each of us may remember what happened when we last visited London but few of us will remember when they learned that it is the capital of England. Staying with capital cities for a little longer, while we know that Paris is the capital of France and if we do not, it is a fact which is readily acquired. However,

---

[1]A video of these little robots in action can be found at https://www.youtube.com/watch?v=NJo5HEdq6y0 [last retrieved 22nd Feb 2016].

in addition to knowing this, I also remember the last time I had a good lunch there, what I had and with whom I had it. Also, when I recall this, I can see (visualise) myself in the scene, the stuffed Stork in reception (for which the restaurant is famous) and I remember that they had sold out of the myrtle flan I had hoped to order. Episodic memory has a meta-cognitive dimension – we know that we know. For example, we all know that some of our memories are more vivid than others but, even when we do not have a very accurate memory of a particular event, we do know that we experienced the event at some point in our past. To do so, we appear to travel mentally back in time to reconstruct and re-experience it.

Mental Time Travelling

Wollheim (1984) has observes that the episodic – semantic memory division may correspond to the differences in the way these kinds of remembering are reported. As we have already seen, semantic remembering is propositional, for example, I remember that X happened. In contrast, episodic remembering is more a matter of I remember X happening. Episodic memories resemble the experiences they represent. When an experience is remembered, this comprises how things looked, sounded like, or smelled like too. In addition, we also recall our thoughts and state of mind, our beliefs and feelings (*ibid*, p. 64). It is for this reason that episodic remembering has been described as "mental time travel" (Tulving 1984). Downham (2009) has also suggested that when we remember events, the remember-er re-enacts their thoughts, feelings, and intentions which they experienced at that time too and it is these components which make up a first-person perspective. It is this time travelling aspect to episodic memory which gives it a distinct enactive character. And as Wollheim notes, it is the intentionality (or about-ness) of mental phenomena 'that allows them to be internally related to one another or that makes for what has been called the "holism of the mental" (Wollheim 1984, p. 37). The intentionality of episodic memory is the narrative glue which creates a stream of consciousness rather than remembering the past as a series of fragments. Again this is evidence that when someone remembers (thinking and feeling) this or that, they are engaged in mental re-enacting the past.

Conway's Update to Episodic Memory

More recently, Conway (2001) writes that episodic memory is "experience-near" contrasting it with the "experience-distant" memories of fantasy or plans. He conceives of episodic memory as a system that contains information which is highly event specific and sensory-perceptual detailed. These memories are only relatively short lived unless linked with the more persistent autobiographical memories. Episodic memories, he tells us, hold records of goal completion. We remember if we have taken a coffee break or brushed our teeth or whether we had abandoned those plans. These memories represent knowledge of the specific actions and the results of those actions derived from "moment-to-moment experience" which he describes as the minutiae of memory. As part of this update, he has listed a number of the properties of episodic memory (*ibid*, table 1, p. 1376) an excerpt of which is as follows:

- Retains records of sensory-perceptual processing derived from working memory
- Contains organizing abstract knowledge derived from goals active during experiences
- Represents roughly the order [of the events] in which they occurred
- Have a short duration (measured in hours)

Conway also presents evidence that episodic memories are represented in those parts of the brain "most closely involved with the processing that took place during the actual experiences" (ibid, 1376). As interesting as this is, how is it relevant to HCI? Well, this reformulation or refinement to the thinking on episodic memory allows us to avoid the problems of the "fourth wall" and to establish (or perhaps even assert) the validity of the use of post use questionnaires which are so popular in, for example, user experience and tele-presence research. It may also play a role in at least one theoretical account of the experience of tele-presence too (Riva et al. 2004).

The Fourth Wall

"The fourth wall" is an expression comes from the theatre. Breaking "the fourth wall" means having a character on stage becoming aware of their fictional nature or stepping out of the narrative to address the audience directly (a device often used by comedians). In HCI research, we can imagine asking someone to experience a digital experience and then assess the extent of their involvement or immersion or engagement. Asking someone how immersed (or engaged – whatever) they are during this is essentially asking them to step out of the experience and to break the fourth wall. So the only practical alternative (excluding the use of biometrics) is to ask people questions after the experience usually in the form of a questionnaire (e.g. Witmer and Singer 1998; Usoh et al. 2000). In addition to the usual problems of establishing that the questionnaire is valid (is it measuring what we think it is measuring) or reliable (is it measuring what we think it is measuring accurately) there remains the issue of determining whether we are eliciting their actual experience rather than the gist or partial memory of what they had experienced. What Conway has established with his work is that episodic memory is available to a promptly administered questionnaire is accessing these "near-experience" memories.

Time Travelling into the Future?

If we can travel into the past, can we do so prospectively? Rabin and her colleagues suggest several different but related explanations for this phenomenon. Firstly, evidence from Buckner and colleagues indicates a "capacity for self-projection" which supports a mental shift to "alternate times, places, and perspectives" (Buckner and Carroll 2007). There is also evidence from amnesic patients, who have severe deficits in episodic memory (as a result of trauma), who also have difficulties imagining their personal futures or novel scenes (e.g. Hassabis et al. 2007). One noteworthy amnesic patient was unable remember a single specific episode from his past, nor could he imagine a single specific episode that might occur in his personal future (e.g. Loftus and Zanni 1975). These and related observations led Schacter et al. (2013) to put forth the constructive episodic simulation hypothesis which argues that critical function of episodic memory is to support the construction of imagined future events based on past experiences, and the flexible recombination of elements of past experiences, into simulations of possible future scenarios. Episodic memory supports the mental simulations or enactment of how the future might unfold (e.g. Schacter and Tulving 1994; Schacter et al. 2011, 2013). While this focuses on the contribution of episodic memory, semantic memory contributes to future thinking too (Irish et al. 2012).

Time travelling into the future need not be a mere pastime as it is the very basis of such techniques as future workshops (e.g. Jungk and Müllert 1987).

6.4   Niche Creation

As enaction tells us, our cognition is self-organising, embodied and is concerned with the bringing forth of our own worlds but what could this latter point mean in practice? From this perspective, we must challenge (and perhaps even reject) the standard position that the brain is concerned with identifying features in a pre-given environment. In the late 1970s cortical cells were found to be extremely specialised in that they responded to a small range of targets. The most famous example of these were neurons in monkeys which showed a vigorous response when exposed to a stimulus in the shape of a monkey's paw (Gross et al. 1969; 1972). But if we are not concerned with identifying predefined features, what could it mean to create our own worlds. In one sense this sounds like make-believe – which we discuss in the next chapter – or possibly, in a very tangible sense, niche construction.

Laland and Sterelny (2006, p. 1751) tell us of niche construction that it is not the "organism-driven modification of the environment per se, but rather modification of the relationship between an organism and its relative niche. Hence the term "niche construction" includes such things as habitat selection, where organisms modify the environment that they experience". Niches are found throughout the biological world, for example, beavers construct dams and in doing so create their own watery landscapes of pools and lagoons. Other examples include the trap-door spider constructs a "trap door" above its burrow allowing it to spring upon an unsuspecting insect; and gorillas building a nest every evening to ensure a safe and pleasant night's sleep and the annual migration, well-trodden paths taken by animals such as the reindeer.

Niches are also found in the various social and cognitive worlds we construct. They are found anywhere organisms manage, optimise and appropriate their local environments. Magnani and Bardone (2008, p. 3) write that we "build models, representations and other mediating structures" and that we are "ecological engineers" engaged in creating what they describe as "cognitive niches". The term "cognitive niche" itself was coined by Tooby and DeVore (1987) who suggested it to explain aspects of human cognition. Stotz (2010) also writes that a cognitive niche presents itself as "a problem-solving resource and scaffold for individual development and learning [...] what is most distinctive about humans is their developmentally plastic brains immersed into a well-engineered, cumulatively constructed cognitive–developmental niche". In a similar vein, Clark (2008) also notes that cognitive niches replace the necessity to plan any task by exploiting regularities in the "agent's motor, sensory and neural systems and the physical and social environment" and with their help they can accomplish tasks beyond the capacity of the "naked brain".

Technological Niches

Elsewhere (Turner 2013) has proposed *technological niches*. Such niches extend beyond the technology itself, and would be constructed to ensure that we feel safe, secure and comfortable in the face of the complexities (and threats) presented by technology. A technological niche is the result of appropriating technology. In many respects these appropriative acts are an active expression of familiarity, we are make technology more familiar. Technological niches are necessarily smaller, simpler, more manageable and more closely aligned to our needs, both personal and professional, than the "world of work".

We are, of course, not the to first describe these technological worlds which we create for ourselves. The language is different but the underlying ideas are similar. Kirsh (1996) has proposed *artefact ecologies* which comprise a number of different elements, including what he calls "species", systems, user groups, practices and the task environment. An artefact "species" might include such things as axes or knives, table or desktop computers which, to use the language of biology, "compete with" and complement each other; artefact systems are collections or constellations of other mutually related artefacts (e.g. knives and forks). Of course, if creating our own niches proves to be too demanding we can even buy an "off-the-shelf" ready-made niche, for example, it has been observed that certain manufacturers create technological niches to ensure that their product range work together seamlessly. Similar observations have been made of social media which effectively shield the individual users from the vagaries of the Web by offering all a user could possibly want within the confines and safety of their own platform. What emerges from this is the discussion of niche creation reflects many of the aspects of Vygotskian scaffolding writ large.

Krippendorff and Butter (2007) agree writing that "It is a truism that we surround ourselves with objects that we are comfortable with and experience as meaningful. This is axiomatic for designers as well as for those who have a stake in their designs. To design artefacts for use by others is to design them to be or to have the chance to become meaningful to these others – not merely in their designers' terms, but according to these others' own and often diverse conceptions." They continue, "Artifacts of different species with synonymous meanings (interfaces) compete for the same ecological niches, while artifacts that have complementary meanings can work together, cooperate, and may develop larger technological cooperatives … Ordinary users may not be aware of the ecological properties of their artifacts, which are brought about by inserting them into contexts of their choice, but to designers, these properties are of central importance for a design to have a chance of surviving in the context of other species of artifacts". They emphasize the contextual and dynamic nature of the affordances associated with artefacts and the meanings attributed to them. Jung et al. (2008) offer yet another complementary perspective, writing of *personal ecologies* of interactive artefacts as comprising all physical artefacts with some level of interactivity enabled by digital technology that a person owns, has access to, or simply uses. Their work identifies *ecological factors* which define connections or commonalties between artefacts which are commonly based on their function, or shared information, or their perceived characteristics. Also propose *ecological layers* which seem to be multiple sub-ecologies, grouped by e.g. context of use or selected features of the artefacts; many artefacts exist in multiple layers. Use of ecologies by individuals may be more or less structured or organised. For example, worth may be a factor: an artefact may be inexpensive or valuable and this may be a factor in the development of ecologies and how objects within them are appropriated.

Surrounding Ourselves with Technology

Finally, from Activity Theory, Bødker and Klokmose (2015) write that "Human beings surround themselves with many artifacts, in many everyday activities, and what artifact is 'natural' for them to use, is highly dependent on their individual past experiences, as well as of the shared practices in which they are part, and the technological possibilities offered to them, in (and outside) these communities of practice." True to the spirit of Activity Theory, such ecologies are necessarily shared by a community, within which individuals develop praxis "There is no user without other users who share their experiences with artifacts and materials, understanding, etc.". Ecologies comprise multiple different devices which serve similar purposes, with no clear means of deciding between them: this is situated and depends on the characteristics of the ecology; both artefacts and activities in constant development, i.e. they are dynamic. This can be analysed through their Human-Artifact model, which "combines analyses of human experiences and artifacts, and addresses the tensions between human skills and capacity on the one hand, and the action possibilities and affordances offered by the artifact on the other". They see no distinction between the physical and the digital in this context "we believe the distinction can be overcome through a dialectical materialist understanding of how our perception is shaped through our artifact ecology." So there we have it, clear evidence that people create their own technological niches. The reason for creating these niches or ecologies is not always clear but it is safe to say that these structures tend to scaffold our broader endeavours.

6.5   Enactive Perception

Visual perception has probably received more attention from within Enaction than any other cognitive faculty. A major theme in this research is that perception is something we do, it is active and it is a skill. This stands in sharp contrast to classical cognitive accounts of perception which often simply treatment as an example of information processing. Noë's (2004) treatment of perception is helpful here. He argues that touch, not vision, should be our model for perception. He does not regard perception as a process in the brain but consistent with enactive theory, it is better thought of as a consequence of the skilful activity of the body as a whole. Thus perception is not merely about the transduction of physical sensations: it is about having sensations and knowing what to do with them. Hutto and Myin (2013, p. 17) write that, "what is necessary for experiencing, in addition to appropriate stimulation is the organism's history and embodied habits of interacting". Not knowledge or unconscious inference but habit. Further, perceptual content is not given "all at once" but should be seen as the product of our "active inquiry and exploration." (Noë 2004, p. 33). So when we skilfully perceive digital technology what do we perceive? The answer, quite predictably, is that we pick up the affordances it has to offer. However, we propose that with our continued use of (and correspondingly increasing skill with) technology we do not merely see the affordances on offer but we are able to see it differently – we see it as.

Seeing As

If indeed perception it is a skill that we learn, we should be able to improve this skill and this has been demonstrated to be the case. By way of an example consider making sense of an x-ray image. Presented with a standard chest x-ray, most people are unable to identify which dark splodge is the heart. The radiologist, in contrast, looking at exactly the same patterns of light and dark is able to identify all manner of unwelcome problems – and, of course, the heart. The same pattern of light produce the same retinal image in novice and expert but different perceptions result. It is the very heterogeneity of skilled perception which opens up possibility as Bucciarelli (1994) observes:

> ...consider this page in front of you. [...] A naïve empiricist would sense its weight and estimate its size; another reader might note its colour or texture; a chemist on the design team would describe its resistance to discoloration, its acidity, and its photosensitivity. A mechanical engineer would be concerned with its tear or its tensile strength, its stiffness, and its thermal conductivity. An electrical engineer would speak of its ability to conduct or hold a static charge. All of these attributes of the object, the same artefact, are understood within different frames of reference, and they might all contend in a design process.... (Bucciarelli p. 71)

Skilled perception discloses opportunities and possibilities that unpractised eye seeing cannot. Perception as a skill has also been explored by Chase and Simon (1973) who have shown that the chess master player perceives patterns of pieces which the novice cannot; similarly the academic is able to locate him or herself in the information space offered by a journal paper more accurately than the less experienced reader (e.g. Dillon and Scaap 1996) and the expert tennis player is able to predict the direction of an opponent's serve better than a novice (e.g. Farrow and Abernethy 2003). Oudejans et al. (1996) have also reported that the perception of an individual's ability to catch a falling object by running to its landing point is improved when observers are permitted to begin running before making their judgments, rather than watching the flight of the ball while remaining stationary.

So, we propose that an inevitable consequence of the extended use of technology is that it discloses something new about it we see it as something else. For example, those of us who have used our email clients for an extended period of time may come to recognise that it can be used as an automatically date-stamped and convenient "to do" list. While we continue to see the affordances the email client offers, we also see it as an application which affords organising the list of tasks we need to complete. Having disclosed a new affordance or a cluster of affordances we are then free to exploit it or them. This exploitation of the new is, of course, appropriation. From this perspective, appropriation emerges as a natural consequence of use. We regard this formulation acts as a kind of bridge between perception – affordance coupling and thinking with things.

6.6   In Conclusion

Enactive cognition is not as well articulated as it might be but it offers a variety of interesting contributions to HCI. It has its own very distinctive formulation just as extended cognition and the different varieties of embodiment have but beyond this, it speaks directly to a number of different aspects of HCI. For example, while memory does have a role in HCI, we can be confident that it is not as a storehouses of knowledge, or disembodied facts. Episodic memory offers a more meaningful, personal perspective. As for the importance of "bring forth a world", which stands in contrast with our dealings with one which is conceived of as objective, pre-existing we can see that it offers a theoretical basis for the many different forms of niche creation. Finally, in recognising the close coupling between perception and affordance we have proposed a theoretically rich means by which we appropriate technology. Although enaction may be a little unfamiliar its potential contribution to HCI is significant.

References

Atkinson RC, Shiffrin RM (1968) Human memory: a proposed system and its control processes. In: Spence KW, Spence JT (eds) The psychology of learning and motivation, vol 2. Academic, New York, pp 89–195

Blakemore C (1988) The mind machine. BBC Publications, London

Braitenberg V (1984) Vehicles: experiments in synthetic psychology. MIT Press, Cambridge, MA

Brooks RA (1999) Cambrian intelligence. MIT Press, Cambridge, MA

Brooks RA, Connell JH, Ning P (1988) Herbert: a second generation mobile robot, Memo 1016. Massachusetts Instituted of Technology AI Lab, Cambridge, MA

Bruner J (1966) Towards a theory of instruction. Harvard University Press, Cambridge, MA

Bruner J (1986) Actual minds, possible worlds. Harvard University Press, Cambridge, MA

Bucciarelli LL (1994) Designing engineers. MIT Press, Cambridge, MA

Buckner RL, Carroll DC (2007) Self-projection and the brain. Trends Cogn Sci 11:49–57

Chase WG, Simon HA (1973) Perception in chess. Cogn Psychol 4:55–81

Clark A (2008) Supersizing the mind. Oxford University Press, Oxford

Clark A (2009) Spreading the joy? Why the machinery of consciousness is (probably) still in the head. Mind 118(472):963–993

Clayton NS, Salwiczek LH, Dickinson A (2007) Episodic memory. Curr Biol 17(6):R189–R191

Conway MA (2001) Sensory-perceptual episodic memory and its context: autobiographical memory. Phil Trans R Soc Lond B 356:1375–1384

Di Paolo EA, Rohde M, De Jaegher H (2014) Horizons for the enactive mind: values, social interaction, and play. In: Stewart J, Gapenne O, Di Paolo EA (eds) Enaction – towards a new paradigm for cognitive science. MIT Press, Cambridge, MA

Dillon A, Scaap D (1996) Expertise and the perception of shape in information. J Am Soc Inf Sci 47(10):786–788

Downham R (2009) Episodic memory as enactive know-how: cognitive, affective, and conative resources of remembered experience. In: Christensen W, Schier E, Sutton J (eds) ASCS09: proceedings of the 9th conference of the Australasian Society for Cognitive Science. Macquarie Centre for Cognitive Science, Sydney, pp 81–83

Farrow D, Abernethy B (2003) Do expertise and the degree of perception – action coupling affect natural anticipatory performance? Perception 32(9):1127–1139

Gross CG, Bender DB, Rocha-Miranda CE (1969) Visual receptive fields of neurons in inferotemporal cortex of the monkey. Science 166:1303–1306

Gross GC, Rocha-Miranda CE, Bender DB (1972) Visual properties of neurons in inferotemporal cortex of the macaque. J Neurophysiol 35:96–111

Hassabis D, Kumaran D, Maguire EA (2007) Using imagination to understand the neural basis of episodic memory. J Neurosci 27:14365–14374

Hutto DD, Myin E (2013) Radicalizing enactivism. MIT Press, Cambridge, MA

Irish M, Addis DR, Hodges JR, Piguet O (2012) Considering the role of semantic memory in episodic future thinking: evidence from semantic dementia. Brain 135(7):2178–2191

James W (1890/1950) The principles of psychology. Dover Publications, New York

Jung H, Stolterman E, Ryan W, Thompson T, Siegel M (2008) Toward a framework for ecologies of artifacts: how are digital artifacts interconnected within a personal life? In: Proceedings of the NordiCHI 2008. ACM Press, New York, pp 201–210

Jungk R, Müllert N (1987) Future workshops: how to create desirable futures. Institute for Social Inventions, London. ISBN 0-948826-39-8

Kirsh D (1996) Adapting the environment instead of oneself. Adapt Behav 4(3/4):415–452

Kirsh D (2013) Embodied cognition and the magical future of interaction design. Trans Comput Hum Interact 20(1):3

Krippendorff K, Butter R (2007) Semantics: meanings and contexts of artifacts. In: Schifferstein HNJ, Hekkert P (eds) Product experience. Elsevier, New York. Retrieved from http://repository.upenn.edu/asc_papers/91

Loftus EF, Zanni G (1975) Eyewitness testimony: the influence of the wording of a question. Bull Psychon Soc 5:86–88

Laland KN, Sterelny K (2006) Perspective: seven reasons (not) to neglect niche construction. Evolution 60(9):1751–1762

Magnani L, Bardone E (2008) Sharing representations and creating chances through cognitive niche construction. The Role of Affordances and Abduction. Studies in Computational Intelligence (SCI) 123. Springer-Verlag, Berlin/Heidelberg, pp 3–40

Maturana HR (1970) Biology of cognition. Biological computer laboratory research report BCL 9.0. University of Illinois, Urbana, 1970. As Reprinted in: Autopoiesis and cognition: the realization of the living. D Reidel Publishing Co., Dordrecht, 1980, pp 5–58

Maturana HR, Varela FJ (1980) Autopoiesis and cognition: the realization of the living. Springer, Berlin

McGann M (2007) Enactive theorists do it on purpose: toward an enactive account of goals and goal-directedness. Phenomenol Cogn Sci 6:463–483

Moravec H (1988) Mind children: the future of robot and human intelligence. Harvard University Press, Cambridge, MA

Noë A (2004) Action in perception. MIT Press, Cambridge, MA

Oudejans RRD, Michaels CF, Bakker FC, Dolne M (1996) The relevance of action in perceiving affordances: perception of catchableness of fly balls. J Exp Psychol Hum Percept Perform 22:683–703

Riva G, Waterworth JA, Waterworth EL (2004) The layers of presence: a bio-cultural approach to understanding presence in natural and mediated environments. CyberPsychol Behav 7(4):402–416

Schacter DL, Tulving E (1994) Memory systems. MIT Press, Cambridge, MA

Schacter DL, Guerin SA, Jacques PLS (2011) Memory distortion: an adaptive perspective. Trends Cogn Sci 15:467–474

Schacter DL, Gaesser B, Addis DR (2013) Remembering the past & imagining the future in the elderly. Gerontology 59:143–151

Stewart J, Gapenne O, Di Paolo EA (eds) (2010) Enaction: toward a new paradigm for cognitive science. MIT Press, Cambridge, MA

Stotz K (2010) Human nature and cognitive-developmental niche construction. Phenomenol Cogn Sci 9(4):483–501

Tooby J, DeVore I (1987) The reconstruction of hominid behavioral evolution through strategic modeling. In: W G Kinzey (ed) The evolution of human behavior: primate models. SUNY Press, Albany

Tulving E (1972) Episodic and semantic memory. In: Tulving E, Donaldson W (eds) Organization of memory. Academic, New York, pp 381–402

Tulving E (1984) Précis of elements of episodic memory. Behav Brain Sci 7:223–268

Turner P (2013) How we cope with digital technology. Morgan & ClayPool, San Rafael

Usoh M, Catena E, Arman S, Slater M (2000) Using presence questionnaires in reality. Presence Teleop Virt 9(5):497–503

Valera FJ (1999) First-person methodologies: why, when and how. J Conscious Stud 6(2–3):1–14

Varela FJ, Thompson E, Rosch E (1991) The embodied mind: cognitive science and human experience. MIT Press, Cambridge, MA

Witmer BG, Singer MJ (1998) Measuring presence in virtual environments: a presence questionnaire. Presence Teleop Virt 7:225–240

Wollheim R (1984) The thread of life. Cambridge University Press, Cambridge

Web Resource

Bødker S, Klokmose CN (2015) A dialectical take on artifact ecologies and the physical-digital divide. In CHI workshop on ecological perspectives in HCI, Korea, April 2015. Available from http://rizzo.media.unisi.it/EPCHI2015/resources/papers/A-dialectical-take-on-artifact-ecologies.pdf. Last accessed 23 Apr 2016

Chapter 7
Epistemic Coping

we walk and read aloud, we get off and on street cars, we dress and undress, and do a thousand useful acts without thinking of them. (Dewey 1922, p. 178)

7.1 Introduction

So far we have treated cognition as a unitary phenomenon, though one which is susceptible to multiple interpretations and extensions, for example, we have seen that it has been prefixed by the "4 E's" – embodied, extended, external and enactive. However, in this chapter we consider the evidence that cognition comprises two types, which have been broadly characterised as the pairs, intuitive – reflective or automatic – controlled or most simply, fast – slow. With these characterisations also comes the realisation that cognition is either conscious or unconscious and that the vast majority of our behaviour and "thinking" is unconscious. If this is so, and this includes our use of interactive technology (and there are no presenting reasons why that should not be the case), we might reasonably describe this use of it as unconscious resulting in "thoughtless interaction".

We begin with a brief review of the technological developments that illustrates and perhaps even exploits this dichotomy in our cognition.

Two Generations of Information Appliances

If the first six chapters of this book have a common theme it is complexity. Interactive technology, it seems, requires a great deal of complex cognitive preparation (which may be in the form of planning (or the manipulation of a mental model) before it might be used. But what if this were not the case? Suppose interactive technology

© Springer International Publishing Switzerland 2016
P. Turner, *HCI Redux*, Human–Computer Interaction Series,
DOI 10.1007/978-3-319-42235-0_7

enabled us to complete one task really well, like pressing a single button to order our favourite pizza or a box of soap powder from an online retailer when we run low?

Raskin (2000) proposed that computers need not be treated as multi-purpose devices capable of managing a variety of tasks such as hosting a web page, or emulating a piano or managing a nuclear arsenal but could instead could be used to do one thing really well and really easily. He used the term "information appliance" to describe such a device. This was elaborated by Norman in his *The Invisible Computer* (1998) and later extended by contributions from Bergman (2000). In an interview reported in Bergmann, Norman tells us that, "The PC [personal computer] attempts to do all things for all people. It is one device: the same design for both hardware and software made to fit everyone in the entire world … [which] I think is too complex". Information appliances were proposed as a potential solution to this problem.

Although there is some dispute over how exactly an information appliance is defined and whether or not any were built to this original formulation,[1] the principles are inherent to the myriad 'apps' available for a wide range of platforms but primarily for smart phones and tablets. Apps seem to be exactly what Raskin and Norman had in mind and have become near-ubiquitous, for example, as of 2014, 70 % of young people in the UK aged 5–15 years owned a tablet computer whose primary raison d'être is to serve as a platforms for apps (Ofcom 2014). The appeal of such devices is that they are portable, powerful, connected and perhaps most importantly they do not require very much in the way of cognitive effort to use.

In parallel with this Eler and Peyser (2016) have written of the "tinderization" of interaction based on the design of the Tinder online dating service. They observe that Tinder is symptomatic of "speeding up and mechanizing decision-making" and it does so by offering choices reduced to simple yes/no, like/ignore responses which "leaves no room for maybe". They claim that "within Tinder, we sort each other into ones and zeroes, flattening away any human complexity, becoming efficient robots." Whether or not this criticism is fair, this kind of yes – no decision making does not require much in the way of reflection as it is verges on the automatic.

Overall, there is no reason to assume that using these technologies is any different from using a microwave oven, or any modern household appliance. It is something children learn to do as a matter of course and it seems unlikely that their behaviour (say when playing *Candy Crush*) is readily captured with a GOMS model or that small children need to consult a mental model of the technology before they can use it. This is also likely to apply to other forms of interactive technology which are used daily in the home, car, office or classroom and which consequently has (to borrow NASA's term) become overlearned and, as such, is also used with a minimum of cognitive effort.

---

[1] The Amazon Dash Button is arguably the best (and perhaps only) example of this being a Wi-Fi connected button that orders items, such as soap powder, with a single press.

7.2   Intuitive *or* Reflective Thinking

The recognition that we are able to think in two different ways may have begun with Kant (1800) when he discussed the nature of (mental) representation. He tells us that of those which are formed consciously, these are divided into either "*intuitions or concepts*". Intuitions are derived from perception while concepts come from reasoning or are (rather mysteriously) *a priori*. Janiak (2012) tells us that, "intuitions are singular, immediate representations, [whereas] concepts are general, mediate ones". Another popular distinction is that cognition can be controlled or automatic. Dewey has argued that most of what we do is a matter of routine or habit and as such our behaviour is not under conscious control. He claims that we employ controlled, conscious thought only when (by definition) we encounter something which we cannot treat routinely. Agre agrees telling us that, "everyday life is almost wholly routine …" which he defines as, "a frequently repeated pattern of interaction between an agent and its familiar environment" (1997, p. 107).

Kahneman (2011) also identifies a distinction in the operation of our cognition which he calls system 1 and system 2 thinking, or more succinctly, *fast* thinking and *slow* thinking. Kahneman, like many two-systems theorists, has presented empirical evidence for two distinct forms of thinking.

While these pairs of intuitive-reflective, controlled-automatic and fast-slow may have common and overlapping properties, they are discussed and developed differently in the literature and we will respect these divisions in this chapter. Finally, while these distinctions appear to apply to cognition as a whole, there are, of course, more localised divisions – memory, for example, is typically described in terms of a variety of stores such as iconic, short-term, and long-term – but for the purposes of this chapter we will not consider these finer grain partitions. It must be said here that there are researchers who have argued strongly against cognition being anything other than a unitary phenomenon (e.g. Osman 2004) while others have proposed that cognition may comprise as many as three different components (e.g. Stanovich 2009). While not everyone agrees and of those who do, they do not agree amongst themselves, within the limited domain of human-computer interaction, this bi-partite division does appear to have merit.

More Kantian Thought

Davidson (1882, p. 304) has developed the Kantian perspective as follows: *"The primary signification [of intuition] follows the etymology. Intuition literally means – seeing though the eye, visual perception… If, then, we ask at this stage what Intuition is, we obtain as answer – the apprehension or discerning of a thing actually present to the eye; and it is distinguished, on the one hand, from the revival of that thing in memory".*

While this may seem a little unfamiliar, there are number of writers who treat perception as other than a means to identifying and locating objects. The most obvious example of this is the work of Gibson and his treatment of affordance. He argues that perception is direct, unmediated and primarily for action. Kirsh (2013) has developed this, writing that the world is perceived relative to the "action repertoire of the perceiver" – that is, we see the world with respect to what we are able do with it. If we change this repertoire then the perceptual world changes too. For Gibson (1977, 1986), this action-perception coupling is not mediated by internal representations instead it has evolved to detect and exploit the opportunities which the environment provides. "We must perceive in order to move, but we must also move in order to perceive" (1979, p. 223). This position has received both support and attention with work in the cognitive sciences (e.g. Clark 1997), robotics (e.g. Schaal 1999), the study of skilled behaviour (e.g. Montagne et al. 2003) and developmental psychology (e.g. Thelen and Smith 1994; Bertenthal et al. 1997). Together this work has underlined the unmediated coupling between perception and action. However, for the sake of the current argument, we wish to highlight a less familiar aspect of perception, namely that it is the product of experience, or to use that Marxist favourite, history.

Wartofsky (1979) has proposed that perception is an historical process. He argues that much of perception is culturally acquired and that it changes with experience. Like Gibson, he observes that there is a reciprocal relationship between the animal and its environment: while the perceived world of the animal can be treated as a map or an image of the animal's activities, the senses of animals themselves are shaped by the purposive interactions which the species has with the environment, or as he puts it, "Rather, the very forms of perceptual activity are now shaped to, and also help to shape an environment created by conscious human activity itself. This environment is the world made by praxis". An excellent example of this may be found in Goodwin and Goodwin's (1998) study of operational staff at an airport. The study demonstrates how perceptions of information artefacts (flight information displays, documentation linking flights, destinations and aircraft) and their perceived properties or characteristics are shaped by the histories of both the personnel involved and the artefacts themselves. The Goodwins further observe that such perceptions are always grounded in particular organisations, tasks and mediating artefacts.

Though this will be an unfamiliar treatment of perception for some, it does resonant quite strongly with much of the enactive perspective as described in Chap. 6.

Intuitive or Familiar?

The appeal of creating technology that is simple and direct has resulted in the claim that it is "intuitive", this having become probably the most misused term in all of HCI. There can be no such thing as an intuitive user interface because intuitiveness is a property of our cognition (Turner 2008, 2013). Indeed, Raskin (1994) argues that a user interface is only "intuitive" in as much as it resembles (or is identical) to something the user already knows, "In short, intuitive in this context is an almost exact synonym of familiar." Noddings and Shore (1984) agree and tell us that intuitive behaviour is characteristic in familiar domains. They also observe that the greater the familiarity the more likely and reliable the associated intuitions. Blackler and her colleagues argue that intuition is an unconscious form of cognition reliant on prior practical knowledge (e.g. Blackler and Hurtienne 2007). So, what is emerging is that intuitiveness relies on prior knowledge or familiarity which a particular domain – whether one is a clinician, chess player, academic, or tennis player.

Finally, intuition also suggests the affective or visceral (as in prompting a "gut feeling"), Westcott (1968) telling us that it is primarily affective rather than rational and its most frequently cited aspect is an individual's sense of what is right or wrong, appropriate or inappropriate in a given context. Following this thought takes us to Norman's account of the kinds of emotional responses we have to digital technology. Norman (2004) claims that these visceral or intuitive responses are both unlearned and are independent of culture.

Familiarity

The lived experience of the world engenders familiarity. Familiarity is a thorough knowledge of something or someone. The word has a common root with family. Familiarity has not received a great deal of empirical attention and it is rare to find the recommendation to "design for familiarity" and, of course, there is no psychology of familiarity.

We define familiarity with technology as the readiness to cope with it (Turner 2013). Familiarity is that practical "know how" which is the result of repeated, often disparate, exposure to technology. Correspondingly, intuitive behaviour is triggered by these self-same familiar situations. Dreyfus (1991, p. 9) tells us that, "Familiarity consists of dispositions to respond to situations in appropriate ways".

Blackler and her colleagues have reported studies of "technology familiarity" which perhaps unsurprisingly they found to be good predictors of subsequent performance with new but similar or related technology. they found that people with good "technology familiarity" began to use the new technology more quickly and used more of its features than those with poorer technology familiarity (Blackler et al. 2003a, b). These observations have been echoed by Dixon and O'Reilly (2002) who have also argued that people almost never learn completely new procedures as they simply adapted their behaviour from prior knowledge. Blackler and Hurtienne (2007) have gone on to consider the role and structure of prior knowledge per se in the use of digital technology. They begin by re-iterating that the, "use of products involves utilising knowledge gained through other experience(s). Therefore, products that people use intuitively are those with features they have encountered before." Hurtienne and Israel (2007) describe a technical system as being intuitively usable if, "the users'unconscious application of pre-existing knowledge leads to effective interaction" (p. 128).

Why Familiarity Is Not a Form of Representation

Familiarity, as readiness to cope, sounds like an orienting schema or perhaps a script which might guide our actions. For example, I have the know-how to touch type, find my way to the local railway station and take a train to work because I am familiar with keyboards and the vagaries and everyday operation of my local train company. I am familiar because I use a keyboard everyday and have to travel on trains most days. I am familiar with these different forms of technology because I have to use them and because I have chosen to use them, and have watched other people use them, both in the real world and in a wide variety of media. I am able to demonstrate my familiarity with these diverse technologies not by having complex, abstract cognitive structures in my head but demonstrating this "know-how" and acting appropriately.

Some of the Consequences of Unfamiliarity

If familiarity, as practical know-how, enables people to use technology "intuitively", then what are the consequences of unfamiliarity? Here I speak personally, I do not own a mobile phone and find their use and attraction difficult to understand. (*Now you are wondering whether it was wise to buy this book.*) I know how they work at a technical level (cells, microwaves, SIM cards and so forth) but I do not have the know-how to use them to any great effect. I can make a call, I can check the weather forecast but beyond that I am completely immune to their appeal. The consequences of this is that I am in a minority; I appear to be on the wrong side of the "digital divide" but my non-ownership seems to say more about who I am (my identity) rather than my cognition.

7.3 Automatic *or* Controlled Thinking

We could describe the performance of routine activities, which involve little or no thought or awareness, as *automatic*. This leads us to the work of Schneider and his colleagues, who have proposed that our everyday behaviour is the result of two processes which they describe as being either automatic and controlled (e.g. Schneider and Shiffrin 1977; Shiffrin and Schneider 1977). This is not to be understood as a mutually exclusive either-or but an intermix, with people alternating between automatic and controlled processing. These researchers also distinguished between the two processes in terms of the demands they made on our attention. Automatic processing is fast, difficult to modify (as it is not under direct control) but makes no demands on our attentional resources. As such, automatic processing is confined to well-developed, familiar tasks. In contrast,

Table 7.1 Some attributes of knowledge versus skill-based actions

Knowledge-based (conscious)	Skill-based (automatic)
Unskilled or occasional user	Skilled, regular user
Novel environment	Familiar environment
Slow	Fast
Effortful	Effortless
Requires considerable feedback	Requires little feedback
Cases of error	**Causes of error**
Overload	Strong habit intrusions
Manual variation	Frequently invoked rule used inappropriately
Lack of knowledge of modes of use	Situational changes that do not trigger the need to change habits
Lack of awareness of consequences	

controlled processing is slow, under conscious control, effortful and capacity-limited. We rely on controlled processing in unfamiliar situations, Shiffrin and his colleagues regarding automaticity as being the result of repeated or habitual exposure and of controlled processes. Ericsson and Simon (1984) agree, telling us that attention is not required when the same cognitive process has been executed many times.

Moors and De Houwer (2006) in a comprehensive and detailed review of the literature on automaticity write that it has a long history within psychology mentioning the contributions of James and Wundt. They also note that "there is no consensus about what automaticity means" (ibid, p. 297). They tell us that approaches to its study have included the investigation of number of pairs of features, namely that it is –(un)intentional,[2] goal (in)dependent, (un)controlled, autonomous, purely stimulus driven, (un)conscious, (non)-efficient, fast(slow).

Other accounts of automatic and controlled behaviour exist, for example, in context of the skilled use of technology, Rasmussen's (1983) *Skill, Rule and Knowledge* model distinguishes between what he describes as sensory-motor performance which, "take place without conscious control as smooth, automated, and highly integrated patterns of behavior" from those which are rule-based or knowledge-based. In the knowledge based mode, the individual uses technology almost entirely consciously. This is easily observed in the novice or when an individual encounters an novel (unfamiliar) situation. It is argued that careful, conscious and effortful control is required when the individual needs to assess what is needed at every step. In contrast, the skill based mode is evidenced by the smooth execution of practiced actions. Such skill based responses are often in response to a specific event such as an alarm. The differences between these two mode of working are summarised in Table 7.1 which has been adapted from Reason (1990).

---

[2] Intentional in the philosophical sense as meaning it is about something rather than it intends something.

Familiarity (Again)

Another related account of automatic behaviour can be found in Norman's Activation-Trigger-Schema (ATS) proposal (Norman 1981). In this he offers an explanation as to how people can encounter a familiar situation, recognise it and act without deliberation. For example, when driving, the appropriate sequences of actions for braking or steering are triggered automatically (at least in the experienced driver) by appropriate conditions as such traffic lights, oncoming traffic and so forth. Norman's ATS model proposes that action sequences such as these are realised by sensorimotor schemata, which are triggered by activated higher level schema. Once triggered these lower-level components complete the action autonomously, without the further need for intervention. The parallel with hierarchical structure of an activity as in Activity Theory is striking. Reason and Mycielska (1982, p. 224) go further by suggesting that familiar objects in themselves will actually trigger automatic behaviour, "… familiar objects possess what we call an immediate controlling region. Once in touch with them, our actions conform to the structural needs of the object." As our actions can become increasingly automatic, so can the manner in which we think (Uleman and Bargh 1989). The more practice individuals have in thinking in a specific way, the more automatic that kind of thinking becomes, to the point where we can do it unconsciously, without any effort. Automatic processing is when individuals think in a way unconsciously, unintentionally, involuntarily, and effortlessly. Finally, work in social cognition has focussed on the explication of automatic and controlled modes of operation, with particular emphasis on person perception, attitudes and stereotyping (Evans 2008). This may go someway to explain why we so readily anthropomorphise (see Sect. 1.3).

Activity Theory and Automaticity

Table 7.2 identifies the three levels of analysis which can be applied to purposive, technologically-mediated behaviour from the perspective of Activity Theory (we saw a more detailed form of this table in Chap. 2).

Table 7.2 Not all levels of activities are under conscious control

Levels of activity	Mental representation	Level of description
Activity	Motive – not necessarily conscious	The social and personal meaning of activity …
Action	Goal – under conscious control	Possible goals, critical
		goals, particularly
		relevant sub-goals
Operation	Conditions of actions – normally not under conscious control	The concrete way of executing an action in accordance with the specific conditions surrounding the goal

Of interest here is the contrast between actions which are under conscious control and operations. Operations are automatic, internalised and triggered by suitable conditions (Kuutti 1996 p. 38). In short, operations are situated. Further, while they are not consciously performed they originally were under conscious control (and, this of course, is the result of learning). This lowest level of analysis concerns how the activity realised. Of this level Activity Theory tells us that this refers to "the concrete way of executing an action in accordance with the specific conditions surrounding the goal". This level is situated, not under conscious control, and approximates to intuitive behaviour and system 1 thinking (discussed later in this chapter).

Habits

A related concept to that of automatic and controlled modes of cognition is that of habit. It was William James (1890, p. 122) who recognised the importance of habits, writing "We must make automatic and habitual, as early as possible, as many useful actions as we can." He even suggested that "the young" will become mere walking bundles of habits. This been echoed by Pollard (2006) who writes that we often use "habit" as an explanation of everyday life, concluding his discussion by observing, "When we consider just how much of our lives we spend exercising habits, rather than subjecting our actions to deliberation [...] thought is very helpful when we are in novel or important circumstances, the rest of the time it rather gets in the way ... we only think when our habits give out" (p. 18). Pollard also asks us to consider how we acquire a habit. He invites us to imagine someone acquiring the habit φ. Initially, she is able to φ but not automatically; instead φ-ing requires thought and concentration. After repetition, φ-ing has become automatic, φ-ing has become part of what she does. Eventually φ-ing is not just second nature: it has become part of the bundle of habits which define her. So, for Pollard, habits begin as deliberate actions and through repetition they become automatic.

Stephen Turner (1994, p. 16) expands on this, distinguishing habits from simple repetitive behaviours, writing that "Habits are acquired, and there is something which persists between manifestations, a mental trace. The same kind of reasoning that we grant in the case of habits with directly visible manifestations, that there is an invisible "mental" element by virtue of which the visible pattern of behaviour persists, may be extended to those "habits of mind", that we can identify and speak of only indirectly, through complex inferences." Norros (2005) describes habits as having three interlinked characteristics. The first of these is the repetitious regularity of behaviour. It is this aspect which we emphasize in our everyday use of the term. The second characteristic of habits is that they "offer[s] the possibility to express meaning in action" (p. 388). She adds that habits are the way of being for most of us and can be understood in terms of *personal habit*. We have individual, habitual ways of thinking, speaking, behaving and so forth. What is being repeated is our way of *coping* with the world. This repetition of the message is the third and final defining characteristic of a habit in that it has a reflexive component.

7.4   Fast Thinking *or* Slow Thinking

Kahneman distinguishes between System 1 and System 2 thinking in his *Fast Thinking, Slow Thinking* (2011). He describes System 1 thinking as "automatically and quickly, with little or no effort and no sense of voluntary control" (p. 20). Kahneman contrasts this with System 2 thinking which involves the "allocation of attention to the effortful mental activities that demand it, including complex computations. The operations of System 2 is also associated with the subjective experience of agency, choice, and concentration" (p. 21). System 2 may also be described, in more familiar terms, as reasoning or deliberation while System 1 is more perception-like, that is, seamless, immediate and unmediated.

Although Kahneman separates perception and intuition in this model, a point with which not all authors agree, he nonetheless identifies a defining property of intuitive thoughts: they come to mind spontaneously – just like percepts. More formally, Kahneman (2002) illustrates the components of these two systems. As can be seen from Fig. 7.1, the perceptual system and the intuitive operations of System 1 generate involuntary impressions of the attributes of objects of perception and thought. The label "intuitive" is applied to those judgments which arise directly from impressions. In contrast, System 2 is involved in all judgments, whether they originate in impressions or from deliberate reasoning. System 1 is the form of cognition common to both humans and other animals. As we have already noted its operation is fast and is responsible to our day-to-day coping with the world. System 1 thinking has a long list of attributes associated with it including being high capacity, associative, contextualised and not conscious. Kahneman (2011) adds to this list "able to complete the phrase, 'bread and …'", being able to answer the question,

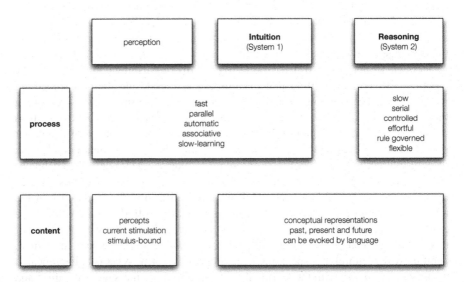

Fig. 7.1 Kahneman's model of cognition

Table 7.3 A selection of the properties of system 1 and system 2 thinking

System 1	System 2
Holistic	Analytic
Automatic	Controlled
Relatively undemanding of cognitive capacity	Capacity demanding
Acquisition personal experience	Acquisition formal tuition
Parallel	Sequential
Evolutionary ancient	Evolutionary recent
Implicit	Explicit
Often unconscious or preconscious	Often conscious
Lower correlation with intelligence	Higher correlations with intelligence
Able to:	**Able to:**
Complete the phrase "bread and …"	Able to identify a surprising sound
Answer the question $2 + 2 =$	Recall & tell someone your telephone number
Read words on large billboards	To compare two washing machines for value
Understand simple sentences	Fill out a tax form

"$2 + 2 =$" and being able to read and understand simple sentences. In reality is probably not a single system, but may comprise to be a set of autonomous sub-systems (e.g. Stanovich and West 2003; Stanovich 2004). Dual-process theorists claim that human beings evolved a powerful general purpose reasoning system – System 2 – which coexists with our older System 1 abilities. Unlike System 1, System 2 is slow, has limited capacity, and is conscious. System 2 thinking is also uniquely human and may have evolved quite recently – perhaps within the past 50,000 years. System 2 thinking is sequential and has a relatively limited capacity; it is also slower than System 1 thinking. However, System 2 permits a number of operations which are not available to System 1 thinking. These include abstract hypothetical thinking and make-believe. Table 7.3 holds a summary of the proposal properties of system 1 and system 2 thinking.

Riva and Mantovani (2012) have reviewed the differences between accounts of the two forms of cognition discussed in this chapter, noting that while their authors may disagree on details and terminology, there is evidence of a broad consensus as presented in Table 7.3.

7.5   Epistemic Coping

We propose a complementary account of our dealings with digital technology, namely, that we cope with it. This is not the coping of dealing with an upset but of absorbed, skilful but essentially thoughtless engagement. We define coping, as adaptive and responsive to the situation we find ourselves in.

The term itself is drawn from the philosophical literature. Dreyfus, for example, describes coping as, "the mostly smooth and unobtrusive responsiveness to circumstances that enable human beings to get around in the world". This practical coping is at work when we eat a meal, write an email, or use an app. In proposing coping we should also recognise that it relies on our repertoire of unarticulated, background skills. Ultimately the Dreyfus position is quite radical, arguing that, "Heidegger's crucial insight is that being-in-the-world is more basic than thinking and solving problems; it is not representational at all. That is, when we are coping at our best, we are drawn in by solicitations and respond directly to them, so that the distinction between us and our equipment vanishes" (Dreyfus 2007, p. 254).

Similarly, Valera (1992) tell us that coping is not concerned with abstract reasoning, as "the proper units of knowledge are primarily concrete, embodied, incorporated, lived; that knowledge is about situated-ness" (p. 7). For Valera, coping is the antithesis of abstract deliberation (*cf.* classical cognition) which may be why he prefers to add the prefix "immediate" to coping. Coping is not merely a response to a stimulus as we might find in Behaviourist accounts as it is dynamic and flexible. The key to this flexibility is our familiarity with digital technology which provides us with a readiness to cope with it rather than to execute a fixed set of responses. Presented with interactive technology we are frequently ready and able to use it. Coping is the how of human computer interaction. It operates at the same "level" as operations (within Activity Theory).

Epistemic and Pragmatic Actions

At this point we need introduce the concept of pragmatic and epistemic actions. Kirsh and Maglio (1994) using Tetris™ as an example, have made an important contribution to this conceptual vocabulary. In Tetris, the falling zoids must be lined up with an appropriate slot in the debris of fallen zoids. As we have already seen, a control button is available to rotate the zoids. In an experiment reported by Kirsh and Maglio (1994) they calculated that the physical rotation of a shape through $90°$ takes approximately 100 ms, and a further 200 ms is required to select the control button itself. While to achieve the same result by mental rotation alone takes about 1000 ms. In all, 700 ms can be saved by offloading the mental rotation into the environment by using the button. Kirsh and Maglio go on to present compelling evidence that physical rotation not only positions the zoid ready to fit an appropriately shaped gap, but is often used to help determine whether the shape and the slot are matched. The latter use constitutes a case of what they call an epistemic action. So, in this instance, the pragmatic actions of recognition and pattern matching are augmented by the epistemic action of manually rotating the zoid. Pragmatic actions alter the world because some physical change is desirable for its own sake while epistemic actions alter the world so as to aid and augment cognitive processes recruited to meet our pragmatic needs. Thus "pragmatic actions" are those things we do to achieve our goals while "epistemic actions" are those actions which we adopt to help us achieve these pragmatic ends. Epistemic actions scaffold, support and offload the cognitive demands of pragmatic actions.

7.6 In Conclusion

Suggesting that the use of interactive technology has an automatic (fast or intuitive) component has a good measure of face validity as we are surrounded by numerous examples of thoughtless interaction. However unlike the intuitive or automatic behaviour, it is argued that coping is a better description as the latter is routinely scaffolded by making use of the situation itself, that is, it makes use of the resources in the local environment, the available information and other computational resources, the technology itself, and other people. We should not forget the capabilities of our bodies in this too. For these reasons, coping is better regarded as *epistemic coping*. Adding a role for the epistemic to coping results in an account which is more closer to what we observe in the day-to-day, routine use of interactive technology.

References

Agre PE (1997) Computation and human experience. Cambridge University Press, Cambridge, MA

Bergman E (2000) Information appliances and beyond: interaction design for consumer products. Morgan Kaufmann, San Diego

Bertenthal BI, Rose JL, Bai DL (1997) Perception-action coupling in the development of visual control of posture. J Exp Psychol Hum Percept Perform 23(6):1631–1643

Blackler A, Hurtienne J (2007) Towards a unified view of intuitive interaction: definitions, models and tools across the world. MMI-Interaktiv 13:36–54. 15, 43

Blackler A, Popovic V, Mahar D (2003a) Designing for intuitive use of products. An investigation. In: Proceedings of 6th Asia Design Conference, Tsukuba, Japan

Blackler A, Popovic V, Mahar D (2003b) The nature of intuitive use of products: an experimental approach. Des Stud 24(6):491–506

Clark A (1997) The dynamical challenge. Cogn Sci 21(4):461–481

Davidson T (1882) Perception. Mind 7(28):496–513

Dewey J (1922) Human nature and conduct. Modern Library, New York

Dreyfus HL (1991) Being-in-the-world: a commentary on Heidegger's being and time, division I. MIT Press, Cambridge, MA

Dreyfus HL (2007) Response to McDowell. Inquiry 50:371–377

Ericsson KA, Simon HA (1984) Protocol analysis. Verbal reports as data. MIT Press, Cambridge, MA

Evans JSBT (2008) Dual-processing accounts of reasoning, judgment, and social cognition. Annu Rev Psychol 59:255–278

Gibson JJ (1977) The theory of affordances. In: Shaw R, Bransford J (eds) Perceiving, acting and knowing. Wiley, New York, pp 67–82

Gibson JJ (1979) The ecological approach to visual perception. Houghton Mifflin, Boston

Gibson JJ (1986) The ecological approach to visual perception. Houghton Mifflin, Boston

Goodwin C, Goodwin MH (1998) Seeing as a situated activity: formulating planes. In: Engestrom Y, Middleton D (eds) Cognition and communication at work. Cambridge University Press, Cambridge, MA

Hurtienne J, Israel JH (2007) Image schemas and their metaphorical extensions – intuitive patterns for tangible interaction. TEI Tangible and Embedded Interaction 2007. ACM Press, Baton Rouge

James W (1890/1950) The principles of psychology. Dover Publications, New York

Kahneman D (2011) Thinking, fast and slow. Allen Lane, London

Kirsh D (2013) Embodied cognition and the magical future of interaction design. Trans Comput Hum Interact 20(1):3

Kirsh D, Maglio P (1994) On distinguishing epistemic from pragmatic action. Cogn Sci 18:513–549

Kuutti K (1996) Activity theory as a potential framework for human-computer interaction research. In: Nardi B (ed) Context and consciousness. MIT Press, Cambridge, MA, pp 17–44

Montagne G, Buekers M, Camachon C, de Rugy A, Laurent M (2003) The learning of goal-directed locomotion: a perception-action perspective. Q J Exp Psychol A 56(3):551–567. doi:10.1080/02724980244000620

Moors A, De Houwer J (2006) Automaticity: a theoretical and conceptual analysis. Psychol Bull 132(2):297–326

Noddings N, Shore PJ (1984) Awakening the inner eye intuition in education. Columbia University, Teachers College Press, New York, p 43

Norman DA (1981) Categorization of action slips. Psychol Rev 88(1):1

Norman DA (1998) The invisible computer. MIT Press, Cambridge, MA

Norman DA (2004) Emotional design: why we love or hate everyday objects. Basic Books, New York

Norros L (2005) The concept of habit in the analysis of situated action. Theor Issues Ergon Sci 6(5):385–407

Osman M (2004) An evaluation of dual-process theories of reasoning. Psychon Bull Rev 11(6):988–1010

Pollard W (2006) Explaining actions with habits. Am Philos Q 43:57–68

Raskin J (1994) Intuitive equals familiar. Commun ACM 37(9):17. doi:10.1145/182987.584629.43

Raskin J (2000) The humane interface. Addison-Wesley, New York

Rasmussen J (1983) Skills, rules, and Knowledge; signals, signs and symbols, and other distinctions in human performance models. IEEE Trans Syst Man Cybern smc-13(3):257–266

Reason JS (1990) Human error. Cambridge University Press, Cambridge

Reason J, Mycielska K (1982) Absent-minded? Prentice-Hall, Inc., Englewood Cliffs

Riva G, Mantovani F (2012) From the body to the tools and back: a general framework for presence in mediated interactions. Interact Comput 24(4):203–210

Schaal S (1999) Is imitation learning the route to humanoid robots? Trends Cogn Sci 3(6):233–242. doi:10.1016/S1364-6613(99)01327-3.42

Schneider W, Shiffrin R (1977) Controlled and automatic human information processing: 1. Detection, - search and attention. Psychol Rev 84(1):1–66

Shiffrin R, Schneider W (1977) Controlled and automatic human information processing: II perceptual learning, automatic attending and a general theory. Psychol Rev 84(2):127–190

Stanovich KE (2004) The robot's rebellion: finding meaning the age of Darwin. University of Chicago Press, Chicago

Stanovich KE (2009) Distinguishing the reflective, algorithmic and autonomous minds: is it time for a tri-process theory? In: JStBT E, Frankish K (eds) In two minds: dual processes and beyond. Oxford University Press, Oxford, pp 55–88

Stanovich KE, West RF (2003) Evolutionary versus instrumental goals: how evolutionary psychology misconceives human rationality. In: Over D (ed) Evolution and the psychology of thinking: the debate. Psychology Press, Hove, pp 171–230

Thelen E, Smith L (1994) A dynamics systems approach to the development of cognition and action. MIT Press, Cambridge, MA

Turner SP (1994) The social theory of practices: tradition, tacit knowledge and presuppositions. Polity Press, Cambridge, MA

Turner P (2008) Towards an account of intuitiveness. Behav Inform Technol 27(6):1–8

Turner P (2013) How we cope with digital technology. Morgan & ClayPool, San Rafael

Uleman JS, Bargh JA (1989) Unintended thought. Guilford Press, New York

Valera FJ (1992) Ethical know-how. Stanford University Press, Stanford

Wartofsky M (1979) Models: representation and scientific understanding. Reidel Publishing Company, Dordrecht

Westcott MR (1968) Toward a contemporary psychology of intuition. Holt, Rinehart and Winston, New York

Web Resources

Eler A, Peyser E (2016) http://thenewinquiry.com/essays/tinderization-of-feeling/

Janiak A (2012) "Kant's views on space and time". The Stanford encyclopedia of philosophy (Winter 2012 Edition), Zalta EN (ed) Available from http://plato.stanford.edu/archives/win2012/entries/kant-spacetime. Last retrieved 22 June 2016

Kahneman D (2002) Maps of bounded rationality: a perspective on intuitive judgment and choice. Nobel Prize lecture. Available from http://www.nobelprize.org/nobel_prizes/economic-sciences/laureates/2002/kahnemann-lecture.pdf. Last retrieved 22 June 2016

Kant I (1800) Logic. Available from https://archive.org/stream/kantsintroductio00kantuoft/kantsintroductio00kantuoft_djvu.txt

Ofcom (2014) http://stakeholders.ofcom.org.uk/binaries/research/media-literacy/media-use-attitudes-14/Childrens_2014_Report.pdf

Chapter 8
Making-Believe with Technology

8.1 Introduction

In Chap. 5 we discussed how we "think with things", that is, how we use technology and other artefacts epistemically, instrumentally and perhaps as part of our cognition itself, to achieve our aims. These perspectives were based on current thinking in the cognitive sciences, but there is another way in which external things and cognition can work together and this is to enable us to make-believe. Continuing this introduction we should note that there is neither an established psychology of make-believe nor has not been considered within the cognitive sciences. There is a make-believe theory developed by Walton (1990) – discussed below – as a means of understanding how people appreciate the Arts. So, within the context of HCI we believe that we are treading new ground. However most would agree that, make-believe involves creating fictional worlds, worlds that are not the case and surely this resonates with virtual worlds created by digital technology and with established HCI/UCD tools such as scenarios. There is also a significant overlap between making-believe and what we mean by mental simulation. Make-believe as a means of creating new worlds may also draw upon (prospective) episodic memory too. We begin by offering some definitions of key terms.

Defining Make-Believe

Our definition of make-believe proposes that it has three components. Firstly we argue that make-believe relies on pretending. Every child can pretend and this ability appears early. It is widely accepted that children are able to pretend soon after their first birthday and this is very much earlier than the full maturation of their cognition. We continue to pretend for the rest of our lives.

© Springer International Publishing Switzerland 2016
P. Turner, *HCI Redux*, Human–Computer Interaction Series,
DOI 10.1007/978-3-319-42235-0_8

Pretending has long been studied within developmental psychology as *pretend play*. Pretending and pretend play are very closely associated so much so that they are often treated as synonyms. This blurring offers useful insights into the nature of pretending, as it has been described as the "voluntary transformation of the here and now, the you and me, and the this or that, along with any potential action that these components of a situation might have", Garvey (1990). Whereas for Rutherford et al. (2007, p. 1025) pretend play is "acting as if something is when it is not". So, we can characterise pretending is "acting as-if" or "behaving as though" (while recognising that this is not intended to be a complete description). This emphasis on acting or behaving is not to be interpreted as Behaviourist but one which identifies pretending as an expression of our embodied or even our enactive cognition and as such it is enabled and constrained by the capabilities and restrictions of our bodies (with the former) or is the means to "bring forth worlds" (with the latter). These aspects of pretending, however, are not widely recognised within developmental or cognitive psychology.

The second component of make-believe involves thinking with an artefact or a piece of technology to create a fictional world defined, in part, by the affordances (and associated conventions) offered by it. A stick becomes a horse with which to ride into battle; a banana becomes a telephone and a call from your boss; shaping your hand in a particular way creates a gun or a "blaster" (sound effects at little extra effort); or a cardboard mock-up becomes a low-fidelity prototype of an interactive system. The banana offers the affordances of being telephone shaped (pre-smart phone) and offering an "earpiece" and "mouthpiece".

We regard this definition as being wholly consistent with Walton's prop theory of make-believe though our vocabulary and our proposed conceptual bases are different. We also suggest that this artefact can be psychological too – so this might include knowledge of the supposed habits of fairy princesses; or the capabilities of wearable technology (real, potentially real or the stuff of a Hollywood movie) or perhaps, most importantly, a story.

Thus we define make-believe as, behaving and thinking with an artefact which might be real, imaginary or psychological (to recall Vygotski). There is one final element to this account of make-believe which is still be to considered and that is *decoupling*. When we make-believe we decouple ourselves, to some degree, from the everyday world to engage with the make-believe world. This decoupling may manifest in a number of different ways and to different degrees. It may take the form of something like a momentary day-dream or it might immerse or transport us to these fictional worlds sufficiently to allow us to share in the adventures of a super-hero in the latest cinematic blockbuster. In essence, this decoupling liberates us from the here-and-now to enable us to explore and engage with these fictional worlds.

Elsewhere (e.g. Turner et al. 2014; Turner et al. 2015; Turner 2016; Turner and Harviainen 2016) we have argued that make-believe is an important though neglected dimension of our cognitive dealings within HCI and here we make the case for its importance. We stress that some of these points are speculative (indeed, verging on the make-believe). We begin by treating HCI from two different perspectives, namely, "HCI as practice" which includes the practices of interaction design, user centred design, and designing for accessibility; and there is also "HCI as an academic discipline" complete with its theories and conceptual frameworks.

HCI as Practice

Within *HCI as practice*, there is abundant evidence of the use of make-believe within HCI but we rarely describe it as such, for example, the Wizard of Oz technique (Green and Wei-Haas 1985) relies on it. In its original form, they describe it as a way of examining user interaction with computers and facilitate rapid iterative development of the wording and logic. They write "The technique requires two machines linked together, one for the user and one for the experimenter. The experimenter (the "wizard"), *pretending* to be a computer, responds to user queries either directly or by pressing function keys to which common messages have been assigned. The software automatically records the dialog and its timing" (my italics). A key component to the success of the technique is that the user must "ignore the man behind the curtain" (the Wizard) who is actually providing the computation. With this technique, make-believe is explicit. Users are asked to behave as though the system were real and to ignore the "computer".

Make-believe can also readily be seen at work within many of the design activities of HCI. Arguably, the design of interactive technology typically relies on the use of stories to depict the envisioned technology being used by the target user to carry out a range of tasks both serious and frivolous in a number of different contexts. This is achieved by means of scenarios (Carroll 1995); personae (e.g. Cooper 1999; Pruitt and Adlin 2010); storyboards (e.g. Truong et al. 2006; Buxton 2007) and, of course, a wide range of different kinds of prototypes. These, of course, can be thought of as different kinds of stories and no matter what their form, they are the product of make-believe: after all, someone, somewhere made them up (even if the components are factual).

A scenario is a little story. It may be purely textual or be more like a strip cartoon in which case it is described as a storyboard. Scenarios, almost by default, are written in plain language as they are intended to be understood by specialist and non-specialist alike. However, Howard et al. (2002) and Svanæs and Seland (2004) are among a number who regard scenarios as something which can be 'acted out' by third-party actors or role-playing users. In addition to taking a number of forms, scenarios have alternate names such as user stories (e.g. Cohn 2004) or design fictions (e.g. Sterling 2009) and even use cases (Alexander and Maiden 2004) depending on their origins or how they are being used. We might also include personae which at their simplest are also stories but in this instances their focus is on the potential user (real or fictional) for whom one is designing. Lene Nielsen (2014) writes that there are four different varieties of personas which she lists as: goal-directed; role-based; her own which are "engaging"; and the final category which are fiction-based. She tells us that advocates of the first three agree that a persona should be based on data, while, the fiction-based perspective is a product of the "designers' intuition and assumptions".

Scenarios, personae, storyboards, no matter what the trope, involve fictional worlds which, we would argue, are the products of – by definition – make-believe.

Finally, a prototype potentially takes this a further stage has it can be (depending upon the implementation) handled and interacted with. It can be used to rehearse an action; it can be used to pretend to complete a task; it can be reasoned with ('it will fit in a purse/handbag but it is too big for a jacket pocket'); it can be used as a prop in role-playing or make-believe. In short, it is an artefact with which we can reason about potential interaction with the real thing. One of the earliest forms of prototyping used in HCI was low fidelity, paper prototyping. This technique dates from a time when prototyping an interactive system was an arduous process which involved writing lines and lines of code just to draw a simple shape on a screen. Paper prototyping was devised as means of mocking up and evaluating an early interface design using paper, cardboard, plastic sheeting and other bits and bobs. A user was then recruited who is then asked to step through a typical interaction with the system. (This process bears a number of similarities with the Wizard of Oz technique described above and these two different methods are often conflated and confused). The designer pretends to be the computer and he or she physically animates the interaction with the make-believe system. In practice, the participants in a these design sessions play act, role play (or as we prefer) make-believe that the prototype they are using will more-or-less behave just like the real thing (e.g. Snyder 2003).

HCI as Theory

We now consider *HCI as theory*. We proposed that make-believe has a significant (though largely unvoiced) role in how we account for the use of interactive technology.

As have seen in chapter one, mental models are a popular means for accounting for our use of interactive technology. Their advocates assume that we have acquired a "working model" of the target system, while knowing it is likely to be incomplete and inaccurate in places, which we "animate" to guide us in the use of the technology itself. This animation may be accompanied by self-talk (e.g. in using a household coffee machine to make a cappuccino "wait until the light goes green before removing the milk capsule and replacing it with the coffee"); or it might appear as an image in one's minds eye; or as a series of gestures reproducing the actions to be taken. In employing a mental model we appear to be rehearsing the steps we intend taking. This *behaving as* is a component of make-believe. Finally, the mental model itself can be described as a psychological tool (following Vygotski) with which to think about the operation of the technology. If the mental model account is correct, there is some underlying form of "everyday reasoning" or problem solving at work but this, as we have suggested, is often accompanied by evidence of make-believe.

Turning to our second example of make-believe we consider the use of *metaphor* within HCI, specifically, at the user interface. A metaphor is a linguistic device of the "my job is a prison" variety. So when we speak of metaphor as a feature of user interface design, we can only assume that HCI has appropriate the term and is using it in a non-linguistic manner. A possible alternative would to be consider this as involving the use of visual metaphor but this tends to be confined to the cinema or advertising. An example of a visual metaphor from the recent movie Gravity (Cuarón 2013) involves an astronaut in the International Space Station curled up in the foetal position with a tube from her suit symbolising, perhaps, an umbilical cord. However, the use of metaphor within HCI generally does not have this form. The use of metaphor dates to 1970s, with the creation of the "desktop metaphor" and, of course, current interactive systems are replete with it. It was devised as a means of providing a familiar interface to computers for the non-specialist. Smith *et al.* (1982) described the first desktop metaphor on the Xerox Star system: "*Every user's initial view of Star is the Desktop, which resembles the top of an office desk, together with surrounding furniture and equipment. It represents a working environment, which current projects and accessible resources reside. On the screen are displayed pictures of familiar office objects, such as document folders, file drawers, in-baskets and out-baskets. These objects are displayed as small pictures or icons.*" Whatever this is, it is not a metaphorical treatment of a real desktop. It is "toy" desktop, perhaps the kind of thing given to a child (who has ambitions to become an accountant) to play with. Indeed, rather than proposing the operation of metaphor, there is a simpler explanation - we simply act as though it were a desktop. An odd desktop, admittedly complete with an anomalous trashcan, but we act as though it were real when we are putting files in a folder which we arrange on its "top". Much the same is true of the other metaphors that are scattered about the landscape of a graphical user interface, e.g. scissors for cutting, a clipboard for pasting, a drawing pin for posting, a paperclip for attaching. We treat these all as though there were what they appear to be.

While we are not suggesting that make-believe is a complete account of how mental models or "metaphors" work in HCI, we believe that it does make a contribution to how we understand how these devices operate. Having made a case for the use of make-believe, we now consider pretending, make-believe and decoupling in more detail.

8.2   Pretending

We all pretend. We develop this ability early in life, Nakayama (2013), for example, has presented evidence of children as young as 7 months old who are able to pretend to cry merely as a means of obtaining "care-giver physical contact" (a cuddle). Pretending presents a number of intriguing, if not downright astonishing problems for the researcher as identified by Leslie (1987, p. 412), "Pretending ought to strike the cognitive psychologist as a very odd sort of ability. After all, from an evolutionary point of view, there ought to be a high premium on the veridicality of cognitive processes. The perceiving, thinking organism ought, as far as possible, to get things right. Yet pretence flies in the face of this fundamental principle. In pretence we deliberately distort reality". In essence, Leslie argues that we can pretend before we have formed a veridical view of the world. He continues with the observation that our ability to pretend should, more reasonably, arise at the end of our intellectual development rather than "at the very beginning of childhood". So, having achieved cognitive mastery of the world one might expect an individual to be able to demonstrate this ability by deliberately distorting our representation of it and then returning to it skilfully. But this does not appear to be the case. Finally, in the language of computer science, Leslie poses the following questions, just how is it possible for a child to think about a banana as though it were a telephone? His point is, if the representational system, which cognitivists claim to underpin cognition, is still in the process of "mapping" the world, how does it manage to tolerate distortions such as this? How is it that our cognition does not "crash" given this arbitrary onslaught? His own solution to this problem is to propose a meta-representational account of pretence, which we discuss below.

The literature on pretending tends to be limited to the study of pretend play in children with a view to understanding its role in child development (e.g. Leslie 1987; Harris 2000; Nichols and Stich 2005). Russ (2004), for example, has argued that the development of a number of cognitive and affective processes rely on pretend play. Pretend play involves the exercise of divergent and convergent thinking and it also facilitates the expression of both positive and negative feelings, and the ability to integrate emotion with cognition (e.g. Seja and Russ 1999; Jent et al. 2011). Early pretend play has also been implicated in creativity in later life (e.g. Russ 2004; Singer and Singer 2005). The focus on pretend play relies on the generally agreed position that it is essential to a child's cognitive, affective and social development and this ability appears quite early in life. Leslie (1987, p. 412) tells us that it can be observed at "the very beginning of childhood", while Harris tells us it appears later and equates it was the development of language. Specifically, play involves the exercise of alternating cycles of divergent and convergent thinking which is the ability to generate different ideas, story themes, and so forth and then to weave them together. When children take on different roles in pretend play it allows them to acquire and practice the skills of communication, problem solving, and empathy (Hughes 1999). Rakoczy et al. (2004) have also reported that children as young as two are able to appreciate the difference between trying to perform an action in the real world, and pretending to perform the same action. This ability is essential otherwise we would be unable to discriminate pretending from any other form of action. Perhaps, what is more interesting, from the perspective of HCI, is how pretending is thought to operate and more importantly, this prepares the ground for a discussion of decoupling. We briefly consider three accounts.

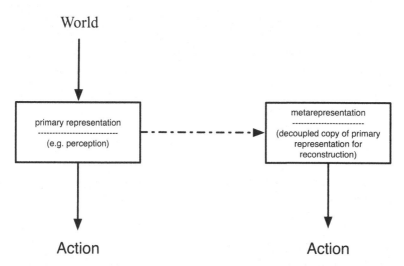

Fig. 8.1 Leslie's metacognitive model

Metacognition

Leslie (1987) begins by supposing that the child is able to create a representation of the world which is accurate and faithful. This he calls the primary representation and this has a direct semantic relation with the world. For pretending to occur the child must make a copy of this representation and change it. This is illustrated in Fig. 8.1. This copy is decoupled from the world being a copy of a copy – or meta-representation and it is this which forms the basis of our ability to pretend. He proposes a semantics of pretence which supports this. He reasons that children need to be able to distinguish between acting/believing in the real world and pretending and this is achieved by quarantining the meta-representation from the real copy (of the world). The key to Leslie's account is the de-coupler which is responsible for making a copy of the primary representation and its subsequent manipulation and quarantining. It should be noted that this model relies upon the supposition of a common representational code governing the whole process (*cf.* Prinz 1984).

Twin Earth

Lillard (2001) rejects the meta-representation account of pretending and offers the "Twin Earth" model in its place. The "Twin Earth" model has its origins with Putnam's Twin Earth thought experiment (Putnam 1973). She tells us that when children pretend, they create another world that shares many of the characteristics of the real world. While much remains the same, there are, of course, significant changes, such as the "child becomes the mother [and] … sand becomes apple pie", (ibid, p. 22). Then the child reasons about the constituent parts of this twin world. Many of the relationships are unchanged, for example, while the child may pretend to be the mother, this (twin) mother treats her children just like the real world version. Lillard notes that both pretend play and Twin Earth are quarantined worlds which are themselves decoupled (see below) from the real world.

Possible World Boxes

Finally, Nichols and Stich (2005) have created an influential cognitive model of pretending which itself is based on a modification to what they describe as the "widely accepted account of cognition as adopted by people working in this field". Nichols and Stitch make it clear that they do not believe that their account is necessarily complete or definitive but that they do think that they have, in contrast to other researchers, described pretending quite fully. Their most frequent criticism of other accounts being that they are "under-described". They begin by noting that the mind (sic) contains two quite different kinds of representational states, namely, beliefs and desires. Beliefs are what we know, true and false, about the world. Desires are what we want, and Nichols and Stitch implicate the bodily systems of being the source of them. To pretend is to create another "world" in the possible world box (a partition) of our cognition. They tell us that pretending begins with a premise ("let's have a tea party") which, if adopted by the pretender, forms the basis for subsequent inference and embellishment. They also recognise that the premise may be bound or constrained by schematic structures, writing: "clusters or packets of representations whose contents constitute 'scripts' or paradigms detailing the way in which certain situations typically unfold" (p. 34) (Fig. 8.2).

The contents of the possible world box has full access to our beliefs and from there to our practical reasoning faculties. An updater mechanism keeps us informed as to the status of the pretend episode. The possible world box is populated with representational tokens which are different from those found in the beliefs and desires boxes. These tokens neither represent the world as it is, nor what we would like it to be, but rather represent what the world "would be like given some set of assumptions that we neither believe to be true (that is, we believe to be the case) or want to be true"(Nichols & Stitch, ibid p. 29). The precise nature of the possible world box in their account is, ironically, a little under-described though we note that this description of possible-world boxes is not unlike a virtual environment.

Logically Similar and Not Confined to Children

Although these three models are quite different in detail they appear to be logically very similar. By whatever means we are able to separate ourselves from the real world, and interact with, reason and emote about another. Although a child may be

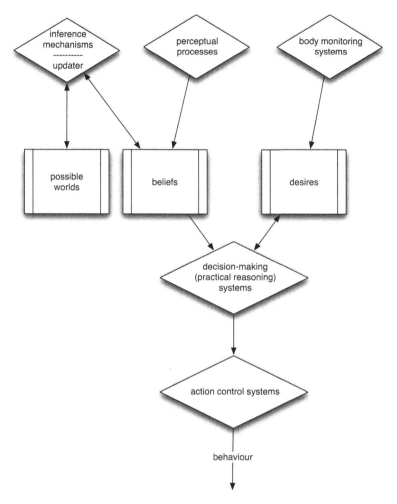

Fig. 8.2 The structure of a "possible world box"

free to pretend as she wishes, we add that these worlds are regular, rule-driven and bounded (Turner et al. 2015) Pretending involves acting as though or behaving as if. So, for example, I can (with difficulty) pretend to like the sound of the bagpipes; I can pretend to be a kangaroo; I can pretend that our department's management makes sense. And evidence of these forms of pretending is my behaviour towards the players of bagpipes, my hopping with both feet held together and my sitting quietly at departmental meetings respectively. To pretend is to act as though. As we have already noted, this emphasis on acting and behaving suggests that pretending is embodied and as such reflects the opportunities, capabilities and restrictions afforded by our bodies.

Indeed Nichols and Stich (2005, p. 20) have commented on the paucity of research into adult pretending. However, from their own work, they conclude that adult and childhood pretending are not very different. We can ourselves report on one instance of adult behaviour where Foley artists (those people who add the everyday sounds to a movie's soundtrack) freely admit to pretending, and making-believe as a part of their work (Carruthers and Turner 2016).

8.3   Making-Believe with Technology

As we seen there is a substantial literature on pretending – as pretend play – and there are a number of treatments of imagination which we will touch upon at the end of this chapter but make-believe itself has been largely left unexplored. Though we should recognise that make-believe is not always described as make-believe and that make-believe does not always involve fairy stories.

Make-believe, as we have seen, is at work in HCI but can also be found at work in domains as varied as storytelling (Ryan 2015); gaming (Mukherjee 2015); scientific reasoning (Toon 2010); aspects of acting on stage (Goldstein and Bloom 2011) and perhaps our propensity to anthropomorphise technology (e.g. Fogg and Nass 1997). And we cannot forget competing in the world "air guitar" championships (BBC 2012).

Dolls and Hobby Horses

Walton (1993) writes, "Dolls and hobby horses are valuable for their contribution to make-believe. The same is true for paintings and novels. These and other props stimulate our imagination and provide for exciting or pleasurable or interesting engagements with fictional worlds. A doll, in itself just a bundle of rags or moulded plastic, comes alive in a game of make-believe, providing the participant with (fictional) baby". Walton calls this "prop oriented make-believe".

His interest in "toys and art" arise from the earlier work of Gombrich (1963) on this very subject. In his *Meditations on a Hobby Horse* Gombrich compares pictures of a horse to that of a child's hobby horse. While a picture may accurately portray a horse, a hobby horse, in contrast, is a substitute for a horse. He rejects the view that the hobby horse is a symbol – standing for a horse – a man-made horse, as it were, he argues instead that it can function as a horse. A hobby-horse can be ridden and more to the point it can be ridden as part of a make-believe game and it is this last point that Walton builds upon. In short, function trumps form –"Any ride-able object could serve as a horse".

Walton introduced the idea of fictional worlds to complete this picture. The child's hobby horse is not just any old horse but can become Black Bess in the fictional world in which the child is Dick Turpin on his way to rob a carriage. Walton proposes that when we look at a picture, say of, Dali's Don Quixote we create a fictional world in which we are looking at Don Quixote. But this is not the Spain of Don Quixote as created by Dali, but a fictional world that includes Don Quixote and the viewer. Ryan (2015 p. 209) agrees by describing the purpose of make-believe games is "to create a world in which to play".

Walton (1990) has made further observations that make-believe games, cinema, and a variety of other media are governed by what he describes as "principles of generation" which are "reality-oriented". This reality principle makes the fictional worlds believable. He also proposes the *Mutual Belief Principle* for fantastic worlds (e.g. the Star Trek® or Marvel® worlds). This principle is based on a tacit agreement between the creator of these worlds (and a set of rules which hold for these fantastic places) and those who experience them. In these worlds, for example, it is "agreed" that alien languages are mutually intelligible, and that space craft can travel faster than the speed of light. And, of course, when the movie, game or VR experience is over, the fictional world disappears and the real world returns.

Mirroring and Quarantining

Pretending/make-believe have also been found to be governed by the same kinds of laws and restriction that we encounter in the real world. Reality may be suspended, but not wholly. Pretending/make-believe mirror the real world. These "rules" make our make-believe believable and when they are broken, as for example, in a movie they may be experienced as a "plot hole".

Let us consider a tea party (non-English readers are free to substitute coffee for tea).

> A child proposes that she and her friends might hold a tea party. They agree to participate and equip themselves with toy tea cups and a toy teapot. The teapot is empty. The children lay the tea set neatly on a tablecloth. One child acting as "mother" (the tea pourer) pretends to pours everyone a cup of "tea". As each child drinks from their (empty) cup of "tea", they may then chat and perhaps share pretend "cake". As the "tea" is drunk, "mother" refills the empty cups. The party reaches its natural conclusion.

Leslie (1994) found that when he "tipped out" and "spilled" the contents of one of the empty teacups, the children regarded this cup to be "empty" and could be topped up with make-believe tea. Non-tipped cups continued to be "full" and could not accept additional tea. The basic laws of tea parties, if not of physics, continue to hold.

Quarantining complements mirroring in that the events which occurred within the make-believe episode are confined to them. Spilling make-believe "tea" will not result in clothing really being wet. Perhaps the most interesting aspect of quarantining is when it fails. The failure to quarantine make-believe attitudes, beliefs and behaviours may be taken to be a symptom of mental illness. This is evidenced in the all too frequent reports of murderous gunmen attributing their behaviour to having played violent games.

8.4   Cognitive Decoupling

So, our account of make-believe relies on our ability to act, behave and emote as if and to think with technology (in a fairly order and rule bound manner) and in doing so we are able to create a fictional world and to decouple from the here and now to enter or engage with it. We regularly experience cognitive decoupling in situations ranging from letting our minds wander or when we actively make-believe. Indeed, we often immerse ourselves and to feel present in these fictional worlds. We will argue that the means by which we feel present in these other "worlds" lies with this ability. These worlds may be not as vivid, immediate or as tangible as the real world, but they can be very engaging. These worlds are not simply the product toys, stories, other people but of digital technology too.

Now we consider the source of these abilities. Firstly, they are likely to be the product of system 2 thinking and here we diverge from Riva et al. (2004) and Riva and Mantovani (2012). They have argued that our experience of presence in the *real world* is a consequence of our system 1 thinking. It is immediate, it is intuitive and it is automatic – all the hallmarks of system 1 thinking. They also argue that our sense of being present in the real world helps regulate our behaviour within it by telling us about the status and effectiveness of our actions. As such, this ability offers us practical advantages in dealing effectively with the world. It is a system 1 response to where and how we find ourselves and it does not require conscious thought or deliberation. They extend this premise to the sense of presence in virtual environments.

Agreed, but feeling present or immersed in a fictional or virtual world is not automatic. We do, to a greater or lesser extent, chose to immerse ourselves and we are able to return to the real world whenever we wish. For example, the success of the movies during the Great Depression of the 1930s in the US is attributed, in part, to being a vehicle by which people could forget their real world worries. People immersed themselves in movies to decoupling themselves form the real world. There are numerous everyday examples of people deliberately decouple themselves (to some extent) from the real world for a variety of reasons including as a means of reducing or managing their anxiety (e.g. listening to music while visiting a dentist), for entertainment at the movies or simply to pass the time with a daydream.

Cognitive Decoupling and Tele-Presence

While the study of tele-presence (presence hereafter), as an academic discipline, dates from the early 1990s with the publication of the first journal dedicated to its research, this is not to suggest, however, that designers, artists and writers have been unaware of the power of their media to create a sense of immersion or transportation or feelings of being present elsewhere, from long before this time. Prehistoric cave art may have been created for this very purpose and the use of stained glass in churches and cathedrals has been recognised as a means of transporting church-goers to other (spiritual) worlds. Indeed stories of all kinds, irrespective of medium – whether a cave painting, a stained glass window, a poem and a myriad of digital technology – have this power to transport, immerse, engage and to create a sense of being other than where we currently are. We might suggest that this is evidence of Coleridge's "the willing suspension of disbelief" but we challenge this double-negative and replace it with a positive statement, "the willingness to make-believe".

So, returning to the examples we have already considered, we do not propose that the people who first gazed on cave paintings actually believed themselves to be in the presence of aurochs nor, while in churches, to be in the company of spiritual beings. Neither do we propose that people believe themselves transported to a "stately pleasure dome" after reading Kublai Khan nor fighting aliens on the surface of Mars with their space marine buddies in a games arcade. What we do propose is that people decouple from the everyday and readily act, think, react and emote as though we were or might be in these situations. These episodes of mediated presence/make-believe are "sandboxed" – or equivalent, in that they are labelled as make-believe and we are able to distinguish between these fictional worlds and the real thing.

Strong and Weak Representation

In addition to the observed behavioural differences between System 1 and System 2 thinking they are also distinguished by different demands they place on our "cognitive resources". System 1 thinking places fewer demands than system 2 thinking. This is nicely illustrated when we consider cognitive decoupling, for example, Stanovich et al. (2011) and Stanovich and Toplak 2012 include "cognitive decoupling" as part of their definition of system 2 thinking. We have argued (above) that cognitive decoupling is an important component the experience of immersion (or the sense of presence) in a virtual environment and this is consistent with how we are able to engage in hypothetical thinking (Evans 2007, 2010). The reasoning here is that in order to reason hypothetically, we must be able to prevent our representations of the real world from becoming confused with representations of the make-believe, hypothetical (or virtual) situation. While this necessarily places greater cognitive demands on an individual's working memory, there is a richer theoretical position proposed by Clark and his colleague (e.g. Clark 1997a, b and Clark and Grush 1999). Clark has introduced the idea of representation being either "weak" and "strong".

A weak representation is an internal state that is capable of bearing information about an external object only when that object is in close proximity. Weak representations are found in what Clark describes as "information and control systems", which provide animals with quick feedback about objects in the immediate environment and thus enable them to interact with such local objects effectively. These systems contain internal states that are "information-bearing" in the sense that they correlate, in a non-accidental fashion, with features of external objects. If the source object of a weak representation becomes distal or absent, however, the representation becomes unavailable. However, such representations can be stored off-line for future use. This is also a description of system 1 thinking – as discussed in the previous chapter.

A strong representation, in contrast, is an information-bearing state that is serviceable even if its source object becomes distal or absent. Clark argues that "a creature uses full-blooded internal representations if and only if it is possible to identify within the system specific states … whose functional role is to act as decoupleable surrogates for specifiable (usually extra-neural) states of affairs" (Clark and Grush 1999, p. 8). According to Clark, if a system does not possess "the capacity to set-up and manipulate inner models instead of operating directly upon the world, it will fail to count as a locus of full-blooded internal representation" (ibid, p. 9). For Clark, strong representations count as genuine representations because agents actually use them as surrogates for other objects. Weak representations, in contrast, do not count as genuine representations, for while it may be convenient to describe these states as representational, agents themselves do not actually use them as representational surrogates. So, as Clark would have it, weak representations are active when the animal is engaged with its world (the world contributing to its own representation) while, correspondingly, strong representations are active when the animal is disengaged from the world. And this is a description of system 2 thinking.

In short, we (epistemically) cope with the world on an everyday, routine and habitual manner but are capable of de-coupling from it to deal with more complex problems *or* to immerse ourselves in a fictional world. This ability to de-couple from the everyday and to immerse in the fictional or can we say virtual, is of interest to any discussion of technologically mediated worlds.

Make-Believe and Affect

Although make-believe is largely governed by mirroring and quarantining, both may be violated. Quarantining breaks down and becomes "contagion" when the contents of the pretence directly affect actual attitudes and behaviour. This is most readily witnessed when these attitudes and behaviour are predominately affective, for example, imagining something scary (for example, as a fierce animal in the kitchen) may "bleed" and give rise to actual hesitation such as reluctance to enter the room. In attempting to explain this Gendler (2008) has proposed a new form of believe – the alief which is "*a*ssociative, *a*ction-generating, *a*ffect-laden, *a*rational, *a*utomatic, *a*gnostic with respect to its content, shared with animals, and developmentally and conceptually antecedent to other cognitive attitudes" (the leading italicised "a's" are hers). An alief is also defined as an habitual propensity to respond automatically and affective to particular stimuli. So, for example, Gendler also tells us that while a person may believe that drinking out of a sterile bedpan is completely safe, she may nonetheless show hesitation and disgust at the prospect of doing so because the bedpan invokes an alief with the content "filthy object, disgusting, stay away". Perhaps more interestingly, Gendler describes the effect produced by walking on the glass-floored Grand Canyon Skywalk as an alief incorporating "the visual appearance as of a cliff, the feeling of fear and the motor routine of retreat" (2011).

This also brings to mind the original visual cliff experiment was devised by Gibson and Walk (1960) as a means of investigating depth perception in small children. Their interest was in whether this form of perception was learned or innate. To test this, they created a "visual cliff" which consists of a board laid across a large sheet of plate glass which was supported above the floor. On one side of the board a sheet of patterned material was used to give the glass the appearance of solidity. On the other side a sheet of the same material was placed on the floor to create a visual cliff. The experiment involved placing an infant at the opaque end of the platform with a parent encouraging them to crawl towards them. If the infant was able to perceive depth (seeing that the transparent space as real drop) then the infant was expected to hesitate. The researchers found that many of the infants crawled over to their mother on the "shallow" side without any problems but a few of the infants were extremely hesitant. However, some infants refused to crawl to their mothers. Although this shows that infants can perceive depth when they are old enough to crawl it does not establish that this ability is innate or, of course, it may tell us that infants may hold the appropriate alief about cliffs.

The relevance of contagion to presence research may also go some way to explaining the successful use of virtual reality in the treatment of phobias (e.g. Rothbaum et al. 1995, 1996; Botella et al. 1998; Emmelkamp et al. 2002). In these instances virtual re-creations of spiders, flying, confined spaces and so forth have been used to de-sensitize those suffering from the corresponding phobias by presenting them with the object of their fear in a safe, managed environment but one which is capable of evoking an affective response. Perhaps even more dramatically, Hoffman et al. (2006) have reported the successful use of virtual reality technology in the pain management of burns treatment. In their study, they reported that the feeling of cold (induced by a snowy landscape) can be used to reduce the pain from real world burns suffered by servicemen. Clearly, at least part of the explanation of the usefulness of virtual reality in treatment and therapy may lie with the contagion aspect of make-believe.

8.5 Imagination

We have not mentioned imagination in this chapter but it undoubtedly has a significant role in the kinds of "what if "thinking we have discussed so far. We argue that as it is sufficiently different from both pretending and make-believe to merit its own treatment, indeed there is some recent evidence to suggest that imagination may depend on its own neural substrates (Zeman et al. 2015).

However, this being said, imagination has proved very difficult to define. Does it, for example, always involve an image (as in visual image) as the name suggests? Clearly not – we can readily imagine the smell of a rose, or roughness of a cat's tongue, the feel of the east wind in Winter or something more abstract and unlikely a competent manager or an sane nationalist.

Walton who, after listing a wide variety of different forms of imagining writes, "What is it to imagine? We have examined a number of dimensions along which imaginings can vary; shouldn't we now spell out what they have in common? — Yes, if we can. But I can't" (1990, p. 19). Similarly Strawson (1970) writes, "The uses, and applications, of the terms 'image', 'imagine', 'imagination', and so forth make up a very diverse and scattered family. Even this image of a family seems too definite. It would be a matter of more than difficulty to identify and list the family's members, let alone their relations of parenthood and cousinhood." One of the problems with defining (much less understanding) imagination is that it might reasonable include day-dreaming, fantasying, visualising, wishing and other slippery concepts.

Interestingly Harris (2000) is happy to describes imagination as the capacity to consider alternative possibilities and their implication. He also tell us that this emerges early and transforms children's developing conception of reality. We note that his position is quite similar to what we have described as make-believe. He does go on to identify three roles for imagination (p. 161) which are (i) to become "absorbed in make-believe or fictional worlds"; (ii) to make "comparisons between actual outcomes and various outcomes" and (iii) to explore the "impossible and magical".

However, our real interest in imagination here is limited to our ability to project ourselves into a variety of situations and into our pasts and our possible futures (mentally) – as we have already discussed in Sect. 6.3 – and thus its relationship with episodic memory. The capacity for self-projection into "alternate times, places, and perspectives" requires a shift or decoupling from the here-and-now and appears to rely on use of episodic memory. These and related observations have led to the formulation of the constructive *episodic simulation hypothesis* which argues that critical function of episodic memory is to support the construction of imagined future events based on past experiences, and the flexible recombination of elements of past experiences, into simulations of possible future scenarios. Thus episodic memory is believed to support the mental simulations of how the future might unfold and lends support to Harris' position.

8.6 In Conclusion

Carruthers (2011) has also argued that these forms of adult creative expression and childhood pretend play are likely to share common cognitive resources and origin, indeed, Vygotski (1978) argued that imagination is "internalised" play. Further, this form of thinking may be a relatively recent evolutionary development which may have first appeared some 50,000 years ago and may have contributed to the flowering of human creative thought which has continued ever since then. Finally, from an evolutionary psychology perspective, Cosmides and Tooby (2000) tell us that being able to pretend is the result of cognitive de-coupling which they define as our ability to make use of contingent information and the artefacts which embody that information. They write, "arguably, one central and distinguishing innovation in human evolution has been the dramatic increase in the use of contingent information for the regulation of improvised behaviour" (p. 53). Thus we pretend when presented with media such diverse as cave art to the latest IMAX movie and in doing so temporarily divorce ourselves from the everyday and mundane and from the here and now.

References

Alexander I, Maiden N (2004) Scenarios, stories, use cases. Wiley, Oxford

Botella C, Baños RM, Perpiñá C, Villa H, Alcañiz M, Rey A (1998) Virtual reality treatment of claustrophobia: a case report. Behav Res Ther 36(2):239–246

BBC (2012) Air Guitar hampionships. http://www.bbc.co.uk/worldservice/learningenglish/language/wordsinthenews/2012/08/120829_vwitn_air_guitar_championships.shtml.   Last accessed 20 Jul 2016

Buxton B (2007) Sketching user experiences. Morgan Kaufmann, San Francisco

Carroll JM (1995) Scenario-based design: envisioning work and technology in system development. Wiley, New York

Carruthers P (2011) Human creativity: its cognitive basis, its evolution, and its connections with childhood. Br J Philos Sci 53(2):225–249

Carruthers L, Turner P (2016) The role of make-believe in Foley. In: Turner P, Harviainen J-T (eds) Digital make-believe. Springer, New York

Clark A (1997a) The dynamical challenge. Cogn Sci 21(4):461–481

Clark A (1997b) Being there: putting brain, body, and world together again. MIT Press, Cambridge, MA

Clark A, Grush R (1999) Towards a cognitive robotics. Adapt Behav 7(1):5–16

Cohn M (2004) User stories applied. Addison Wesley, Boston

Cooper A (1999) The inmates are running the asylum: why high tech products drive us crazy and how to restore the sanity. Sams Publishing, Indianapolis

Cosmides L, Tooby J (2000) Consider the source: the evolution of adaptations for decoupling and metarepresentation. In: Sperber D (ed) Metarepresentations: a multidisciplinary perspective. Oxford University Press, Oxford

Cuarón (2013) Gravity, Warner Bros. http://gb.imdb.com/title/tt1454468/. Last accessed 20 Jul 2016

Emmelkamp PMG, Krijn M, Hulsbosch L, de Vries S, Schuemie MJ, van der Mast CAPG (2002) Virtual reality treatment versus exposure in vivo: a comparative evaluation in acrophobia. Behav Res Ther 40:25–32

Evans JSBT (2007) Hypothetical thinking: dual processes in reasoning and judgement, vol 3. Psychology Press, Hove

Evans JSBT (2010) The psychology of reasoning. In: The science of reason: a Festschrift for Jonathan St BT Evans. Taylor & Francis, Hoboken, p 423

Fogg BJ, Nass C (1997) Silicon sycophants: the effects of computers that flatter. Int J Hum Comput Stud 46:551–561

Garvey C (1990) Play. Harvard University Press, Cambridge, MA

Gendler TS (2008) Alief and belief. J Philos 105:634–663

Gendler TS (2011) Imagination, intuition and philosophical methodology. Oxford University Press, Oxford

Gibson EJ, Walk RD (1960) Visual Cliff. Sci Am 202:67–71

Goldstein TR, Bloom P (2011) The mind on stage: why cognitive scientists should study acting. Trends Cogn Sci 15(4):141–142

Gombrich EHJ (1963) Meditations on a hobby horse and other essays on the theory of art. Phaidon, London

Harris P (2000) The work of the imagination. Blackwell, London

Hoffman HG, Richards TL, Bills AR, Van Oostrom T, Magula J, Seibel EJ, Sharar SR (2006) Using fMRI to study the neural correlates of virtual reality analgesia. CNS Spectr 11(01):45–51

Howard S, Carroll J, Murphy J, Peck J (2002) Using 'endowed props' in scenario-based design. In: Proceedings of the second Nordic conference on Human-computer interaction. ACM Press, New York, pp 1–10

Hughes FP (1999) Children, play, and development, 3rd edn. Allyn and Bacon, Boston

Jent JF, Niec LN, Baker SE (2011) Play and interpersonal processes. In: Russ SW, Niec LN (eds) Play in clinical practice: evidence-based approaches. Guilford Press, New York

Leslie A (1987) Pretense and representation: the origins of "theory of mind". Psychol Rev 94(4):412–426

Leslie AM (1994) Pretending and believing: issues in the theory of ToMM. Cognition 50(1–3):211–238

Lillard AS (2001) Pretend play as twin earth: a social cognitive analysis. Dev Rev 21:495–531

Mukherjee S (2015) Video games and storytelling: reading games and playing books. Palgrave MacMillan, London

Nakayama H (2013) Changes in the affect of infants before and after episodes of crying. Infant Behav Dev 36(4):507–512

Nichols S, Stich S (2005) Mindreading: a cognitive theory of pretense. Oxford University Press, Oxford

Nielsen L (2014) Personas, Available from https://www.interaction-design.org/literature/book/the-encyclopedia-of-human-computer-interaction-2nd-ed/personas. Last retrieved 3 March 2016]

Prinz W (1984) Modes of linkage between perception and action. In: Prinz W, Sanders AF (eds) Cognition and motor processes. Springer, Berlin, pp 185–193

Pruitt J, Adlin T (2010) The persona lifecycle: keeping people in mind throughout product design. Morgan Kaufmann, San Francisco

Putnam H (1973) Meaning and reference. J Philos 70:699–711

Rakoczy H, Tomasello M, Striano T (2004) Young children know that trying is not pretending: a test of the 'behaving-as-if' construal of children's understanding of pretense. Dev Psychol 40:388–399

Riva G, Mantovani F (2012) From the body to the tools and back: a general framework for presence in mediated interactions. Interact Comput 24(4):203–210

Riva G, Waterworth JA, Waterworth EL (2004) The layers of presence: a bio-cultural approach to understanding presence in natural and mediated environments. Cyber Psychol Behav 7(4):402–416

Rothbaum BO, Hodges LF, Kooper R, Opdyke D, Williford JS, North M (1995) Virtual reality graded exposure in the treatment of acrophobia: a case report. Behav Ther 26(3):547–554

Rothbaum BO, Hodges L, Watson BA, Kessler GD, Opdyke D (1996) Virtual reality exposure therapy in the treatment of fear of flying: a case report. Behav Res Ther 34:477–481

Russ SW (2004) Play in child development and psychotherapy. Earlbaum, Mahwah

Rutherford MD, Young GS, Hepburn S, Rogers SJ (2007) A longitudinal study of pretend play in autism. J Autism Dev Disord 37(6):1024–1039

Ryan M-L (2015) Narrative as virtual reality 2: revisiting immersion and interactivity in literature and electronic media. JHU Press, Baltimore

Seja AL, Russ SW (1999) Children's fantasy play and emotional understanding. J Clin Child Psychol 28:269–277

Singer DG, Singer JL (2005) Imagination and play in the electronic age. Harvard University Press, Cambridge, MA

Smith DC, Irby R, Kimball R, Verplank B, Harlsem E (1982) Designing the star user interface. Byte 7(4):242–282

Stanovich KE, Toplak ME (2012) Defining features versus incidental correlates of Type 1 and Type 2 processing. Mind & Society 11(1):3–13

Stanovich KE, West RF, Toplak ME (2011) The complexity of developmental predictions from dual process models. Dev Rev 31(2):103–118

Sterling B (2009) Design fictions. Interactions 16(3 May + June):20–24

Strawson PF (1970) Categories. In: Wood OP, Pitcher G (eds) Ryle. Doubleday, New York, pp 181–210

Svanæs D, Seland G (2004) Putting the users center stage: role playing and low-fi prototyping enable end users to design mobile systems. In: Proceeding of the SIGCHI conference on human factors in computing systems. ACM, New York, pp 479–486

Snyder C (2003) Paper prototyping: the fast and easy way to design and refine user interfaces. Morgan Kaufmann, San Francisco

Toon A (2010) Models as make-believe. In: Frigg R, Hunter M (eds) Beyond mimesis and convention, Boston studies in the philosophy of science. Springer, Dordrecht, pp 71–96

Truong KN, Hayes GR, Abowd GD (2006) Storyboarding: an empirical determination of best practices and effective guidelines. In: Proceedings of the 6th conference on designing interactive systems. ACM Press, New York, pp 12–21

Turner P (2016) A make-believe narrative for HCI. In: Turner P, Harviainen J-T (eds) Digital make-believe. Springer, New York, pp 11–26

Turner P, Harviainen J-T (2016) Introduction. In: Turner P, Harviainen J-T (eds) Digital make-believe. Springer, New York, pp 1–9

Turner P, Turner S, Carruthers L (2014) It's not interaction, it's make-believe. In: Proceedings of 2014 European conference on cognitive ergonomics. ACM Press, New York, pp 22–28

Turner P, Hetherington R, Turner S, Kosek M (2015) The limits of make-believe. Digit Creativity 26(3–4):304–317

Vygotski LS (1978) Mind in society: the development of higher psychological processes. Harvard University Press, Cambridge, MA

Walton KL (1990) Mimesis as make-believe: On the foundations of the representational arts. Harvard University Press, Cambridge, MA

Walton KL (1993) Metaphor and prop oriented make-believe. Eur J Philos 1(1):39–57

Zeman A, Dewarb M, Salac SD (2015) Lives without imagery – congenital aphantasia. Cortex 73:378–380

Web Resource

Green P, Wei-Haas L (1985) The wizard of Oz: a tool for rapid development of user interfaces (Technical report) available from https://deepblue.lib.umich.edu/bitstream/handle/2027.42/174/71952.0001.001.pdf;jsessionid=2F1E8C62D57043FF1408B24686312163?sequence=2. Last retrieved 23 June 2016

Chapter 9
Post-cognitive Interaction

In the beginning, the computer was so costly that it had to be kept gainfully occupied for every second; people were almost slaves to feed it (Shackel 1997, p. 97)

So here we are at the end of this review of the current thinking on cognition and how it might impact how we use and think about interactive technology. We have seen the early enthusiasm for cognitive models of various kinds, which attempted to capture and predict human problem solving and behaviour, has waned in the face of challenges to their basic assumptions and a whole raft of, frankly, better ideas. HCI has followed the same pattern as artificial intelligence research and for similar reasons. Treating cognition as something which is confined to what goes on in our heads is clearly not enough.

9.1 Embracing the Post-cognitive

The subtitle of this book, "the promise of post-cognitive interaction" really refers to everything we have discussed beyond Chap. 1. The cognitive revolution ushered in an appreciation of cognition as involving the manipulation of mental content alone. A post-cognitive understanding of how interactive technology is used requires an appreciation of something broader than brain and technology: as we have seen abundant evidence for the role of the external too – including the body, gesture, language, representations, tools, artefacts, niches, scaffolding, other people and all manner of psychological tools. It appears that the initial formulations of cognition had over enthusiastically and uncritically adopted the "brain is a computer" metaphor a little too literally. Unlike a computer it learns, it is plastic, and it is intentional. This intentionality is key as it means that the things we think about and act upon refer, in the broadest sense, to things in the world. Thus, with only a few exceptions, our mental states have the property of "about-ness". In contrast, the contents of a computer's memory or in the registers of the CPU are not intentional,

© Springer International Publishing Switzerland 2016
P. Turner, *HCI Redux*, Human–Computer Interaction Series,
DOI 10.1007/978-3-319-42235-0_9

they are not about things. They are simply ones and zeros and it is the intentional status of cognitive contents and structure which allows us to rely on all manner of other stuff to achieve its ends. The brain may be a little like a computer but not in any of the important ways.

HCI needs to recognise that cognition is constantly being redefined in the light of the latest thinking, research findings and vogue. The accounts of cognition we have unpicked in these pages were unknown 30 years ago and there is every reason to believe that they will look pretty quaint in a further 30 years. Although Newell and Simon may have hoped to pin down the essence of cognition when they formulated their physical symbol hypothesis, they did not, not because cognition is such a slippery concept but because Neisser might have been right when he wrote that "every psychological phenomenon is a cognitive phenomenon" and as such is subject to redefinition as we learn more about it.

Avoiding (or at Least Postponing) a Synthesis

At this point it is reasonable to expect a synthesis of what we have encountered so far. Integrating the findings of the previous seven chapters (we exclude the substance of Chap. 1) is surprisingly simple as there are only a small number of recurrent themes, for example, embodiment, various forms of mediation, the situated nature of our actions, scaffolding and off-loading, and (say) the social distribution of cognition. We have also learned, for example, that the fact of our embodiment has consequences for the regulation of our cognition (through, for example, somatic markers); while the presence of a body schema invites the opportunity to enhance our cognition by means of tools and, of course, our bodies are situated as Gallagher tells us, "the body [...] is always situated in so far as it is a living and experiencing body. Being situated in this sense is different from simply being located someplace in the way a non-living, non-experiencing object is located. That the body is always situated involves certain kinds of physical and social interactions and it means that experience is always both physically and socially situated".

So, while a synthesis of the *post-cognitive* accounts of cognition is fairly straightforward, it is not necessarily very meaningful – as we might struggle to identify roles for each of these while playing angry birds on our cell-phones. Indeed when we consider the everyday use of cell phones and tablets an appeal to system 1 thinking may be sufficient (particularly, I would argue, system 1 thinking in the form of epistemic coping). We may only need to invoke system 2 thinking when we are dealing with the unfamiliar or complex.

So, rather than bringing everything together in one unlikely and unwieldy edifice, we might simply conclude that HCI is essentially a form of thinking and behaving with things (which is another way of saying Vygotski was right). Things of all kinds mediate our actions; things mediate the ways in which we work with others; we off-load aspects of our cognition onto things; and we engage in make-believe with things. With HCI, these things just happen to be interactive. In many ways this definition is unsurprising as technology and our cognition have co-evolved, indeed this is at the very heart of the definition of the concept of techné which is the origin the word technology (so, in addition to Vygotski, the ancient Greeks were prescient too). However, there is something still missing, and that something is the means by which we makes sense of these very disparate elements and that is a narrative.

9.2   The Case for Narrative: The Other Aspect of Our Cognition

Extravagant claims are frequently made for narrative and for the power of stories, for example, Haven (2007, p. 3) writes that "Humans have told, used, and relied on stories for over 100000 years" while noting that written communication began only approximately 6000–7000 years ago. The dating of the Epic of Gilgamesh (arguably the oldest text in existence) is c.2700 BCE which is less than 5000 years ago, making the figure of 100,000 years a little speculative.

Oral storytelling has recently been reliably dated to the Bronze age.[1] Da Silva and Tehrani (2016) have found evidence to suggest that some common fairy stories originated then. To date them, they employed phylogenetic analysis, which allowed them to establish the evolutionary relationships between different Indo-European languages. They found, for example, the story of the Smith and the Devil may be 6000 years old. This is the story of an ambitious blacksmith who sells his soul to the Devil (or Bronze age equivalent) in exchange for superior metal working skills. The story has been retold over the millennia not least by Marlowe and Goethe (though I do wonder about the existence of blacksmiths in the Bronze age).

Anthropological and philological evidence aside, the writer Kathryn Morton has observed that, *"The first sign that a baby is going to be a human being and not a noisy pet comes when he begins naming the world and demanding the stories that connect its parts. Once he knows the first of these he will instruct his teddy bear, enforce his worldview on victims in the sandlot, tell himself stories of what he is doing as he plays and forecast stories of what he will do when he grows up. He will keep track of the actions of others and relate deviations to the person in charge. He will want a story at bedtime."* And this, in a sense, is what is missing in our many treatments of the cognition underpinning HCI – a connecting story. Just how do the bits fit together? Fortunately there is a growing body of research which argues for narrative as a means of integrating a body of knowledge such as this. This integration may take place at an individual's level of comprehension or across a discipline (e.g. Bruner 1986, 1991; Peterson 1999 to name but a few). The power of narrative has been identified in a number of different ways. Hirsh et al. (2013) offer a number of examples, they tell us, for example, that Schank and Abelson (1977) have used

---

[1] Dating the Bronze age depends upon which part of the world we are discussing. In the Near East it is dated at between 3200 and 1200 BC or approximately 5200–3200 years ago. In China it was about 1000 years later.

narrative to capture the planning and order of events; while Oatley (1992) has written of the emotional significance of an event. Sarbin (1986) was, of course, the pioneer of this approach when he wrote of the "storied nature of human conduct". Sarbin has argued for the use of stories rather than logical thought or derived "laws" to capture and study human behaviour – after all, that is what all people do all of the time – listen to and tells stories about their experiences. He argued that the root metaphor of psychology should be narrative rather than the range of other metaphors which have been adopted over the years.

A similar line of thought can be found in Bruner's work too. In his *Actual Minds, Possible Worlds* (1986) he argued for the narrative construction of reality, that is, the world is best understood by and through the stories we tell about it rather than through scientific reasoning. Bruner shows that there are, basically, two kinds of thinking which he describes as paradigmatic and narrative, which represent the world in different ways and they obey different laws. One is concerned with reasoning and produces rational arguments based on knowledge, facts and is often abstract. The other involves narrative and produces stories with human experience at its core. Bruner points out that while we have developed sophisticated analyses of how to think in the paradigmatic way, we have relatively little to say about how to write good stories. However he suggests that narrative thinking incorporates two dimensions: the "landscape of action" (the plot) and the "landscape of consciousness" (the motivations). The former outlines the actions and the actors, the latter outlines their mental states (such as goals, beliefs and emotions).

We have always been able to consider the human condition through the mirror of both great literature and popular media. For example, it is now widely suggested that as people age that they should not be reaching for the self-help book ("fifty tips to stay active") but to novels. Novels report on the experience of aging more accurately and appropriately than any self-help manual. And I can't avoid mentioning Star Trek® here, which along with other "what-if" TV series, has been exploring the human condition through the lens (or mirror) of science fiction for the last 50 years. In addition to being credited with having "invented" a number of technological innovations, the TV series has revealed much about the Cold War stereotypes, the arms race, and the importance of inter-racial (and inter-species) cooperation. This is not just a "trekkie" fantasy as it has emerged that no less a figure than Martin Luther King persuaded Nichelle Nichols (who played the part of Lt. Uhura) to stay with the show when she had considered leaving (Star Trek 2011). So, where shall we look for the story of HCI? An answer may lie with technology itself.

9.3   The Disclosive Nature of Technology

While we happily speculate about, and examine the role of cognition in interaction, we rarely consider the role of technology as such. Technology is almost always treated as though it were neutral and interaction as something we do to it or with it. Essentially, we treat technology simply as a means to an end. In response to this, we suggest that technology, at least in the context of HCI, often discloses something about ourselves. We have already seen evidence presented at the end of Chap. 6 that some people are treating interactive technology as an extension to their cognition and that it is changing how we think and estimate our understanding and knowledge. As Turkle (1995, p. 26) writes, "Computers don't just do things for us, they do things to us, including our ways of thinking about ourselves and other people".

Heidegger has a great deal to say about technology most of which is pretty obscure. He tells us that the true nature of technology is its ability to disclose. His argument begins with the observation that techné, which is the root of the word technology, was originally used to describe both process and product, that is, the skills required to use or make the tool as well as the tool itself. More than that, techné stands in opposition to physis (nature) which implies "a natural self-genesis" unlike techné which has a role for reason and the hand of man. This division, he argues, lies behind the everyday understanding of technology. He tells us that to regard technology as purely a means for an end is limiting as it hides its essential meaning which is as a fundamental mode of revealing.

By way of example, he argues that technology reveals the world as a "standing reserve" or as a body of raw materials ready to be extracted, transformed and exploited. So, while we may enjoy the natural beauty of a scene, technology orients us to see, for example, the opportunity to mine the coal, oil or minerals lying beneath our feet. We extend his argument to propose that technology also reveals something about its users too. We focus on one aspect of this disclosure, namely, that we appropriate technology. We customise, modify, and personalise it to more closely suit our needs, whims, fancies and as a vehicle for self-presentation. So, technology discloses not only that we are intrinsically tool users but, more importantly for the current argument, that we are disposed to appropriate it too.

Hassenzahl (2004) agrees. He writes that our experience of interactive technology can be divided into pragmatic and hedonic aspects. The former are concerned with users' goals (and hence requires utility and usability) or as Heidegger might have put it, as technology is a means to our ends. The hedonic attributes of technology, in contrast, are primarily related to the users' sense of self, which Hassenzahl further subdivides into stimulation and identification. The stimulation aspect of technology is, more or less, a measure of how much fun it is to use and how much fun we can have with it (think engagement). Identification is a little more interesting as it is concerned with the "human need to express one's self through objects". This self-presentational function of products is, he tells us, entirely social; individuals want to be seen in specific ways by relevant others. Using and possessing a product is a means to a desired self-presentation, that is, communicating important personal values to relevant others.

A Long History of Appropriation

A number of compelling stories have been told about the appearance and development of our species to complement the scientific findings from the fossil record. Perhaps at this point it is timely to recall that Nye (2006, p. 5) proposed that that storytelling and tool creation may have co-evolved. Religion may have started this with creation myths. These stories, of course, have ebbed and flowed over the centuries in step with the rise and fall of their associated religions. More recently, a new raft of stories have been told to do much the same. These stories have variously attributed to our response to dramatic climatic changes (Trauth et al. 2006); the acquisition of "symbolic cognitive processes" (Tattersall 2006); brain specialization (Calvin, *ibid*); genetic mutation (Klein, *ibid*); the development of projectile technology (e.g. Ambrose 2001); and, or the appearance of complex social relationships (Hare 2007). To this list we now add the appropriation of tools and technology.

Having picked up a stone to crack a nut, an ape separates kernel from shell and drops their stone tool. Our ancestors are likely to have done something similar at least initially, but then learned to shape the stone to make a better axe or scraper or knife or perhaps a tool which fitted our hands a little better. At some point we learned to retain the tool for the next time we found a nut. While we used to boast that our use of tools distinguished us from other animals (McKee et al. 2016) – we now know that this is not so – but at least we are almost certainly the only animals who retains a tool from one episode of use to another. For the sake of completeness, we should note that chimpanzees do carry sticks which they use to "fish" for ants from one mound to another but this is probably limited to one feeding episode only. We also invented that most underrated of tools – the bag which we use carry other tools around – and the great apes are yet to do this.

The first hominid was Homo habilis which means quite literally, the handy man, then came Homo ergastor – the working man. These classifications seem to recall the Biblical curse of Adam, and the different species are defined not just with respect to teeth or morphological clues from fragments of fossils but by the tools these people made. Tool use is not just a matter of producing a neater way to butcher game, as Burke and Ornstein (1997) tell us, when humans began to make tools we changed the process of natural selection. The "axe introduced an artificial change … for the first time, people who were good at sequencing their actions found these talents in demand and were rewarded" (p. 19). We are, in a very real sense, all self-made men and women.

Domestication

Silverstone and Haddon (1996) use the term "domestication" to describe appropriation as the way in which technologies are integrated into everyday life and adapted to match the demands of daily practices. They based these ideas on the parallel they draw with the domestication of wild animals for their use as sources of food, for clothing, for work and for protection. Dourish (2003) re-iterates this view by describing the practical and situated aspects of appropriation writing that, "Appropriation is the way in which technologies are adopted, adapted and incorporated into working practice. This might involve customization in the traditional sense (that is, the explicit reconfiguration of the technology in order to suit local needs) …" (*ibid*, p. 467). These sentiments have been echoed by Jennie Carroll (2004) who has suggested that appropriation is an extended process which occurs after the introduction of a technology and between the two states, "technology-as-designed" and "technology-in-use." Her model highlights the importance of actual use over projected or intended use. More recently, Belin and Prié (2012) have described the appropriation of digital technology in similar terms writing that it is the process by which people continuously integrate artefacts into their practices. These are examples of appropriation as "design-in-use" (or artefact evolution) which occur in response to the demands of the situation users encounter.

A frequently cited theoretical treatment of appropriation is the work of Salovaara (2008). He claims that appropriation can be understood as being the result of interpretation (or re-interpretation) in which an individual perceives new opportunities for action (more commonly described as affordances) with the artefacts. In doing so they acquire a new mental usage schema. This schema holds both the new conceptual knowledge (that is, knowledge of the new uses to which the artefact can be put) and the practical, "know-how" allowing the individual to put the artefact to this new use. To achieve this, Salovaara proposes modifying Neisser's perceptual cycle. This cycle, which is classically cognitive in structure, has at its heart a schema – a mental representation – which mediates and directs interaction with the world, and in this instance, digital technology. In essence, Salovaara has argued that appropriation involves modifying both our conceptual and practical understanding of technology. As affordances have a key role in this, there may be something of a conceptual mismatch between affordance and schemata. Our own account of appropriation does not rely on mental representation, instead we begin with use. We defined *use* as the active, purposive exploitation of the affordances offered by, in this instance, technology. In activity engaging with technology we exploit what we find. However an inevitable consequence of this exploration is that everyday use routinely reveals something new, we quite simply see it as something else. Having disclosed a new affordance (or a cluster of them) we are then free to exploit it or them. This exploitation of the new is how we define *appropriation*. From this enactive perspective, appropriation emerges as a natural consequence of use.

9.4   The Promise of Post-cognitive Interaction

… is, I propose, one of unbounded technological appropriation, and as we have just seen, appropriation is consequence of use, rather than disembodied, disengaged reflection (Flint and Turner 2015). Appropriation ranges from the "cosmetic" personalisation of the cell phone and other individual technology to the other end of the spectrum with instances of "ensoulment". Ensoulment is a distinctive and striking form of appropriation which has been identified by Nelson and Stolterman (2012) to mean "promot[ing] an aesthetic of well-loved designs in which the meaning and value of a design is taken in as a feeling of being deeply moved and as a consequence, a feeling of being significantly changed". Research into ensoulment has tended to focus on it as an indicator of sustainability though it is recognised that the concept has a widely applicability. Ensouled things are things which are and have been cared for, cherished and valued. Between these extremes is everyday appropriation. Apple introduced iPad in 2010 describing it as "a revolutionary device for browsing the web, reading and sending email, enjoying photos, watching videos, listening to music, playing games, reading e-books and much more" (Apple 2010). They also described it as a "magical device". Since its launch it has been the object of regular everyday appropriation – it has become a replacement cookery book in the kitchen; a replacement digital radio; second monitor for a personal computer; an expensive cat toy (there are apps for this); a back seat, in-car entertainment centre; a musical instrument; a medium for finger painting for small children – we could go on. Just to show that everyday appropriation is not limited to Apple products, we consider the work of Dalton et al. (2012) who offer a nice example of *ad hoc* tangible interaction in a study of their Kolab system. They describe Kolab as "a nomadic TUI [tangible user interface] that takes advantage of the fact that the world is full of potential tangibles and that people appear to be comfortable in improvising with them". In a field trial they found that people readily appropriated a range of available objects (including teabags, mobile phones, jewellery and drinks containers) to act as tangible tokens to be used within the system.

Of the myriad of potential examples of technological appropriation, we limit ourselves to a further three specific instances. We begin with an unavoidable technology – Apple's iPhone. iPhone is arguably the most successful technological product in history (in terms of sales, at least) but consider for a one moment how people have made it their own. This is at the heart of what we mean by *appropriation* rather than the more quirky interpretation which is taken to mean finding an unusual or unexpected use for it which Dix (2007) quite rightly regards as oxymoronic. Our interest here is in the stories of its everyday use. Here is one. I witnessed the following outside a café in Padua. I saw a group of three teenage boys appearing to take turns to gesticulate wildly at a fourth who was holding something. All of this was done with great energy but in silence. It took a moment to realise that they were using sign language to communicate with a third party by way of the iPhone's videoconferencing ability (this was the something which was being held).

The second example dates from the 1990s and again is drawn from personal experience. The Web was invented in 1989 (webfoundation), and the EU funded project UNOM – *users, network operators and manufacturers* which ran from 1992 to 1995 – was tasked with exploring a number of networking issues not least of which was establishing uses for it (sic). Banks from Madrid and Milan, an electronic manufacturer and telecoms companies sought to work together to find practical applications for ISDN connectivity running speeds up to 56 kbs. In truth we couldn't find any convincing applications despite our best efforts to create a multiservice terminal for the end users. In retrospect, if we put people on the spot and ask them to find uses for a new technology (such as high speed connectivity) it is really rather very difficult. Better to give them access for an extended period and they will "domesticate" it.

The final example concerns the "everyday" use of a Sony video camera. This study was reported by Terrence Turner (1992), an anthropologist working with the Kayapó people who live in the Amazon basin in Brazil. These people used a video camera to make their own *indigenous* videos. At this time the Kayapó were faced with the building of a dam to which they were opposed (the damming of the river would have resulted in the loss of several of their villages). So, rather than being the object of an anthropological video, they appropriated this technology to make their own videos of their everyday lives in order to influence public opinion and the decision makers who would disrupt their homes.

It is stories of use, both everyday and extraordinary and the almost inevitable appropriation which follows which will provide us with the complementary narrative to a post-cognitive HCI.

References

Ambrose SH (2001) Palaeolithic technology and human evolution. Science 291:1748–1753

Belin A, Prié Y (2012) DIAM: towards a model for describing appropriation processes through the evolution of digital artifacts. In: Proceedings of DIS '12: proceedings of the designing interactive systems conference 2012, Newcastle, pp 645–654, 11–15 June 2012. doi:10.1145/2317956.2318053

Bruner J (1986) Actual minds, possible worlds. Cambridge University Press, Cambridge

Bruner J (1991) The narrative construction of reality. Criti Inq 18(1):1–21

Burke J, Ornstein R (1997) The axemaker's gift. Tarcher Penguin, New York

Carroll J (2004) Completing design in use: closing the appropriation cycle. In: Proceedings of European conference on information systems, pp 337–347

Dalton N, MacKay G, Holland S (2012) Kolab: appropriation & improvisation in mobile tangible collaborative interaction. In: DIS 2012, Newcastle, pp 21–24, 11–15 June 2012

Da Silva SG, Tehrani JJ (2016) Comparative phylogenetic analyses uncover the ancient roots of Indo-European folktales. R Soc Open Sci 3:150645

Dix A (2007) Designing for appropriation. In: Proceedings of BCS HCI group conference, pp 27–30

Dourish P (2003) The appropriation of interactive technologies: some lessons from placeless documents. Comput Supported Coop Work 12:465–490

Flint T, Turner P (2015) Enactive appropriation. AI & Soc 31:1–9

Hare B (2007) From nonhuman to human mind: what changed and why? Curr Dir Psychol Sci 16(2):60–64

Haven K (2007) Story proof: the science behind the startling power of story. Libraries Unlimited, Westport

Hassenzahl M (2004) The interplay of beauty, goodness, and usability in interactive products. Hum Comput Interact 19:319–349

Hirsh JB, Mar RA, Peterson JB (2013) Personal narratives as the highest level of cognitive integration. Behav Brain Sci 36(03):216–217

McKee J, Poiner FE, McGraw WS (2016) Understanding human evolution, 5th edn. Routledge, New York

Nelson HG, Stolterman E (2012) The design way: intentional change in an unpredictable world. The MIT Press, Cambridge, MA

Nye DE (2006) Technology matters. MIT Press, Cambridge, MA

Oatley K (1992) Best laid schemes: the psychology of emotions. Cambridge University Press, Cambridge

Peterson JB (1999) Maps of meaning: the architecture of belief. Routledge, London

Salovaara A (2008) Inventing new uses for tools: a cognitive foundation for studies on appropriation. Hum Technol 4(2):209–228

Sarbin TR (1986) Narrative psychology: the storied nature of human conduct. Praeger/Greenwood, London

Schank RC, Abelson RP (1977) Scripts, plans, goals and understanding. Earlbaum Associates, Hillsdale

Shackel B (1997) HCI: whence and whither? J Am Soc Inf Sci 48(11):970–986

Silverstone R, Haddon L (1996) Design and the domestication of information and communication technologies: technical change and everyday life. In: Mansell R, Silverstone R (eds) Communication by design. Oxford University Press, New York, pp 44–74

Tattersall I (2006) How we became human. Sci Am Spec 16(2):66–73

Trauth MH, Maslin MA, Deino A, Strecker MR, Bergner AGN, Dühnforth M (2006) High- and low-latitude forcing of Plio-Pleistocene African climate and human evolution. J Hum Evol 53(5):475–486

Turkle S (1995) Life on the screen: identity in the age of the internet. Touchstone, New York

Turner T (1992) Defiant images: the Kayapo appropriation of video. Anthropol Today 8(6):5–16

Web Resources

Apple (2010) http://www.apple.com/pr/library/2010/01/27Apple-Launches-iPad.html

Star Trek (2011) http://www.npr.org/2011/01/17/132942461/Star-Treks-Uhura-Reflects-On-MLK-Encounter

Web Resources

Apollo 11 Flight Journal. Available from http://history.nasa.gov/afj/. Last retrieved 3 September 2015

Apple (2010) http://www.apple.com/pr/library/2010/01/27Apple-Launches-iPad.html

Bødker S, Klokmose CN (2015) A dialectical take on artifact ecologies and the physical-digital divide. In CHI workshop on ecological perspectives in HCI, Korea, April 2015. Available from http://rizzo.media.unisi.it/EPCHI2015/resources/papers/A-dialectical-take-on-artifact-ecologies.pdf. Last accessed 23 Apr 2016

Buzzfeed http://www.buzzfeed.com/charliewarzel/heres-the-cold-hard-proof-that-we-cant-stop-checking-our-pho#.ddKwzN8aK

Carr N (2008) Is Google making us stupid. The Atlantic magazine. Available from http://www.theatlantic.com/magazine/archive/2008/07/is-google-making-us-stupid/306868/. Last retrieved 3 March 2016

Charniak E (1972) Towards a model of children's story comprehension. Technical report 266. MIT Artificial intelligence laboratory report. Available from ftp://publications.ai.mit.edu/ai-publications/pdf/AITR-266.pdf. Last retrieved 29 July 2015

Eler A, Peyser E (2016) http://thenewinquiry.com/essays/tinderization-of-feeling/

Facebook (2016) Available from http://www.bbc.co.uk/news/technology-36021889

Fitts PM, Jones RE (1947) Psychological aspects of instrument display. Analysis of 270 "pilot-error" experiences in reading and interpreting aircraft instruments (Report No. TSEAA-694-12A). Aero Medical Laboratory, Air Materiel Command, U.S. Air Force, Dayton. Available from www.dtic.mil/cgi-bin/GetTRDoc?AD=ADA800143

Green TRG (no date) Cognitive dimensions of notations and devices http://homepage.ntlworld.com/greenery/workStuff/res-CDs.html. Last retrieved 28 April 2016

Green P, Wei-Haas L (1985) The wizard of Oz: A tool for rapid development of user interfaces (Technical report). Available from https://deepblue.lib.umich.edu/bitstream/handle/2027.42/174/71952.0001.001.pdf;jsessionid=2F1E8C62D57043FF1408B24686312163?sequence=2. Last retrieved 21 June 2016

Ilyenkov E (1977) Problems of dialectical materialism (trans: Bluden A). Progress Publishers. Also available from http://www.marxists.org/archive/ilyenkov/works/ideal/ideal.htm. Last retrieved 21 June 2016

Janiak A (2012) "Kant's views on space and time", The Stanford encyclopedia of philosophy (Winter 2012 Edition), Zalta EN (ed) Available from http://plato.stanford.edu/archives/win2012/entries/kant-spacetime. Last retrieved 21 June 2016

Kahneman D (2002) Maps of bounded rationality: a perspective on intuitive judgment and choice. Nobel Prize lecture. Available from http://www.nobelprize.org/nobel_prizes/economic-sciences/laureates/2002/kahnemann-lecture.pdf. Last retrieved 21 June 2016

© Springer International Publishing Switzerland 2016   161
P. Turner, *HCI Redux*, Human–Computer Interaction Series,
DOI 10.1007/978-3-319-42235-0

Kant I (1800) Logic. Available from https://archive.org/stream/kantsintroductio00kantuoft/kantsintroductio00kantuoft_djvu.txt

Kaptelinin V (2014) Affordances. In: Soegaard M, Dam RF (eds) The encyclopaedia of human-computer interaction, 2nd edn, Interaction design foundation https://www.interaction-design.org/literature/book/the-encyclopedia-of-human-computer-interaction-2nd-ed/affordances. Last accessed 27 Apr 2016

Kennedy JF (1961) Available from http://www.jfklibrary.org/JFK/JFK-Legacy/NASA-Moon-Landing.aspx

Luria AL (1928) The problems of the cultural behaviour of the child. J Genet Psychol 35:493–506 Available from https://www.marxists.org/archive/luria/works/1928/cultural-behaviour-child.pdf

Microsoft (2016) Available from http://www.bbc.co.uk/news/technology-35927651. Last retrieved 31 March 2016

Minsky M (1974) A framework for representing knowledge, MIT-AI Laboratory Memo 306. Available from https://web.media.mit.edu/~minsky/papers/Frames/frames.html. Last retrieved 6 July 2015

MIT (no date) http://tangible.media.mit.edu/projects/Tangible_Bits

Nielsen L (2014) Personas. Available from https://www.interaction-design.org/literature/book/the-encyclopedia-of-human-computer-interaction-2nd-ed/personas. Last retrieved 3 March 2016

Ofcom (2014) http://stakeholders.ofcom.org.uk/binaries/research/media-literacy/media-use-attitudes-14/Childrens_2014_Report.pdf

Ramachandran VS (2000) Mirror neurons and imitation as the driving force behind "the great leap forward" in human evolution. Retrieved from EDGE: The third culture. http://www.edge.org/3rd_culture/ramachandran/ramachandran_p1.html

Self-models (2007) http://www.scholarpedia.org/article/Self_models

Shortcliffe EH (1976) Computer based medical consultation. Elsevier, New York. Available from http://people.dbmi.columbia.edu/~ehs7001/Shortliffe-1976/MYCIN%20thesis%20Book.htm. Last retrieved 29 July 2015

Telegraph (2015) http://www.telegraph.co.uk/news/11408986/Why-we-should-bowl-the-little-green-men-a-googly.html. Last retrieved 15 February 2016

Telegraph (2016) http://www.telegraph.co.uk/technology/facebook/7879656/One-third-of-young-women-check-Facebook-when-they-first-wake-up.html

Vygotski LS (1930) The instrumental method in psychology. Available from https://www.marxists.org/archive/vygotsky/works/1930/instrumental.htm. Last retrieved 3 July 2015

Webfoundation http://webfoundation.org/about/vision/history-of-the-web/

Printed in the United States
By Bookmasters